What is Fascism

Discourses and Polemics

Giovanni Gentile

Translated By Richard Robinson

Sunny Lou Publishing Company
Portland, Oregon, USA
http://www.sunnyloupublishing.com

1st Edition: April 18, 2023

ISBN: 978-1-955392-36-5

* * *

This translation from Italian is based on
the Vallecchi Editore edition of
Che cosa è il fascismo, Firenze, 1925.

Contents

Note to the Reader

In keeping with our desire, the author has consented to the publication of this collection of discourses given by him recently on various occasions in order to illustrate fascist thought, and of articles and other short writings with which he has participated in recent polemics on the topic of fascism. It seemed to us that this collection could be very useful for the political education of Italians, fascist and non-fascist alike, that this book could steer the conversation away from daily gossip and toward contemplation on the profound passions and lofty spiritual interests that are the essence of fascism.

In the Appendix is reproduced a piece of writing from 1920, which was no longer in print. It can serve to demonstrate to certain critics how the author has felt and spoken since then.

– *The Publisher*

Part the First:
The Ideas of Fascism

I. What Is Fascism

Gentlemen,

I have to confess that I do not begin speaking here without a certain preoccupation. I came to Florence to give a lesson at the Fascist Cultural Circle, where one reads, studies, and discusses among fascists who are desirous of manifesting and clarifying their own ideas; and I had in mind for that a discourse specific to that place and to that audience. Instead, to my great surprise, I am tasked with speaking before thousands of listeners variously prepared and disposed, in this solemn and magnificent hall of memories and glories where one could not come to give a "lesson" without giving proof of overly bad taste; nor, of course, could words be tolerated that did not re-echo the lofty sounds of history and that did not preconize a generous faith in the fatherland. Fortunately, the selfsame argument of my discourse is about those who stir up ardent and universal passions, who rouse and nourish in everyone an interest provoking adherence or polemics and setting the spirit and mind to work to solve the essential problems of the fatherland and human life itself in general. And together with the quality of the argument, your cordial reception encourages me to speak sincerely, frankly, about those things of fascism that I have meditated on for a long time, and that I feel strongly about from the bottom of my heart, in the hope here also of succeeding at being understood by everyone, or at least at not being misunderstood. Where there is sincerity there is also a good disposition to understand beyond what is said and what can be said, discovering the correct and underlying motives that inspire whoever speaks. To understand in good faith: which does not always succeed in happening.

On the other hand, what I have to request of you, I would have had to request it even of the brief circle of friends whom I would have found at the cultural circle. Even when speaking of fascism to fascists, like any other fascist, I would have needed to make a preliminary disclaimer. And to say: take care, the fascism I speak about is my fascism. Indeed, its being so large a movement, which presses together around the same standard, and in one common faith, hundreds of thousands of Italians, and its being for everyone one single movement, and therefore one same life, one same ideal, does not mean that everyone who agrees with it sees it with the same eyes, understands it with the same intelligence, feels it with the same spirit. Unity results from this multiplicity, from this infinity of temperaments and psychologies and cultural habits and conceptions of life. The strength of fascism derives from this very rich and inexhaustible source of inspirations and joint needs and spiritual energies. And it would dry up and grow arid in the mechanical monotony of empty formulas if it could be defined and restricted in articles of a determinate credo. Moreover, our great Gioberti,[1] in the fragmentary book of his which was however strewn with genial thoughts, by which he sought to induce the Catholic Church to adopt those reforms that appeared indispensable to him in order to renew and re-

[1]Gioberti: Vincenzo Gioberti (AD 1801-1852), an Italian priest, then later a statesman, philosopher, and writer.

vive the marvelous millennial institution, even of Catholicism which is the type of religion composed of rigidly objective characteristics, he correctly said that every Catholic has his own [version of it]. – But the Pope, it could be objected, was not of this opinion. – "And yet," Gioberti replied, "it is exactly as I say." – And it was not sophism. Because for however much effort is made to renounce one's own personality and adhere to a common belief, that belief will never be accepted if to a certain extent it is not understood; and it cannot be understood. beginning with the same words in which the ideas are expressed, unless one avails oneself of the culture and feelings and tendencies and ultimately the entire complex of elements in which our personality is organized and concretized. Around fascism, as around any well-specified and identified thing, which everyone equally knows what it is, we are all gathered, however many Italians we might be in our day to work and fight: for or against, it does not matter. Even our adversaries have been constrained by the same fascist intensity of the movement to take up a position with respect to it. Each will have a clear or obscure, and more or less obscure, idea of it: but everyone, exalting it or condemning it, equally speaks about fascism; everyone, the violent or the nonviolent, are faced with the problem that is the argument of this discourse: what is fascism? But fascists, of course, conceive of fascism in a very different way than their adversaries do; and for the same reason, however incomparably minor the difference might be, the concept varies from fascist to fascist; and the solution to the central problem, which all strive for, turns out to be palpably diverse. To dissimulate or conceal these differences, like every hypocrisy or falsehood, would be an indication of little faith and obtuse intelligence in the life that belongs to every great spiritual movement. For life is always development and consequently continuous and incessant change: therefore unity, but also variety and the internal conflict of discordant elements whereby life is induced to take on new forms. And where there is the calmness of stagnant water, the air is infected and life dies.

Which might sound bad to someone who coarsely imagines the discipline of a party or the steadfastness of a school as the stultification of men who adhere to this or to that. But neither brutes nor men turned into brutes have ever made history. And all that which is great in the world of men, political platform and philosophical doctrine, has always been great in that same way in which I imagine fascism: a fundamental structure, a nucleus, which is a vivid idea and therefore a direction of thought, an inspiration and a tendency, in which various spirits meet and come to agreement and participate in the same life which is, the greater the number of those who engage in it, all the more vigorous and powerful; and around that nucleus, through the spontaneous generation of so many seeds of thought that in history gradually come to maturity, a varied blossoming of reflections and systems, which are new organs and because of which the central organism grows stronger while receiving and appropriating to itself, from the atmosphere in which it vegetates and lives, always new energies. In that nucleus is unity and faith. In it is the essential thing, the root of life and strength.

I come to fascism from my studies, from history, from philosophy. Others from art. Others from the squadrismo of the daily political battle. Others from the polemics of journalism. Others from the art of the parliamentary game. Others from other origins. Each with his soul, with his culture, with his habits, his life, his personality. But all arrive at the same point, and all meet on the same path: which is the path on which fascism today is fighting its beautiful fight in Italy and in the world in order to impress its form onto the State, and through the State onto the whole spirit. Everyone: even those who, like me, have always lived at school and at their studies, and who, outside the militant politics of every day, have contemplated national problems through history and philosophy. Because there is philosophy, and then there is philosophy, Gentlemen. And the ancient, famous story, now become a proverb, of the philosopher who was looking up at the sky and not watching where he was walking on the ground and for that reason fell into a ditch, – that philosophy which, since Aristophanes, men of common sense make satires of and laugh heartily at, outside life and extraneous to the fight in which life consists, without seeing the concerns that nourish the fight and for which all men live, play, and hope, or suffer and torment themselves, and know that life is a fatigue, an effort, a personal sacrifice, abnegation, passion, and the inexhaustible desire for the goal that is always to be sought but never reached; that philosophy is dead for a stretch[44] now. Our philosophy is thoughtful, yes, but because life is thoughtful; it is a reflection on life, but because true life is a reflection on itself, its luminous activity, which is explained in a way all its own, because it consciously makes it so, knowing where it goes and how it can arrive there. And what will today be a philosophy worthy of our time will be unable to be an impoverished and denatured life, almost vanished in the pale reflection of an abstract thought; on the contrary, it will be the same life but more intense, more energetic, almost boosted and lifted by the vigilant awareness of the laws themselves.

Let me try, then, to respond in my own fashion to the question that we have put to ourselves: what is fascism. And we will endeavor together to approach what could be called, as I hinted at earlier, the living and unique nucleus of fascism, which we are all looking at, but which we all have interest in seeing precisely.

The Two Italies

And to begin with, I invite you to consider whether it cannot be said that from history comes down to us as if two distinct and different images of the Italy that we are examining. Everyone of us is examining it, to be honest. History is not a past that interests only the erudite: it is present, alive in the minds of everyone. However many Italians there are, they all feel it: they feel that they belong to this Italy, which is not just the azure of its sky, its hills and its seas, nor the desolate and alpine land that alternates with its fertile plains and its smiling gardens. Let us close our eyes, let us leave to the side the horizons of its landscapes, so varied in beauty and light: and Italy remains in our mind, indeed it grows big and becomes huge in the glory of what it is in the mind and heart of all civilized men, who render it its justice or at least recognize it as the nation of intelligence and of a never-setting millenarian culture and of the arts, its solitary thinkers, and its hard civil life amidst internal difficulties, of a national society slow in its laborious process of organization and unification amidst external powers fighting in the vaster organizational process of modern Europe. Everyone, seeing more or less, or more or less penetrating and understanding and feeling, have in themselves, without being able to remove it, this historical Italy, alive, but of a life that prolongs itself and is dug into the centuries by the roots, and there you have Italy, with its national characteristics that make themselves ever more evident around the eleventh century when, after the destroyed Empire, the Communes teem with the impetus of their freedom and their arts, and lay the groundwork for that Renaissance, which will be the most genial creation of the Italian spirit, the brightest beacon of light to men in every part of the world, when the Italians of the Renaissance themselves doubled in number, searching for the port of new science, new art, new thought, new faith, and ultimately the modern Age. This Italy, which everyone carries in his heart, which forms in fact the substance of our being and of our character in the world, if we look at it intensely today, with the gaze made sharper by our current passion for a loftier and stronger national life, with this passion that broods within us after the trials of the great war,[2] ever since we felt the anguish of conflict and the pride of victory, we see this Italy present itself now in one aspect, and later in a more diverse one. We see two Italies before us: an old one, and a new one: the Italy of many centuries, which is our glory but is also a sad heritage, which weighs on our shoulders and pulls on our soul: and which is even, to be frank, a shame, which we want to wash ourselves clean of, which we must make amends for. And it is precisely that great Italy that has so great a place, as I said, in the history of the world. The only Italy, it can be said, that is known and studied and investigated by all civilized peoples, and whose history is not a particular history, but an epoch of universal history: the Renaissance. In which there is so much light, yes, and so many titles to national pride for Italians, but there is also so much darkness. Because the Renaissance is also the period of individualism which led the Italian nation through the splendid dreams of poetry and art to indifference, skepticism, and the nonbelligerent indolence of men who have nothing around themselves to defend in the family, in their fatherland, in the world where every human personality conscious of its own valor and its own dignity pours out and plants itself, because they believe in nothing that transcends the free and happy game of their own creative fantasy. Whence the frivolity of a habit that is decaying and rotting little by little as the active feeling of nationality fades away and minds grow weak; whence a literature in which carnivalesque songs and burlesque bizarrerie of every sort are mixed into a comedy that draws its material and its spirit from mocking, face-

[2]Great war: World War I.

tious, and cynical novellas; a comedy that is never for all that a true art, wherein even beneath the laughter the crying can be heard, or rather the seriousness of the spirit that knows the misery of its deficiencies, that one must free oneself of with effort in order to ascend to that ideal, where alone there is life; and the academies are transformed into gatherings of cultivated but idle geniuses, in whom dissertation degenerates into gibberish, reputations, once minted in the antique metal of ingenuous but serious and profound humanism, compete in wittiness and strangeness of invention, ludicrous allusions and analogies; religion becomes exterior and lifeless form, philosophy is persecuted with torture and burnings, and science languishes in intellectualistic practice, capable of kindling the passions of *literati* (as scientists are also called), but inept at jolting minds and instilling therein the goad of those problems, in which man is armed with all his strength to move against mystery and destiny. Empty literature, superficial, soulless. Sonnets, canzoni galore: but one man, who sings and expresses his passion, never. Academies that seem like masques. As much culture as one wishes; but infecund, dead. Men without will, without character; life without plans, which are those of the particular individual who thinks of himself, but nothing more. The Italy therefore of foreigners, and not of Italians. Italians without faith, and for that reason absent. Is not this the old Italy of decadence?

Residues of the Old Italy

That Italy, for us, is dead; and there is another, thank heaven. And one can say, in a certain sense, as I will soon explain, that the first is dead for two hundred years now. But it is not so dead that we do not find it now and then in front of us even today, in this year of grace 1925. There are as yet too many people in Italy who believe in nothing and laugh at everything, and yearn for the Arcadia and other Academies; and they grow resentful of anyone who disturbs their digestion. Do you remember the tremendous Italian vigil of the great war, when the few who believed carried the many who shrugged their shoulders, repeating the foreign insult that Italians don't fight? Or when the young felt quivering in their chest an obscure instinct and abandoned themselves to it, certain, blindly trusting in the national destiny, in the strength of the race, in the necessity of a great cruel proof which however cemented the recent national unity, more thought about than believed in, or more believed in than attempted and achieved, and tempered in battles, which every free people must always be ready for, the Italian fibre? And mature men, the wise, smiled and calculated, and were horrified at the thought of pointless sacrifices, as they said, and feared the dangers, which by virtue of calculations were never encountered, and which never are encountered by whoever is not animated by an indemonstrable faith? Today that pavid and myopic and skeptical neutrality is synonymous, for a great many Italians at least, with the ineptitude of feeling about Italian problems in an Italian way; am I not right? But that kind of old style spiritual temperament, which does not dare because it does not believe, runs away from courage because it does not see any advantage in sacrifice, measures national fortune by individual wellbeing, and always loves for that reason to walk on solid ground, not compromising oneself, never getting excited, and leaves idealism to poets, women, or philosophers at best, and voluntarily brushes to the side every question that could endanger harmony and a quiet life, and is satisfied to joke about everything and everyone, and always throws the cold water of prose on the enthusiasms of poetry, and recommends moderation at all costs, and feigns a sacred horror for polemics and violence, and inculcates in his neighbor all the maxims of egoism, and reflects, studies, understands, and "knows the story" like the quintessence of cleverness and wisdom; isn't this still for too many people the *non plus ultra* of the finesse all their own of the Italians? There are Masons who, it is known, have planted the nail of the famous laicity which is neither for religion nor against it; but even non Masons, insofar as Italians, do they not prefer to remain silent on things religious, and show restraint and modesty in revealing and defending their own convictions, when they have any? All that is the old Italy, the Italy of individualism, the Italy of the Renaissance; even when the martyrdom of philosophers was infecund because unhonored, and unhonored because conformant with the logic of their own doctrines, all individualistically closed within a world without connections with that life, in which there was concrete reality and in which one bumped up against one another because it was necessary, and therefore martyrdom was encountered there. Men at that time didn't feel their personality grafted onto the social world which each person belongs to, in which alone he can live with his own human interests, with his family, with his faith as a moral person who has duties, a plan to realize, a truth to profess. Seeing as nothing lives within the secrecy of our own mind that does not drag us to come out from within, to preach what is our truth, to communicate it to someone else, to enable it with all the energy that can assemble there through collaboration, through cohabitation, for the community of our moral life. Every faith brings men together.

The Italians of the Renaissance up to Galileo

Men of the Renaissance, o Gentlemen, could so tower in art because art is a dream that abstracts from reality in which there are also other men and the world to which our life is bound and which we share with others, and he wanders about in the free world of fantasy where the individual is creator and absolute lord of his own creations. The greatness of artists, which is its defect; because in this free life that releases itself from every bond, the hard sense of what may be called historical reality is lost, where our family, which has so many needs, which are really our own personal needs in that it is up to us to satisfy them and morally we cannot do otherwise; and there are all the other men, with whom the same necessity to satisfy our needs binds us in an indissoluble bond, with common duties in a social organism that our person has been bound to and which even all our fortunes are tied to, and for whose salvation consequently we need to make every effort and to risk our life even. And yet those poets and artists and thinkers of ours, cultivated and refined men, did not have any feeling for the fatherland. And Italians could be admired and at the same time disparaged; and their cities could be conquered with gesso; and the Challenge of Barletta[3] was possible, for example, because personal valor is not lacking in Italians, and even in the art of training and leading armies they knew how to excel, and many of our captains were famous: but there was never an Italian army, there was never a battle that could be said to have been won by the Italians.

Art itself finally was bound to decline. For not even art can live outside that moral world, which we call ideal: that world that man creates by the effort of his mind, placing himself above life which he would be compelled naturally to live, together with all other living people; and he realizes it because he begins to yearn for it like that better reality, which does not exist but which he can make exist and must: the more he does, the higher its worth. Now, all the merits, no one sees them and appreciates them and idolizes them like something that belongs to the closed secret of his conscience; but rather always like something universal, to which all men aspire, and which is certainly the patrimony of everyone. Art itself becomes a game; and it

[3]Challenge of Barletta: a tournament fought on February 13, 1503, in Apulia, between thirteen French knights and thirteen Italian knights, after Charles de la Motte disparaged the Italians and was challenged. The Italian knights won the tournament.

is because of Italian literature, that genre, which had so much success in the fifteenth century: Bernesque poetry.[4] It is since the fourteenth century that art and culture could be considered "vanity": those vanities, against which the heroic soul of Savonarola rebelled, who paid with his life, here in this piazza, on account of his repugnance for the frivolous and skeptical spirit of the Renaissance. He took life too seriously, when not one of the representatives of the Italian spirit took it very seriously. He asked too much of men, when men were lacking.

And they were lacking for centuries, men were, while the Academy expanded. From which, I repeat, we have not yet succeeded in recovering. Is not the great Galileo also an academic, a man of letters? Whose innovative genius, whose rigorously scientific thought, we kneel before. But when we study the trepid and wary life of his, when we read those so very obsequious letters of his, when we see him, him, the greatest Italian among coetaneous men, prostrating himself before lords who give him the stipend and leisure time to study, or contriving and faking it at the feet of the Inquisitors that they might leave him be to meditate and write and cultivate his literary glory, and never a hint or a scornful gesture at those rights, which were infringed on, never a proud reclaiming of his dignity as a thinker and as a man, never an allusion of any sort to the great sadness of the times and of the fatherland, never a generous sentiment for the great thinkers who were persecuted, dead or alive, and whose thought his own was closely connected to

[4]Bernesque poetry: poetry after the style of Francesco Berni (AD 1498-1535), which is satirical, mocking, and burlesque in tone.

however, consequently we have to feel that something essential was lacking even in this great Italian: and that the man was inferior to the scientist. And even he indulges in the frivolity of the aforementioned contemporary poets; and he jokes and laughs in Bernesque chapters against his scientific adversaries. Not even in the great Galileo is there a faith.

Vico and His Times

Between Galileo and Vico what an abyss! At the distance of less than one century behold a new spirit appearing. Compared to Galileo, whom he admires even, and to the entire Renaissance, which in many respects he is also related to, Giambattista Vico appears to belong to another people, another history. He too wanted to be a man of letters and is extremely jealous of his literary glory; but he is unable to conceive of any other goal for his studies than to "cultivate a kind of divinity in our soul." His thought, his life, the entire man is absorbed in a religious vision of history, which is the new world discovered by his philosophy. Obscure philosopher, a stranger in many eyes, a writer of books that he himself vaguely felt were a revolution in everything that had always been thought before, and which were a new epoch in the human spirit, but which nobody wanted to print, and when he printed them with great sacrifice to himself and to his large family, nobody understood, and those friends and colleagues of his, to whom he gave them as gifts, they didn't make any mention of them, and slipped away when they ran into the author, so as not to be constrained to talk with him about them. Then, for a long time, admired, but sometimes for the least important aspects of his thought, which was misunderstood: solitary, like a tall tower in a desert. And he never laughed. When he attempted laughter, satire transformed it into invective, and he felt the great bitterness of a mind troubled by the mean and unintelligent adversaries of his lofty vision of the divine, which nobody cared about. With Vico, the Italian religious consciousness rises up again, one begins to feel that life is taken seriously; one beings to hear a voice that, when it is listened to, will penetrate minds deeply, and will bring them to face problems that one hadn't heard about for centuries in Italy.

Vico is of the XVIIIth century, even though one could say that he is against everything belonging to the XVIIIth century: the century of abstract rationalism, the Enlightenment, materialism, individualism. In the second half of the same century, behold another great, solitary, and exceptional mind: another precursor or prophet (as he himself calls himself) of an Italy opposed to that of the Renaissance: Vittorio Alfieri. Another Italian who does not laugh: and he writes satires and comedies, but he is no less proud of his tragedies; and he too holds "letters" in high regard, but in order to resolve this problem, which is his problem and the problem of Italy of the Eighteenth century and the beginning of the century following it: the problem of man. He feels that anyone who is not literate is not a man, a character, a will. To will, to be oneself, to affirm oneself proudly consequently, to advance in the world conscious of oneself, in jealous tutelage and defense of oneself, with one's own thought, however obscure, and one's own program, however modest: to carry oneself as a free person and one's own master, to be one's own person, but also with the consciousness of being a citizen, an Italian, and a true man: this is Alfieri's literary problem, which is also the moral problem of all men, and the problem of Italians who begin to recover from their torpid spiritual subjection to foreigners, to feel Italian, and to pay attention to what is happening to them so as not to remain beneath other nations: not to remain there morally, so as not to remain there politically. The influence of Alfieri's personality and teachings on the successive generation, which is the generation of '21 finally, is huge.

Cuoco and the Reawakening of National Consciousness

But already in the first years of the XIXth century, in Milan, the center of the new Italian life, under the impulse that the French Revolution and Napoleon gave to national consciousness, there is a writer, unknown until only recently and not appreciated in adequate measure to his historical importance: a writer, who did not succeed in any work of his at giving a mature and complete form to his thought, but with an admirable historical essay of political acumen, philosophical profundity, and historical sense of the Italian soul, with a kind of historical romance, artistically mistaken but rich in thoughts eloquently expressed, and above all with a journalistic activity of copious vein, lofty inspiration, and great efficacy, he succeeded in planting in the minds and hearts of Italians, his contemporaries – to begin with the greatest, Foscolo and Manzoni – the idea and feeling of a new Italy. Which was already dawning on the horizon, but could be promoted with a new moral, political, military, and philosophical and literary education. An Italy aware of its glorious past, not in order to be proud of it vainly, but to draw subject matter and new hope from it, and with virile intentions of a revival of national dignity. Vincenzo Cuoco, historian, thinker, writer, picks up Vico's thought, clarifies and popularizes some fundamental concepts of it, uses it to enlighten the mind of contemporaries, makes an instrument of it for a new moral and political ideal of the Italian people; and lights a big torch at the head of the road, on which the people prophesied by Alfieri will march along in the new century. After him, the mostly moral problem of the Astigiano[5] becomes political: and it becomes the secret of our Risorgimento. To remake the temperament, the conscience, the character of Italians; who will never be able to obtain what they did not deserve or conquer by themselves. The Italians, who had learned how to fight with Napoleon, begin to feel how one might give oneself also a life worth living; at least in order to live that life which is necessary to a man who takes it seriously. Religious sentiment revives. Our patriots, in one way or another, conceive of life religiously.

[5]The Astigiano: in reference to Alfieri who was born in Asti.

Mazzini

Gentlemen, the model of Italian patriotism, who gave us a fatherland; he whom we always turn to with reverent and grateful spirit, because he was the loftiest and truest prophet of the Risorgimento, the Ezekiel of the new Italy, which because of him has finally risen up among nations, and is now on its feet, and knows and affirms that there is also Italy in the world, with its duties but also with its rights, and it will not fall, it will not lie down anymore because the old Italy which we have spoken about, if it is not already dead, must die: he was Giuseppe Mazzini. He instructed Italians how to love themselves, and how to acquire a nation for themselves; he taught what life is when the nation can love itself and redeem itself, and what men's duties are as a result. Or rather, he (as a youthful notebook of his has recently revealed to us) read, transcribed, and meditated on the more admonitory articles by Vincenzo Cuoco to Italians, without even knowing who the author was. And he forms a bond with him. Which unites all the architects of a national Risorgimento, in that everyone directly or indirectly felt the influence of his spirit or they built on a basis that he had created, with the ardor of his faith and with the fervor of his untiring industriousness, giving a principle, an orientation, and a concrete plan to the conspirers teeming all over Italy before him. And it reaches us, and closes in on and concludes in an idea and in a faith, all the history of this new Italy that was won at Vittorio Veneto,[6] annihilating its ancient ad-

[6]Vittorio Veneto: the name of a town in northern Italy where the Battle of Vittorio Veneto (AD October 24 – November 4, 1918)

versary in a blaze of light.

Now, the Mazzinian gospel survives the marvel of the Risorgimento, because it is the faith of Italy which came out of it; that youthful Italy that Mazzini evoked. It is the fascist gospel, it is the faith of the youth of 1919, of '22, of today: of the ideal youth of this Italy, which is made and must be made again; and remains for that reason young also in the heart of old men, who felt the truth of the faith that was prophesied by Giuseppe Mazzini. Few are the articles of this faith; and because they are few, and sparse, not woven into a laborious and solid philosophical system, to be taken all or nothing, they could be grasped easily and understood by the multitudes of well-disposed spirits. And it was taught to thousands of young hearts and took root there, and germinated and bore fruit, so that many young people could then dissociate themselves from Mazzini for those accessory things that men so often insist on considering essential; and they can forget having once been partisans of Mazzini; but they brought back with them [from the war] the remade heart and the fortified breast.

Mazzini's Concept of Freedom

The first article of faith was and is this: fight materialism. Mazzini, without being a philosopher by profession, like a Rosmini or a Gioberti, fought materialism all his life, tenaciously, proudly, efficaciously. It was

was fought and won by the Italians against the Austro-Hungarian army in WWI (which ended November 11, 1918).

in fact the first root of that weakness and infirmity that Italians had to free themselves of in order to really feel the nation and therefore to create an Italy. The nation is law and religion, which demands the subjection of the particular to a general and perennial interest, to an ideal that is superior to all that has been and is, in past and present individuals, and that for every single individual is all that exists or holds value. But for the materialist there is nothing else than the particular individual, with his instincts, with his attachment to his particular life, as to a supreme and absolute good, with his need to enjoy; to enjoy himself, and others inasmuch as their enjoyment becomes part of his and augments it; the individual, spoken of by old Guicciardini,[7] the "wise" man of the Renaissance, and old-style Italian. And Mazzini felt that this materialism is unworthy of the thinking man; he felt that no man can really live a life worthy of the name human while being inspired by materialism, which was for him synonymous with individualism.

In truth, o Gentlemen, turning one's eyes away even, on account of the vile desire for one's own comfort, from the high ideals of the fatherland, from duty, from the moral ties of fraternity which bring all men together in a similar life, who is the man that can also lazily close himself off in the narrow ambit of his own thoughts and in the egotistical life of mean and misanthropic passion without thinking, at least, and confiding in his own thoughts? And can a person think without being certain of the truth

[7]Guicciardini: Francesco Guicciardini (AD 1483-1540), a Florentine statesman and historian, author of *The History of Italy* (*Storia d'Italia*).

that he is thinking about? And can a truth be so subjective that it is valid only for the person who is satisfied with it, without giving him the right to affirm it and proclaim it whenever he wants to, like the truth that everyone ought to admit, provided they see it from his same point of view? And can a word be spoken even in the silence of our mind, which, if uttered out loud, does not have, nor is expected to have, any meaning for others? Or do we not all feel just the opposite? The thought bursts out irresistibly and is affirmed and expands and propagates; because we think it, but as a thought held by everyone, which in fact unites men of distant places and times in the truth. And the word does not sound within us without tending to be spoken on its own, and to rouse deep within ourself always vaster waves of spiritual movement, which it is the expression or living form of. And that same word that remains shut in the secret of our heart is one link in a chain: it is part of a discourse begun long ago and that will be continued, and was expressed by others and will remain in our mind, if it does not leave a trace at least (on a par with all words that we may sound in others' ears) in our soul, where it will no longer be erased, even though forgotten, and it will re-echo in the words and actions that we engage other men with. So, the word always binds us together, like a thing of our own, and not our own: our own and others'. Others who are and will be; and others who have been; for the word has a history, is national, i.e., it is of the many who speak only in our tongue. And then? The particular individual is a product of the imagination, by means of which each of us represents himself as one among many, in the crowd, circumscribed within the extreme limits of birth and death and in the brief confines of his own physical body. While what is a part of each of us, he feels it deep inside himself inasmuch as he has a right to be affirmed, a feeling to be expressed, a memory to be remembered, a word to be spoken, a luminous image to be added to the song, to the sound, to the color, and to the eternal form finally: and in general a faith, whatever sort of faith it is, lofty or humble, to be seized on in order to palpitate in the incessant rhythm of the spiritual life, from which it is impossible, through games of the imagination, ever to grow estranged totally.

Even at the time of Mazzini, there were liberals who put the individual above everything; liberals whom we still have in our way, and they kick and oppose the irresistible movement of history. And liberalism raised, at the time of Mazzini, a blazing banner, that banner of freedom that even Mazzini adored, and which he too fought for. And freedom was needed then, politically, by the nation against foreigners and by the citizens against the State; it was the main problem. But Mazzini also said that true freedom is not that of individualistic liberalism, which does not recognize the nation above individuals, and does not consequently understand the mission that depends on people, nor the sacrifice required of individuals. And against this liberalism he launched the accusation of execrated, blind, and absurd materialism.

The Concept of Nation

Freedom, yes, we say it ourselves today, but within the State. And the State is the nation; that nation that appears to be something that limits us and subjects us to it, and makes us feel and think and speak and above all be in a certain way: Italians in Italy, children of our parents and of our history, which stands behind us and puts a heart in our breast, and speech in our mouth, in the same way that nature, in general, with its laws, has us given birth to us with a certain form and face and destiny for a certain, well-defined, and fundamentally irreformable life. So it appears, but it is otherwise. Another one of Mazzini's articles of faith, another immortal glory of his, is this concept: that a nation is not a natural existence, but a moral reality. Nobody finds it therefore at birth, everyone must work to create it. A people is a nation not inasmuch as it has a history, which is its materially-certified past, but inasmuch as it feels its history and appropriates it to itself with a living consciousness like its own personality; that personality, whose edification it must work at, day after day, forever; which, for that reason, one can never say that one possesses it yet or that it exists in the same way as the sun and the hills and the sea exist; but, rather, it is produced by an active will that directs itself constantly toward its own ideal; and for that reason it calls itself free. A people is a nation if it conquers its freedom, assessing its value and braving all the suffering that such conquest requires, and it assembles its dispersed members into one body, and redeems itself, and founds an autonomous State, and does not presume, but creates its own being with the help of God who is revealed and acts in its same consciousness.

This high Mazzinian concept of nation, which could in fact rouse the nationalistic feeling of Italians, and position our national problem as a problem of education and revolution: that revolution, without which not even Cavour would have been capable of constructing Italy. This is the nation for which Italians cannot help always feeling affiliated with the Mazzinian *Giovine Italia*[8] and who today call themselves fascists. The nation is, really, not geographical or historical: it is a program, it is a mission. And for that reason it is a sacrifice. And it is not, and never will be, an accomplished fact. It will never be that grand museum that Italy once was for Italians, who guarded over it and exploited it, and for the foreigners who came to visit it, tossing a few coins into the hand of the custodians. Yes, museums, galleries, monuments of ancient greatness and splendor: but provided we feel worthy, provided we want to be worthy, and don't just stand around catching butterflies under the Arch of Titus or sit unmindful at festive gatherings and academic commemorations on Campidoglio; provided we stand proudly in defense of memories with works that revive the oldest traditions and noble past in the present and future. And the memories are a patrimony to defend not with erudition, but with new work, and with all the arts of peace and war, which might preserve that patrimony, renewing it and augmenting it. And to the monuments we will add even new ones if you wish. Let us erect them on our piaz-

[8]*Giovine Italia*: Italian for "Young Italy," the name of a group founded by Mazzini in the early 1830s.

zas to reinvigorate the temperament, to honor the living more than the dead in the consecration of recent memories, more glorious really than Italian history possesses, and, by the admonition of generous memories, to elevate our consciousness as free citizens of a great nation. Because when one says nation, one also means freedom, which is more than a right, it is a duty: a lofty conquest, which is not obtained unless through abnegation of the citizen ready to give his all to his country without asking for anything in return.

Return of Fascism to the Spirit of the Risorgimento

Even this concept of the nation, on which we insist today, is not a fascist invention. It is the soul of that new Italy, which little by little must get the better of the old. Fascism, with its vigorous feeling of the national enthusiasm that dragged Italians into the fire of the great war and made them victoriously undergo the tragic trial, with its energetic reaction to the materialists of yesterday who tried to undercut the value of that trial and prostrate the soul of citizens in the discouragement, desperate by fatigue and anxiety, of a wellbeing all the more impatiently desired the more difficult it was to obtain; fascism waved before the eyes of the people the greatness and beauty of the accomplished sacrifice as its greatest legacy for the future. And so it shook again with a powerful hand the consciousness of Italians so that they might remember to be children of Italy and remember the conditions that made this Italy possible, since its first Risorgimento; the conditions that gave our fathers the means to be ashamed of the old servitude, to escape inertia, to free themselves of the old habit of rhetoric and literature so as to begin speaking seriously about freedom.

Fascism has returned to the spirit of the Risorgimento with the greatest vigor that could derive from the new consciousness of the great trial undergone with so much honor by the Italian people and by the certitude of its capacity to fight and win and count for something finally in the history of the world. It has returned to that spirit with a passion that is intolerant of any weariness or cowardice, in an unstoppable ardor to wake the nation out of the recent and certain momentaneous dimming and drowsiness of its consciousness, so that the fruit of immense sacrifice be not dispersed, so that the position finally deserved and already almost reached of a great power, or of a nation that has its own will, be not lost at all from view, rather that it become the object of this will, to be conquered and firmly held onto.

Fascist Violence

In this impetuous ardor, fascism has resorted to violence when it thought it necessary. Because of which, men of the old Italy at a certain point have looked scandalized. To a certain point; because in a first instance that violence served something even for them: when the State seemed to be going to ruin and was not up to the task of guaranteeing public safety. Which also, as is natural, presented something of an embarrassment for those who were disposed to letting the same moral values of the war be done away with and trod on, continuing to smile at the Mazzinian religion of the nation provided that the individual was assured of public safety by public authorities, from work to thought, for the full range of natural liberties; in other words, provided that every gentleman who thought of himself and of his family was allowed to live his life, once and for all, after all the privations and the *corvées* of the war! And for the first time also the bludgeons of the squadristi appeared as a grace of God. But once the State was back to order, the security of normal life reacquired, and the causes that made the violence necessary forgotten – and how easy it is to forget past annoyances! – it was not enough that the Head of the Fascist Government should announce that from now on the cudgel was going back into the attic, and that from now on there was the State, having issued from fascism, to promote and defend the ideals; it was not enough that the squadristi should become a regular militia, albeit voluntary, of the State; it was not enough to protest every day that not everyone in fascism wanted to be a force outside the State anymore: the cudgel, in its physical brutality, became the symbol of the violent fascist soul *extra legem*. And with evil perfidy every offense was exploited, every abuse of power, every prepotency that was perpetrated by delinquents of the fascist party (for a party that tends to invest and permeate, and thus to educate the masses, and numbers more than several hundreds of adherents, it is not surprising that it include within its fold even delinquents, profiteers, bullies, on whose account it could be mistaken, and whom it succeeds in recognizing alas too late and to its own detriment) in order morally to wound this fascism which by now was becoming an ire of God. And behold a predication of Franciscan gentleness and charity toward one's neighbor, that had never before been felt in Italy. Behold a Quakerism which Italians hadn't had an example of. Behold the usual moral question, with which in Italy one has always tried to tear down strong governments, which had a certain awareness of what the State is, that if it is not strong, it is not a State. I don't want to insist on this point. This time, old Italy must have patience, and as to the moral question it must wait for the judgment of history. Fascism is not conflated with the men that, here or there, today or tomorrow, can represent it: it is an idea, a spiritual movement, that draws its strength from itself, from its own truth, from its own correspondence with profound needs, historical and national. And what everyone can note today is this curious fact: that its adversaries, knowing that fascism is an idea, don't get upset with this or that fascist, but with all fascists, without distinction. Or at least with those who stand out and fight for fascism. At these preachers of Franciscan charity – who now call themselves liberals! – they throw punches from morning to evening: ridicule, invective, fantastic accusations, defamations, calumnies that they know to be such. A violence of language and a calculated cynicism, with methods of fighting to dishonor a brigand. And not one of them has a scruple about it: not even the literati and philosophers that anti-fascism abounds in, for obvious reasons, just as old Italy always abounded in, against which fascism rose up. To say to a gentleman: you are a beast, or a profiteer or a violent man, a contractor of crimes or an instigator of misdeeds, this is not violence for our most innocent liberals. Because, printed, violence is not violence. Such is the magic of the sincerest worship of the freedom of the press.

Now, o Gentlemen, let us be clear, once again, for all men of goodwill. There is violence, and then there is violence; and no fascist ever, who is worthy of marching under a pennon, has ever gotten them confused. And whoever had gotten them confused is not worthy of standing with us; and will be expelled when found out. There is the violence of a private citizen, which is abuse, anarchy, social disintegration; and if fascism is not a word empty of meaning – something not even its adversaries will pretend – this violence has never found a more resolute, more frank, or more formidable enemy than fascism. But there is another kind of violence, which originates with God and with all men who believe in God, in the order and in the law that God clearly wants in the world: the violence for which there is no equality between the law and the delinquent; and it is impossible to admit that he might freely be persuaded to accept or, better yet, to ask for that punishment, which even, as a great philosopher correctly observed, is his right. The will of the law annuls the will of the delinquent: that is, it is a sacred violence. And men, beginning with Jesus, always resorted to acts of violence when they firmly believed that they represented the law, or a superior and universal interest. In the Catholic Church, not only the Dominicans, but also the followers of St. Francis. In the State, always all the armed forces. When the State was in crisis, always the men of revolution which is the establishment of a new State. Is fascism a revolution? Its idea is certainly revolutionary. To deny it a revolutionary character there are those who speak with enormous error about the peaceful ways, and perhaps they mean bloodless ways, of the march on Rome, but who are every day busy deploring and denouncing *urbi et orbi*[9] the bloody and irreducible violence of fascism.

Vico's Recurrent Barbarism

We have recalled among the memorable initiators of the new Italy the great Neapolitan philosopher Giambattista Vico. Well then, our most deep-rooted opponents will perhaps smile to hear that the good Catholic philosopher of the *New Science* is among the spiritual masters of fascism. But I refer them to the study of Vico's "heroic morality" in the age when, under the terror of gods, the first men abandon pretty Venus for shame, and, with force and violent passions conformant to the designs of Providence, they found families and therefore society and the State; I refer them to his doctrine of recurrent barbarism whereby eternally (and therefore not only in specific epochs, but whenever it occurs and always) one returns to violent force in order to reorder and revive degenerate

[9] *Urbi et orbi*: Latin for "everywhere" (literally "in the city [of Rome] and in the world").

and States corrupted by the freedom particular to more civilized nations where pervasive rights have gradually produced a regime of absolute civil equality. How many times has fascism been accused, with unintelligent malevolence, of barbarism? Well, yes: understand the right meaning of this barbarism, and we will boast about it, as destroyers of false and fatal idols by means of wholesome energies, and restorers of the nation's health in the power of the State, conscious of its sovereign rights, which are its duties. Our barbarism will scorn the false, misleading, and falsifying intellectualistic culture, indulgent and prone to individualistic whims and anarchistic egoisms, just as it will scorn false piety and hypocritical brotherhood and even the rules of etiquette that wean men from rude and wholesome frankness and accustom them to reciprocal deceit and every intolerable tolerance; but we will ignite in the Italian soul an inextinguishable thirst for knowledge which is hard work, and the interior reform of the man, and the conquest by moral and material means of a life always more lofty, always more fecund, for the individual and for the nation, indeed for humanity and for the world, which is ours, o Gentlemen, because we live in it and of it; and we will educate our children, the young who are around us vibrating with enthusiasm, to feel that life is not pleasure, but duty, and that one loves one's neighbor not by procuring for him and making easy for him the quiet life but rather helping him and training him for work, for sacrifice. In this way, parents really show their love for their children: not by caresses and cajoling, but by provident, strict, vigilant, and active care, so that each child is ready and equal to the needs of life, to the laws of the world, to duty.

Fascist Doctrine of the State

From our Mazzinian consciousness of the sanctity of the nation, as a reality that is realized in the State, we draw the motives for that exaltation which we are used to having for the State. Exaltation that appears as a new rhetoric to old-style skeptics, who look at us, wink, smile, among the half-wits and the cunning; and they keep murmuring: statolatry! It is the usual fixation of liberalism, which Mazzini called individualistic and materialistic! I'm reminded at this moment of what a worthy fellow said in 1882, who was also a liberal, but a genuine liberal, one of those who truly believed in liberty, and loved it seriously. "We are at the point," he said, while lamenting the disorders of parliamentarianism and the arrogance of radicals toward the State, which was reduced by them to an instrument of their caprices and the voluble demands of crowds and cliques; "we are at the point where the memory even of the etymology of the Italian State has been lost." – The State, with respect at least to individual judgment, must exist; it must rule, as something firm, solid, indestructible. Law and strength; law that asserts itself and does not cede every time it does not please a single individual or turn in favor of this or that category. And because this strength exists, it must be power, internal and external; capable of realizing its own will. Rational or reasonable will, as all those who, unable to stay at the stage of simple whim, express themselves through action, and triumph; but a will that cannot admit others who might limit it. So, sovereign, absolute will. The legitimate will of citizens is that which coincides with the will of the State which organizes itself and manifests itself by means of its central organs. With respect to foreign or international relations, war, in the ultimate instance, tests and guarantees the sovereignty of the single State in the system of history, which all States take part in. And the State demonstrates in war its proper power, which is, so to speak, its proper autonomy.

Ethical State

This State that wants, indeed is, the only concrete will, – because all others can be called will only abstractly, inasmuch as it essentially ignores indissoluble relationships so that every individual is bound to society and practically breathes in like atmosphere its language, custom, thought, interests, and aspirations: – this State, I say, would not be will if it were not a person. Since through will it needs to have consciousness of what it wants, the ends and the means; and in order to have such a consciousness, before anything it needs to have consciousness of itself, to distinguish itself from others, to affirm itself in its own autonomy, as the center of conscious activity; all in all, to be a person.

But whoever says person says moral activity: which means an activity that wants what it must want, according to an ideal. And the State, which is the national consciousness and will of this consciousness, attains from this consciousness the ideal that it aims for and directs all its activity at. For which reason the State cannot not help being an ethical essence. Allow me this philosophical terminology. The meaning is transparent when every one of you appeals to his own conscience and senses there the sanctity of the Fatherland that demands, with an order that is unquestionable, to be served without hesitations, without exceptions, until death. The State has an absolute moral value for us, like a person from whom all others derive their value, which, coinciding with that of the State, is absolute too. Think about this: human life is sacred. Why? Man is spirit, and as such he has an absolute value. Things are means, men ends. And yet the life of the citizen, when the laws of the Fatherland demand it, must be sacrificed. Without these evident truths, planted then in the heart of every citizen, there is no social life, nor a human one.

Ethical state? Liberals balk at it. They do not come to clear grips with this concept; so they raise the loudest protests, and appeal to traditions whose principles are the negation of every moral reality, even if they derive from a concern for moral order; and they run headlong after that materialism which belongs precisely to the century in which the liberal doctrine was formulated.

Liberals are opposed to morality as an attribute of concrete individuality, which is the only true will, the only personality in the true sense of the term; and the State is nothing if not the external limit of free individual personalities, whose activities it must conciliate, forbidding that the one be realized at the expense of the other. This negative and empty concept of the State, it rejects fascism resolutely; not only because it presumes placing the State above the individual; but because, according to the already mentioned teaching of Mazzini, it is not possible to conceive of the individual in an abstract atomism that the State should then compose into an impossible synthesis. We think that the State is the same personality as the individual, divested of accidental differences, removed from abstract preoccupations with particular interests, not seen and not taken into account in the general system in which their reality is, and the possibility of their effective guarantee; personality brought back and concentrated in its deepest consciousness, where the individual feels the general interest as his own, and wants therefore what is equivalent to the general will. This deep consciousness that every one of us realizes and must realize within himself as the national consciousness in its dynamism, with its juridical form, in its political activity, this very basis of our individuality, this is the State. And to conceive of it outside of the moral life is to deprive the individual himself of the essence of his morality.

The fascist's ethical State, of course, is no longer the agnostic State of old liberalism. Its ethical nature is spirituality: personality which is awareness; system which is will. And by system is meant thought, program. It means the history of a people brought together in the living flame of an actual and active consciousness. It means the concept of what is, can, and must be; it means mission and proposition, in general and in particular, far and near, mediate and immediate, totally determinate. The State is the great will of the nation; and consequently the great intelligence. It is aware of everything; and does not keep aloof from anything that touches on the interest of the citizen, which is its interest: neither economically, nor morally. *Nihil humani a se alienum putat.*[10] The State is neither a great facade, nor an empty edifice: it is man himself; the house is built and inhabited and made live by the joy and sorrow of the work and all the life contained within the human spirit.

Against the Accusation of Statolatry

Is it statolatry? It is the religion of the spirit, which has not run headlong into the abject blindness of materialism. It is the torch shaken by the young fascist fist in order to ignite a vast spiritual fire in this Italy that has woken up suddenly, I repeat, and fights for its own redemption. But one cannot be redeemed if one does not restore one's moral strength internally, does not habituate oneself to conceiving of one's entire life religiously, does not train oneself in the virile simplicity of a citizen who is always ready, without hesitancy, to serve the ideal, to work, to live, and to die for the Fatherland, as the most important idea, venerable, sacred; and does not like the military life and school which make people strong, or work as the source of every national and private prosperity, the gymnasium of will and character.

[10]*Nihil humani...*: Latin for "it deems nothing related to man as alien to itself."

Fascism and the Proletariat

And fascism, rebellious in a more intransigent way to the myths and lies of the internationalist socialism of those without a fatherland and without duties, exacerbator of the feeling of rights and therefore of individuality in the name of an abstract and empty ideal of human brotherhood; fascism, which this strong ethical State conceives of not as the suffocating lead weight of every germ that ferments in the spontaneous life of the nation, but rather as the supreme form and the conscious and present unity of all national forces in their greatest successive development; fascism does not turn around and chase from the political scene the proletariat, who was introduced there and exalted by socialism. The ethical State must rise up from the same reality and as a result adhere to it; and from this adherence it must derive its strength and its power. So today fascism works hard to reorganize the proletariat on the foundation of the nation and in perfect accord with its moral concept of the State; and longs for a form of government that, removing the State from the conventional lie of the old parliament of professional politicians, erects in its place a structure that is all the more lasting and solid as all the social, economic, and intellectual forces are more dynamic, whence the country's healthy and wholesome political currents arise.

I will not go into particulars, which could be corollaries to the fascist doctrine, but which are not fascism. It is not the corollaries that give historical significance to our movement. Its importance is in the idea, in the animating spirit; that spirit against which, we are sure of it, *portae inferi non praevalebunt.*[11]

Fascism is Religion

Gentlemen, fascism is a party, a political doctrine. But fascism, – and this is its strength; those who as yet have not wrapped their head around it, they know it; this is its great merit, and the secret of the prestige that it exercises on all minds that are not victims of the malicious and interminable chatter of certain journals – the more it is a party, a political doctrine, the more it is above all a total conception of life. One cannot be a fascist in politics and not a fascist at school, at home, at work, as I just now reminded people at the local branch of the Fascio. As a Catholic, if one is a Catholic, one invests one's entire life with religious sentiment, and, whether speaking and working, or being quiet with oneself and thinking and meditating, or whether welcoming and nourishing feelings, if one is truly a Catholic, and has a religious sense, one will always be reminded by loud bells going off in one's head to work and to think and to pray and to meditate and to feel like a Catholic; so too the fascist, he goes to parliament, or he stays within his Fascio, he writes in his journals or he reads them, he attends to his private life or he converses with others, he looks to the future or he remembers his past and the past of his people, but he must always remember to be a fascist!

[11] *Portae inferi...*: Latin for "the gates of hell will not prevail."

Thus one fulfills what can truly be called the characteristic of fascism: taking life seriously. Life is fatigue, it is effort, it is sacrifice, it is hard work; a life in which, as we well know, there is nothing to be amused about, one has no time to be amused.

Ever before us stands an ideal to be realized; an ideal that does not let up. We cannot waste time. Even asleep, we must respond with the talents that have been entrusted to us. We must make them bear fruit, not for ourselves who are nothing, but for our country, for the Fatherland, for this Italy that fills our heart with its memories and with its aspirations, with its joys and with its travails, which reprimands us for the centuries that our fathers wasted, but which recomforts us with recent memories, when the Italian effort appears a miracle; when all Italy is concentrated in one thought, in one sentiment, in one desire of sacrifice. And it was precisely the young, it was the young Italy of the Prophet, who were ready, ran to the sacrifice, and died for the Fatherland. Died for the ideal that only men can die for, for which men can feel the seriousness of life. And thinking of these recent memories in which all the memories of our race are concentrated, in which and from which all hope for our future takes its origins, we who have Italian consciousness, fascist consciousness, we feel incapable of not seeing our six-hundred thousand dead always before our eyes, having risen up to admonish us that life must be taken seriously, that there is no time to lose, that Italy must be made great as they saw it in their last dream, as it must be great and will be great, if we too sacrifice ourselves for it, day after day, forever and always.

II. Fascism and Sicily[12]

Gentlemen,

As a Sicilian Minister, on this electoral eve, I wanted to come and speak in Sicily, not to defend the Government and fascism here, which here also are presented with the confident awareness of encountering the inevitable recognition of time well spent for the fortunes of the Fatherland; but rather, in Palermo, to fascism and the Government, I mean to the entire nation which has placed all its trust in the Government and is now convinced of the fatal necessity of reinvigorating its power by means of the normal historical guarantee of its constitutional forms, and of increasing therefore the effectiveness of them with the explicit manifestation of universal consensus, to defend, I say, Sicily.

You know this: it is said too often about our Sicily, as with the rest of Southern Italy, that it was not spiritually prepared for fascism; that the national party has consequently superficial roots and a miserable life here, not responding to a real demand by the country. Here indeed it would not have been preceded by those social and political movements that elsewhere corrupted public life, and in reaction to which fascism rose up; the stronger and more vital the movements, the greater the upheaval it reacted against. It is said that that long and insistent corrosion

[12]Original footnote: Discourse held at the Teatro Massimo di Palermo on March 31, 1924, on the occasion of the general political elections.

of the State and of the national consciousness, which was exercised in other Italian provinces by socialism in all its forms and degenerations, is missing in Sicily. The malady is absent; so how can the medicine have any effect? And why should anyone resort to it? Fascism, I have heard it stated with great confidence on multiple occasions, does not exist in Sicily because the enemy didn't exist there, which fascism was born to combat. – Simplistic judgment, and for that reason unjust; against which Sicilians must rebel by that indomitable pride, by that proud dignity that has always been the generous note of their character.

Against this judgment I protest with the disposition of both a Sicilian and an Italian: as a Sicilian who recognizes the spirit of this land, and that of the entire Risorgimento, throughout the entire exhausting journey of this new Italy, which still shivers with youthful eagerness and longing for its future, it has always despised being in second place, and aspires to march at the forefront; and now this spirit, even from a distance, has felt a daily palpitation around itself, impatient of delays, desirous of moral renovation and political reconstruction, not only in the near interests of the region, but for that of the great Fatherland, always more dear to the Sicilian than his island itself.

But I protest also as an Italian, who has studied the formation of the national soul, who knows in what solid structure the old regional forms are united, cemented, and fused together in the unique and compact temperament of a new consciousness, present in every province, dominating over every particular tendency: the entire Italian soul, and as such working for everyone equally in what can be called the history of the nation.

It is a simplistic judgment for various reasons. In the first place, socialism, which fascism is opposed to, is only one of the forms of the democratic degeneration of contemporary political society and represents in fact only one of the mental forms that the fascist spirit runs up against. Nor can it be said that all socialism is the target of the violent blows of fascism; and one must clearly distinguish between socialism and socialism, indeed between ideas and ideas of the same socialist conception, in order to see in that its opposite and the enemy of the fascist movement. In fact, it is noted that Sorelian[13] syndicalism, which is without a doubt one of the sources from which fascism's thought and political method derive, wanted to be the genuine interpretation of Marxist communism. And the dynamic conception of history and function which is contained in it is owing to strength as well as to violence, and is all of a pure Marxist origin; even if it is connected with other trends of contemporary thought, which by other paths has arrived equally at the justification of that ruthless but absolutely rational kind of reason of State, which is the historical necessity of the spiritual dynamism that realizes it. Fascism combats Marx's abstract classist conception of society, shaking off the antithesis on which the artificial myth of class struggle rested: conception already demolished by critical theory, which Marxism succumbed to with the same rapidity that earlier it had come into so high and vast a consideration, but which

[13]Sorelian: after Georges Sorel (AD 1847-1922), the French revolutionary syndicalist.

loudly it had given the lie to, later, in practice, by the most imposing fact of war which, constraining individual societies to abandon all ideology in order to adapt to reality and the internal and indeclinable logic of its own organic structure, demonstrated the moral and economical solidarity and intimate unity of the constituent classes of the social and statal organism.

Fascists fight then that [aspect] of Marxism that Mazzini had already fought with apostolic ardor: Mazzini, the prophet of our Risorgimento and, through multiple aspects of his doctrine, the teacher of today's fascism: the utilitarian, materialistic, and therefore egotistical conception of life, understood as a field of rights to be claimed, instead of the palestra of duties to fulfill, with the sacrifice of oneself for an ideal. This Marxism that restricted the horizons of thought and the human heart and represented history like a great theater of economic interests, Fascist doctrine has the merit of combatting it precisely with Giuseppe Mazzini's method: not by words and with abstract theoretical arguments, but with action, with the ideal that actuates and inculcates in young hearts.

In any case, it is wrong to characterize the socialist party as the generically anti-nationalistic and subversive adversary of the fascist party. It is only one of its adversaries. Every socialist is anti-nationalistic, but not every anti-nationalist is socialist. And if a socialist was and is subversive due to presumption, it may be that socialists are or were in fact less subversive than certain presumed men of order, who declared themselves registered with one of the thousand and one categories of the great, too great, liberal party. Socialism, which we combat principally, is that doctrine for which socialists come to find themselves on the same terrain as the many who call themselves their enemies: that doctrine, for which on so many occasions recently we have seen them look at each other with very eloquent smiles of reciprocal understanding, the socialist cherishers of the communist regime and deniers of the family on the one hand, and the ardent supporters and champions of property rights and the institution of the family, like the popularists, on the other. That doctrine, whereby the political party that boasted among its major titles the patronage of religious interests and in particular national Catholicism, could very often become allied with that old radical brand of inferior democratism, entirely based on Free Masonry, or rather on generically irreligious and specifically anticlerical abstract rationalism. Smiles and alliances of equivocal significance and of sure and rapid failure, but born of a common principle of the valuation of social and political life and from the same doctrine: that doctrine, which led Italian parliamentary socialists to the absurd extreme of fighting for the defense of parliamentary institutions, appropriate forms of guarantee of the liberal bourgeois society, and which led all the grey mediocrity of the detritus of various parties of Montecitorio in the insistent search, many times failed but always renascent, of a common denominator, by which they could become united and form a majority and a governing class of some sort: the denominator of democracy.

Who, in recent times, outside the House, succeeded more in following all the democratic formations and distinctions and subdistinctions that every day came to form within it? Each faction strove to rescue I don't know what unqualified principle, which meanwhile resigned itself to drowning in the vast vortex of the substantive: social democracy, liberal democracy, Italian democracy, with the first being wrong not to call itself liberal and Italian, and the second to refuse the characterization of Italian and social, and the third, that of social and liberal: while they were all lumped together under one banner, which so many other factions in the House who preferred the appellation of liberals were wrong to gather under. Since what they all obscurely meant by democracy was what everyone knew: what by now must be quite dead, or which must at all costs die in the field of Italian political life: the subjection of the superior interests of the nation and the State to the various, contrasting, chaotic interests of classes, of categories, – in fact, speaking in the absolute sense, – of single individuals, constituting, little by little, the greatest number and however the greatest pressure on the legislative and governing bodies of the State. The individualistic doctrine, in summary, of the disintegration of the State and of all the moral forces of the nation. Among the supporters of that doctrine, whoever makes an accurate examination of Italy's most recent history, will find that they were subversives who were more antinationalistic than the socialists; and they were the main culprits of the same socialist errors, the main culprits of that senseless arrogance that it evolved into, against every interest needless to say of the same class that it presumed to represent, the socialist party, above all in the years following the war, when every star in the sky of the Fatherland appeared to fade.

But the judgment of fascism's supposed lack of roots in this sacred soil of our fearless island, whose vigorous voice has also responded in powerful chorus, by all the youthful breasts, to the call of the fasci, is also simplistic by another class of considerations. Too simple in fact is the story that explains the origin of a political or moral and, in general, spiritual movement in simple contrast to or negation of the preceding movement. The contrast can explain to us the form that is assumed by the new movement, its polemical attitude, the method of fighting that it resorts to, and so on: not the substance, not the profound motive that draws the life and the strength of the victorious principle from the innermost consciousness. Nothing is born from nothing; and from the democratic slime, where no seed is hidden, it would never be possible to see some living plant sprouting and growing, no vital shoot of political renewal appearing. The origins of fascism are diverse and much more complex than this schematic reason of contrast to the so-called Bolshevism that overflowed from the socio-political corruption of the post-war years, when nations, exhausted by enormous effort, appeared on the verge of collapsing to the ground, desperate to live again for a magnanimous idea.

To understand the reasons for fascism seems to me the best way to discredit the vile legend of Sicily being deaf to the fascist inspiration. And I entreat you, o Gentlemen, to allow me a quick look at the spiritual energies that have flowed into this vast drama, which by now assails us all, and drags us with it;

and sometimes with the greatness of success and the amplitude of consensus and enthusiasms it fills the same authors and leaders with astonishment. Drama, I'd like to call it even, which interests not just Italian life; because the secret of its passions and its significance exceeds the specific confines of one State and the historical determinations of one people, however lofty the characteristics of this people are in the hierarchy of universal history; and they touch on general human interests.

Since to become aware of this historical fact, which holds in the eyes of every spectator the certain miraculousness that the Sicilian Vespers[14] had, o Palermitans, or the triumphal battles of the Mille, which our heroic faith, in a delirium of popular exaltation, consecrated on May 29 in Piazza Pretoria,[15] the invincible martyrs of a providential idea, and which witnessed and will witness those events in every period in which, through a gifted man's intuition, faith, will, and genius, great spiritual movements ripen – one must not stop at the daily news article, at the ephemeral and occasional contingencies out of which illuminating scintillas of consciousness radiate, ready and disposed for creative action. One needs to look at the remote sources of current ideals, which slowly converged to form these consciousnesses.

[14]Sicilian Vespers: in reference to the Sicilian overthrow of French-born king Charles I of Anjou and his rule there, in AD 1282.

[15]*Mille*... May 29: in reference to the assistance given to Sicily in AD 1860 by Giuseppi Garibaldi and his Thousand (Mille) volunteers intent on, and successful in, overthrowing the Bourbon rule there.

I have heard it said that fascism is not a doctrine, does not have a philosophy; that, being opposed to the disintegrating forces of popular and socialist demagogy, fascism, with the energy of a moral force, to which great merit is attributed, and which everyone in fact appears disposed to recognize in it, is a return to liberal doctrine, to its wholesome concept of the strong State, ready to subordinate individual interests to all general interests, and to oppose the inviolable rule of law to the will of individuals. I am not of this opinion; because I make it a point primarily not to confuse doctrine or philosophy with systematic explanations that can be made in words in well-constructed treatises; in fact, I am convinced that true doctrine is what, more than in words or in books, expresses itself in action, in the personality of men, and in the attitude that they assume when faced with problems; and which is a much more serious solution to the problems themselves than someone who disserts in the abstract and preaches and theorizes. False theory. True theory is always a praxis, a form of life: and the man himself is committed, not for a blind fatality of instinct certainly, but for conscious convictions and matured propositions supported by an intuition made certain of the end to which he needs to tend; committed by a yes or by a no, much more effective in each clearer affirmation or negation than speculative philosophy. What more resolute negation of the value of life is there than suicide? And what more energetic affirmation of its value, than the solitary sacrifice of the citizen who dies for the Fatherland, which is the perpetuation of a concrete ideal of life?

Let us leave books to the side then, and let us

look at animating ideas and at the consequent meaning of facts, which are before us in the great book of history with a much greater impressiveness than any more elaborated doctrinal description. And first of all let's exclude, if anything, that the fascist doctrine of the State coincides with liberal doctrine. This doctrine, which it is high time that our adversaries decided to specify the scope and principles of, given that it is true that there is a liberal doctrine that coincides with the fascist doctrine of the State; but it is also true that many liberals today refuse to recognize this coincidence, and in so doing they demonstrate that there is a way of speaking about another kind of liberalism, that it would be better for them to distinguish absolutely from the other, which it is at least licit for fascism to approach. Even if we limit ourselves to considering the history of Italian liberalism alone, from 1820 or '21, when the principle of a doctrine that could be called liberal began establishing itself in a positive way, until 1922, during the entire period in which it developed in the ascending and descending parabola of its internal development, we now find ourselves before very different forms and types of liberalism. There were liberals in the old Italian parliament, after Cavour, to the left and right: conservatives or moderates, as they were called; and progressives, who held out their hand later to the radicals. To the right and to the left, all liberals, and even amongst themselves proudly divided and adverse, to the point where men of the right, like Spaventa and De Meis, could be offended and scandalized after March 1876 by what appeared to them the rashness of their very dear De Sanctis, friend of Ricasoli and now the supporter of a Cairoli.[16] And on the same historical right, between a Catholic and Catholicizer like Massari or Bonghi and a rationalist like Spaventa, did the disagreements and contrasting ideals not prevail perhaps over affinities and a common direction? And to return to the first fathers of the Italian liberal doctrine, is it possible perhaps to associate, as animated by an identical political credence, Gioberti, the restorer of civility in religion and of religion in civility, and Cavour the first champion of the theory of absolute separation between Church and State, which is even a form of political agnosticism of classical liberalism? And Ricasoli, with his Tuscan dictatorship and his theory of freedom in the rigid constraint of public legality, is himself comparable perhaps to his great precursor, Camillo di Cavour, fervid believer in a system of individualistic liberalism in the English way, and on the basis of the liberalistic conception of economists? And in our days, the conservative liberalism of a Salandra is perhaps comparable to the democratic and socialistic left-leaning liberalism, i.e., utilitarianistically oriented and accommodating, of a Giolitti? When I said several months ago that true liberalism was that of Mussolini, I saw that my statement caused great displeasure to many self-styled liberals; but those gentlemen were wrong to be contented by a phrase that, by having too much signification, will finish by no longer having any at all.

Which liberalism do we wish to talk about? I distinguish two main forms of this doctrine; for one of which – and I want to borrow the same words used

[16]Cairoli: Benedetto Cairoli (AD 1825-1889), an Italian politician, prime minister of Italy from 1879-1881.

by the Hon. Mussolini in his discourse at the Teatro Costanzi – freedom is a right, and for the other it is a duty; for the one it is a generous gift, for the other a conquest; for the one it is equality, for the other a privilege and a hierarchy of values. One liberalism locates the root of freedom in the individual, and contrasts consequently the individual against the State, which does not have an intrinsic value any longer, but serves for the wellbeing and improvement of the individual: a means and not an end. It limits itself to the maintenance of public order, resting outside of every spiritual life, closed in the interior sphere of individual consciousness. This liberalism is, historically, classical liberalism, of English origin. And, I immediately add, false liberalism, or containing only a half truth. It was fought amongst us by Mazzini with a criticism that I consider immortal.

But there is another liberalism, matured by Italian and German thought, which calls this fantastical antagonism between the State and the individual absurd, observing how everything that has value in the individual and that can claim to be guaranteed and promoted, by the very fact that it is put forward as a right, has universal reach and expresses a will and an interest superior to the will and to the interest of the individual; what matters is a will and a common personality, which comes to be the ethical substance of the individual. For this liberalism, freedom is indeed the supreme end and the norm of every human life: but only insofar as individual and social education completes it, actuating in the individual this common will, which manifests itself as law, and therefore as the State. Which is not for all that a superstructure that imposes itself from the outside on individual activity and initiative in order to subject it to restrictive coercion; instead, it is its very essence, at the head of a suitable process of formation and development: as is proper for everything that constitutes the greatness and glory of man, which is never a natural and immediate quality, but the result of a persevering effort whereby the individual, overcoming his natural inclinations that drag him down, elevates himself toward the heights of his dignity. The State and the individual are, in this respect, one; and the art of governing is the art of conciliating and unifying the two terms, in such a way that the maximum extent of freedom is conciliated with the maximum extent, not only of the purely external public order, but also and above all of the consented sovereignty of the law and its necessary organs. In that the maximum extent of freedom always coincides with the maximum extent of the force of the State.

What force? The distinctions in this area are dear to those who are not satisfied with this concept of force, which is also essential to the State, and therefore to freedom. And they distinguish between moral force and material force: the force of the law freely voted on and accepted, and the force of violence that rigidly opposes itself to the will of the citizen. Ingenuous distinctions, if in good faith! Every force is a moral force, because it always refers to the will; and whatever the adopted argument might be – of preaching by the bludgeon[17] – its effectiveness can

[17]Original footnote: this phrase ["preaching by the bludgeon"] has struck the fantasy of many good people, who got it from the preceding and following periods and put it into circulation as the

be none other than what finally solicits a man internally and persuades him to consent. Whatever the nature of this argument might be, it is not a topic of abstract discussion. Every educator knows this perfectly well, that the means of acting on the will must vary according to temperaments and circumstances. The key thing to acknowledge seriously is that freedom cannot be had outside the State, and that the State is not the will of the first person to come along, but a living norm, that reins in all wills, and realizes in so-

---

motto characteristic of I do not know what apology of violence. Thus, the phrase has had some success; and for the many who do not read, or it seems like they do not read, or they take pleasure only reading satirical newspapers or the funnies, I have for some time now become the champion of I do not know what "philosophy of the bludgeon." It must be a phrase then that lends itself to equivocation; and I would definitely suppress it if I did not fear other, even more annoying equivocations. The material force to which I attributed a moral value – the context is clear – is not that of the private citizen, but that of the State: the force that everyone has acknowledged and respected as moral under the species of the armed force of the State, which is not armed in order to make sermons. The bludgeon of fascist squadrismo wanted to be and was the vindicating force of the State unacknowledged by the central organs themselves and categorically denied of its constituted powers. It was, that is, the necessary surrogate of the same force of the State in a revolutionary period, when, according to the logic of all revolutions, the State was in a crisis and its power gradually shifted from its fictitious and legal organs to real and illegal organs but tending to legality. Therefore it happens that on the day after the March on Rome the first problem of fascism was the suppression of squadrismo, which became the voluntary militia: that is, the same armed force of before, but accepted among the legal forces of the State. And the bludgeon was put back into the attic with the hope that it no longer needed to come out. Just as it will never come out again if all Italians, fascists or not, convince themselves of the necessity and duty to come together, altogether, in the consolidation of the regime that is in the process of realization and therefore moving past the revolution.

ciety and in the very consciousness of every citizen the irresistible dominion of an iron law.

Let us place a hand over our bosom and confess that this concept of the State stands before us like an ideal; and that ordinarily we are disposed to recognize from the bottom of our heart that this ideal is too high, unreachable; and that the law is, yes, the law if it responds to a general interest and if it makes itself respected absolutely – but all that in abstract and, in other words, when it does not harm our particular interest. Which instead, when harmed, it is only too natural that we should have the right to request an exception for ourselves. Therefore, the *exhortation!* Liberal gentlemen, be honest: this was your freedom; this was your law, this your State, fallen and sullied through lauded liberal institutions, in the deplorable abuses of parliamentarianism: extreme prostration not only of our public life, but, indirectly, of our entire national consciousness. Yes, fascism, on this point, coincides with liberalism – with this second form of liberalism, which sees no individual a subject of freedom other than he who feels the higher interests of the community and the sovereign will of the state beating in his heart. But, all the same, between liberalism and fascism there remains this difference: that fascism says these things in earnest, in other words it does them; while liberalism, in its reduced capacity, only said them. Which is a big difference.

But what gave to fascism the energy that the same liberalism of the strong State was missing, on this point of common doctrine? First of all, the masses, which almost immediately rallied around the pennants of the Fasci; whereas the theory of the strong State was a more or less intellectual dogma of some solitary thinker lost among the sparse ranks of liberals, misunderstood by them, conveniently left to subside in the indeterminate and empty formula of abstract freedom. Fascism is a mass movement, and that liberalism was a simple philosophical doctrine, not always clearly formulated, in the head of some cultivated politician. That is the difference, which is not to be considered simply quantitative; because an idea that animates a mass of people is an idea that has become a passion, capable consequently of communicating itself to the many: and it became a passion, because it is not simply an idea accommodated in a logical system, inside a brain; but it is the energetic consciousness of a personality: it is this same personality that in its universal human value becomes the center of spiritual irradiation. In this way passion breaks out into action, which is life, the manifestation of the personality, and invests reality, and enters into its weft, and becomes intertwined and fuses indissolubly with all the forces living and operating in the world. For this reason fascism recognizes a leader, as no other party does: a leader, who is a living doctrine, a highly gifted and privileged soul; in whom the formula is transformed into action, but it is always a formula, an ideal, universal thought, which unifies and disciplines a multitude of men and consequently creates a powerful social and political force.

And how did a doctrine become passion and action?

What precisely is the immediate origin of fascism? Fascism is the child of war; and for this reason, which I have already mentioned, that the explanation of fascist doctrine is to be found more in events than in books: in events, which are ideally more meaningful than the much-better constructed theories. Since war, o Gentlemen, has many aspects; and for that reason it is very easy to see it in a light that represents it as a simple historical fatality, as a prosaic consequence of inevitable economic contrasts of State or plutocratic groups, as the collision of civil society and ideology, etc., etc.; like everything, except that great spiritual event, which has profoundly roused all the clods, so to speak, of the people's mentality and feeling, and tossed into souls the new seeds of life and new needs; new ideas and new beliefs, in other words. But this is precisely, if well reflected on, the historically more important aspect from which the war is to be viewed. It is immediately seen from this observation, which I think is obvious, this: that if out of the war came both vanquished and victors, and victors who won and victors who lost, with very notable effects on the economy undoubtedly, and on all the rather diverse or contrary lives of the various peoples; everyone, nevertheless, out of the war, both vanquished and victors of every sort, derived a new spirit. We Italians, we who exited as victors of the war, we who were the first architects of the victory of the Entente, we found ourselves, who could deny it? with a new soul: and I say "we," thinking of the Italians who wanted the war, and wanted it with faith, and lived it, and felt the sacred value of it day after day, through the most bitter sorrows and the jubilation of victory. But reflect, o

Gentlemen: even if fortune had been inimical to us, even among the misfortunes that would have fallen on the shoulders of the Italian people, do you believe that morally this war, this great heroic proof, this trial of sacrifice which was voluntarily confronted by thousands upon thousands of youth, whose memory will always be present in our hearts as the venerable holocaust of the best part of us, do you believe that it would not also have produced its great moral benefits anyways?

O Sicilians, remember your Crispi.[18] I remember him as I saw him in my young mind and with the soul in tumult for the grief of shame suffered on March 1 of '96, and for the indignation and the nausea of vile Italy, represented by the demagogues of Montecitorio cursing at the Crispian megalomania, as they called it, and by the women who, having thrown themselves across the railroad tracks, obstructed the departure of troops dispatched for the redemption and revenge of national honor; I remember him and I see him again, Crispi, alone, towering above all the craven mediocrity of little Italians; alone in believing in a great Italy, in affirming the duties and the rights; great also in adversity for magnanimous intentions and worthy of a people that had a consciousness of itself.

And the Italian people will not forget your Vittorio Emanuele Orlando for his speech delivered to the House after the ill-fated day of Caporetto;[19] because in his words Italy, then oppressed by a heart-

[18]Crispi: Francesco Crispi (AD 1818-1901) an Italian statesman and two-time prime minister.

rending anguish, refound itself and all its faith, and towered as on a day of triumph. Since people can be small in victory, and great in defeat. Their greatness, this is, their strength, that indomitable strength which is the secret source of the entire life of a nation, is born by the faith that the people, as individuals, have or must have in themselves. War exalts the soul of a people, educates it, and puts it in contact with that reality, which in war and in peace it needs to have present, and it needs to fight, in order to live and to occupy a place in history.

This war, in which six hundred thousand Italians immolated themselves, is also the first one that Italy fought with the material and moral forces of the entire nation: the first that had truly united all the Italian people under one banner, at the crossroads between life and death, where there was not only existence, but honor at risk; that is, all the tradition that a people has need of, just as every gentleman has need of his name, and the entire future whose darkening would be despair even, and the end of every plan, every action, every palpitation of life. And young Italians have felt it and lived through the war in this way. And they have confusedly felt, in the forced and pensive silences of the trenches, a new life, a new Italy, dawning in their chest and pullulating: a young Italy, already a beautiful idea in the generous heart of the Genovese apostle, but now become a reality; a living reality, full of potential; a pulsating life of feelings and new needs to be satisfied. The incoercible needs of a people who have demonstrated how to vote for a

[19]Caporetto: the Battle of Caporetto, Oct. 24, 1917 – Dec. 19, 1917.

luminous idea, how to stand on its own two feet even improvisatorially, even unprepared, ready for the call of the Fatherland, prepared for every more difficult discipline, for death even. Italy, which Mazzini had correctly predicted as the future Italy, gathered altogether in a religious conception of life and firm in the profound conviction of the formula: "thought and action;" i.e., in the belief and in the feeling that true thought is action, and that the old Italy of saying one thing and doing another is moreover quite dead, the Italy of cultivated intelligence and bright ideas, but without a will, without a character, without the dignity of a people, without a national feeling, without a virile religious faith.

The hymn to Youth intoned by fascists, young and old, has this signification, o Gentlemen: it is the exaltation of this moral youth which does not distinguish between poetic theory and prosaic practice, and it does what it says, and believes, and seriously wants, and keeps the faith. Not all fascists, I am quick to admit, feel the youth they sing within themselves in this way. But tell me, o Gentlemen: who would have rallied and led the Blackshirts[20] to Rome, and what force of cohesion would have animated millions of Italians and kept them united, who now want to remain in Fasci, if an obscure but powerful sentiment had not seized their minds? A unique sentiment, all the more powerful the more obscure it is, that is, the more felt and lived it is: a feeling that is not egotistical, in that it is capable of associating and fraternizing, but root-

[20]Blackshirts: the voluntary militia or paramilitary groups that organized for national (originally local) security, aka the squadristi. Called as such for the black-colored shirts they wore.

ed in that universal faith in an ideal of moral beauty, in that spring of beauty, that stirs and inebriates hearts?

All this psychology, which is also a doctrine, sprang out of the war. And for that reason we all have the sensation that a new life has begun for Italy. The which has fulfilled its revival not by closing a historical period, but by paving the way for a new one, in which we realize and feel that the revival really is not complete: that we are now at the start of our national life, and that we must work, that we must arm ourselves, in our mind and in our heart; we must restore and promote our scientific knowledge, we must remake our soul, we must gain full consciousness of our mission. Imperial mission, not so much outside the country, – where Italy, this great mother of the people, must also expand in order to live, – as primarily within the country, in the national consciousness that must be raised to its level, which our patrimony of civilization and culture, and our huge treasure of human strength, gives us not only the right, but also the duty [to fulfill].

This fulfillment of the Mazzinian prophecy is a fact that the war was moreover able to produce because, spiritually prepared in Italy more than in other countries by a new national education, by the new orientation of minds, produced by the conception of life, it prevailed over the positivism of the preceding century for twenty-five years or so now. A sort of natural elective affinity made socialists reciprocally in the past seek out every sort of demagogue on the one hand, and positivists on the other. Some intellectual of socialism, rather versed in the history of the Marxism, like Antonio Labriola, grew indignant at these connections and recalled the Hegelian origins of so-called critical communism, unintelligible of course to anyone inexpert in the history of absolute idealism. But, to be honest, Marxism was born from Hegelianism by reason of contrast, turning, as Karl Marx liked to say, the idea on its head. And with all his false dialectic there was a naturalistic doctrine of the human world: a vision of history from a mechanistic point of view, which is a category in certain respects adequate for the understanding of economic facts. All which ideas are justifiable only on the positivistic terrain. A close kinship bound socialism and positivism together. And propped up that rationalistic conception, the unadulterated legacy of the XVIIIth century, that a vast association, insinuated into all Italian public life since 1860, counterposed to clericalism by defense of the sovereignty of the new liberal laical State, incapable of piercing the outer skin and discovering the kernel of religiosity within, which is essential to the human spirit, and without which every faith withers and life becomes a game of brute force. Italy, on the day after the formation of the Kingdom, having only just exited the heroic period of the Risorgimento, had quite a strong spiritual leaning; and the Italian culture of between 1860 and 1880 appeared to lift itself up to an admirable height, making the presence of this people felt in all the world of international knowledge, who had formerly thought themselves withered after the great flowering of the Renaissance. But this outburst began gradually to decline and become attenuated. The Italian soul appeared to turn inward and close itself in a passive imitation of foreign knowledge, without any originality. The heroic poetry of Carducci gave way to an art of reflection, in the manner of the decadents. Faith languished in the political arena and in the innermost consciousness [of the people].

But in the three lustrums preceding the war things had already changed. I don't want to suggest, and even less do I wish to praise, this or that philosophical system. It is enough for me to point out the spiritual reawakening of the faceless multitude of youth who began then to grow passionate and to discuss idealistic conceptions of life, who began to feel a disgust for the vulgar bourgeois positivism of their fathers, not enjoying anymore, as a low and vile thing, that socialism which had already warmed so many hearts, wishing instead for a lofty purpose in life, thinking highly of the fatherland, putting the enduring nation above the citizens who die; respecting religion as a serious thing and something to be studied. The atmosphere had changed: it came alive and was bracing, already reinvigorating youthful lungs. People asked about ideas; they wanted to understand; they aspired to noble things; they felt that real life, which encourages us to live finally, is not what one finds opening one's eyes to the light, but what must be created hour after hour, by our will, by our intelligence, by our heart: an ideal that shines a great distance, and which it is up to us to draw near to, moving toward it.

This redemption of the belief in the values of the spirit was the great youthful reserve, which the government of Antonio Salandra could rely on in 1915; it was the flame that lit up and sustained souls with its heat during the war; when the arrogance of skeptics, of good or bad faith, could never be right about that solid belief in the final victory; and it is the fundamental doctrine of modern fascism, that did not permit, will no longer permit that Italy should fall into the skeptical bureaucracy of the antebellum period again, that the glorious banner should be lowered, and that Italians might return to smiling with rhetoric and practicing it, and that they might be content giving proof of their superiority of mind by shrugging their shoulders.

This, according to me, is the great novelty. This, the novelty that since October 1922[21] the Italian nation feels more or less like an incontestable and intangible conquest of the Italian people. The which conquest, I immediately add, for the tranquility of the usual adversaries who have grown tired of that type of forced march that the Prime Minister Mussolini's legislative and governmental action has in some cases seemed like, is not a beautiful and foregone conquest; to the effect that some among them keep repeating in a low voice that the mission of fascism is already fulfilled or close to being fulfilled; with the consequences, of course, which these benevolent critics love to draw from their thesis and which remains in their heart perhaps even more than their thesis. No. The work of fascism cannot be measured merely by laws enacted, by provisions adopted, by reforms put into action; ar-

[21]October 1922: scil., when the March on Rome occurred.

eas in which the fascist government has worked a great deal, as you know, and with so much passion and ardor to restore the State's finances, to discipline the bureaucratic organs, to restore order, to give life and motion and fresh air to education and a truly spiritual content and moral dynamic to the instruction of new generations, to give a solid unity and an adequate efficiency to the army and navy, to endow the nation with a well trained system of aerial defense, to reorganize and guarantee the administration of justice, to give back freedom and energy to the national economy, to reinvigorate and improve public services. But in all these areas, in which Italy has made perhaps more legislative progress in the last year than it had made in the sixty or more years of the Kingdom, the work of the Government has been only a launch, a vigorous stimulus given to the administrative life of the State. The details may require some revision. But what matters most is that the work be continued, that it be assisted, watched over, and governed always with a spirit that will give life and productivity to the mechanisms employed: without which these mechanisms could early on be allowed to rust in order to demonstrate that they can function poorly and that hope was placed in them in vain; and then one would begin to dismantle them in order to return to the old [mechanisms]. Those mechanisms will have need of modifications and adaptations; but that will be possible provided the same plan, the same mindset, continues to employ them and to direct them to the goal, which can be none other than the goal of fascism.

The which plan, more than in a certain number of determinate ideas, is a tendency, a doctrine, a spirit. Tomorrow this spirit will be able to use different means than today; but it will guide them to march down the same path, which it resolutely pursues today with the entire nation. The fascist doctrine and system is likened to the moral education of the human race: a perpetual education, an eternal education, for whoever does not possess the faith, because the work of education can never be complete; indeed, one of its essential characteristics is this, to be accompanied by the awareness that it can never be considered complete. If it is truly only the ideal, as the poet said, then the great artisan will never be able to put the final touches on his masterpiece; and the nation will need perpetually to renew its youthfulness, with its vigor, its ardent aspiration for something better, its eyes filled with its visions, with untiring arms extended toward the goal. I do not consider this a privilege for fascism: but rather duty, mission, which cannot be renounced without betraying itself in its most characteristic value.

It will be said that by assuming such an attitude fascism is not a party, but identifies itself with the very essence of the State in its universality; and it becomes immortal in fact, because the State is immortal; whereas parties fade or change, representing various interests that the State embraces and various points of view whereby these views can be dealt with. – An observation that is both true and false at the same time, which, all things considered, can be said as much about fascism as about every other political system and party. True for the man who positions himself above parties, or presumes to put himself above them in order to have a means to judge and condemn the opposite party: but false for the man who actually puts himself in a position to judge a party by living it, but also by belonging to it, if only ideally. The man who actually puts himself above all parties does not have a party: he is not a political man. To be such, he ought to take, if nothing else, a part for himself, like Dante: which is another way of joining a party; which, it also, for whoever wants to join it, will be the only true party, and therefore deserving of always prevailing. Even this history of parties, all true and all false and destined as such to change, is antifascist doctrine, by those who do not have a belief to defend and cannot admit that others have one.

Fascism will undergo transformation; as everything does that is alive, it will change. But fascism must continue and will continue to develop its plan as long as Italians remember their young men who died for the Fatherland; that is, died for them: died, while believing that the life of every one of us is bound to the life of others, of the children and nephews in perpetuity of the Fatherland, which alone lives, and survives, and merits surviving. It will last as long as Italians feel that the youth cut down on the Carso, on the Isonzo, or on the Piave, teem again at the bottom of their heart like a duty to be fulfilled.

This, o Gentlemen, is fascism. And do we want to doubt that even on this initiative island of ours, on this land that has always given everything to the Fatherland, generous like youth, and has almost never asked for anything in return, this island that has always been among the first regions in Italy to pay and among the last to gain, among the first always to say that the ideal is true and that the individual must sacrifice himself for it – o heroic souls of the Trabia brothers, flowers, most noble symbol of the old and glorious Sicilian soul! – do we want to doubt that fascism has found the terrain already tilled and ready to receive and nourish the seed of this new national life? Must I tell the story of the not only numerical, but moral, contribution of our island to the great war, in which all nations and all regions gave proof of their temperament? Or must I illustrate how profoundly Sicilian the pre-fascist Francesco Crispi was at heart, and how alive with Crispian soul Sicily is in the more illuminated and respected and authoritative part of the Sicilian ruling class; especially here, in Palermo, where his shadow has never departed?

Even in Sicily, up to now, are opposed, as in nearly every other Italian province, strata still thick with the old detritus of the corrupt politics of parliamentarian or parochial clientelism; and around them halos of political prejudices diffused by the current, pseudo-democratic mentality of the period before the war. In every city, in every village, the young find themselves faced with a certain number of old men, who smile and tell stories, rigid in their adherence to the usual manipulators and traffickers who do not admit defeat. At times, unfortunately, the young are relatively few.

Gentlemen, even the Mille were few; but they were strong; and their strength was entirely moral; there was an idea; a true idea; one of those ideas that cannot perish. Young Sicilians, do not count yourselves, and do not count your adversaries. You are the bearers of a renovating spirit, that will make them numerous, armed with an invincible faith, the phalanges that will sweep away, have no doubt about it, all these worm-eaten carcasses that still encumber circles and plazas. Raise your pennons high; that they might be seen by everyone against the backdrop of our very pure sky, where your soul ranges, unaware or contemptuous of transactions and business affairs, enamored by what makes men and people great, through their tenacious work, animated by a noble aim, without feminine weakness, without laughable vanity, without swindles, without cunning, with the fierce pride of meriting and conquering.

Our Sicily, superabundant in every most powerful energy, the fountain of every richest intellectual and moral reserve for the Italian fatherland, in the first half of the century of national life it lifted itself up by virtue of its elders, wishing at the cost of any sacrifice not to appear to be less than other more fortunate, sister regions. But in industry and agriculture, in systems of communication and in the organization of public safety, in the fight against malaria and in the instruction of the people, it hasn't yet had the time or the means to reform, to reconstruct, or to consolidate the base, on which nearly every people must erect every superior moral structure. Sicily, in such regards, continues to wait for its redemption. The national government for this reason extends a hand. But the salvation rests with you, o Sicilians; primarily with you, young fascists, who give us a young, strong, hard-working Sicily, firmly resolute on resolving its problems. You will start by casting your ballot on Sunday: but remember, your part will not be discharged by the vote at the electoral box. Always remember, o youth, the Man who works day and night at Palazzo Chigi, in the toil of a passion blazing for the greatness of the Fatherland, with open eyes intent, turned on you, on all Italians. To him your soul, for the future of yourselves, for the fortunes of this island, sacred to every civilized people after twenty-five centuries, for the glory of the new, victorious Italy!

III. Freedom and Liberalism[22]

Gentlemen,

My discourse will sound more like a lesson than a conference; and it will speak more of philosophy than politics. I say this up front because I don't want you to be disappointed later; because this crowded auditorium makes me think that the announced topic of my conference may have given you the impression that a targeted polemic against antifascist opposition would be heard here tonight; which would certainly be a much more interesting discourse than what I have instead proposed to give. Although I must also confess that I will be unable to speak to you without having before my mind the gentlemen of the opposition; and that all I can say is ultimately directed at them; and that the entire matter of my conference can be reduced in fact to demonstrating one thing (which could be the entire scope of the most radical polemic against liberals, who today use newspapers like soapboxes to give lessons to fascism); which is that the more they speak about freedom, the more evident it becomes that they are ignorant of the meaning of this word.

Since if this word is on everyone's lips since the beginning of time, it does not mean to say that everyone knows what it means. Does it not appear to

[22]Original footnote: [For] a conference held at the fascist University of Bologna on the evening of March 9, 1925.

you a sophistical paradox if I tell you that the words that everyone commonly uses are precisely those whose meaning is the least known. They correspond, that is, to concepts that are therefore more difficult to define. They refer to those fundamental relationships of human life that give material to the most assiduous, most intense, broadest, most systematic reflection: they are, according to philosophers, categories of thought, in other words the principles that will be adopted through the understanding of human life, as it unfailingly presents itself to everyone, and as it ought to be understood by everyone, even if in the most obscure and confused way, so that it might be experienced humanly. Thus everyone speaks about laws, about birth and death, and moving and working and thinking and wanting, and so on and so forth, which seem the clearest and most obvious and honestly within everyone's grasp; and everyone thinks himself capable of proposing determinate and particular theoretical and practical problems, primarily because he has those selfsame fundamental ideas at his disposal, without which none of the data on any such problems would be conceivable in any manner. So a person will seek out how he must act in a certain situation; but he gives no thought to understand what "action" means. And yet, at every step of the way, disputes are hidden among men and in the same practical life that they live together; and what at first appeared as clear as day becomes a matter of dispute. These ideas already employed like monetary currency have a need for examination. They become an object of reflexion, of criticism, whereby one seeks to remove difficulties; as is typically done, putting all the ideas in agreement with one another, into a coherent whole. Philosophy is born. And given that all men more or less reflect and are aware of what they say and force themselves to think without incurring contradictions, everyone more or less practices philosophy. Which has never had a definite form however, like an almost good piece of money that is worn down over time and can be put into circulation only for a certain amount of time, while the imprint lasts. No. Philosophy is an incessant and inexhaustible criticism. And one cannot say he has reached or achieved a philosophy without immediately feeling dissatisfaction, seeing the incoherences in it, being drawn to a deeper critical revision in search of a loftier philosophy. And so all men are philosophers; but the majority, constrained by the necessities of life to be content with an initial and fragmentary reflection, make use of its ideas in a way that, to the more serious reflection of those who are discontented with this vulgar and summary philosophy, cannot fail to appear arbitrary and therefore false. And if a secret instinct, an obscure but profound and universal intuition didn't assist in the weak and inadequate reflection whereby men guide themselves practically in the management of such ideas relative to the fundamental relationships of their life, if, to put it in theological terms, a divine Providence did not intervene in social events *oltre la difension de' sensi umani*,[23] this civilized world, abandoned to the incoherent and discordant and destructive forces of error, would surely go to pot. If men effectively put into practice all the errors that their intelligence leads

[23]*Oltre la difension de' sensi umani*: Italian for "beyond the reach of human understanding." It is a quote from Dante's *Inferno*, VII 81.

them to, pulled here and there by that philosophy of the hour, which is responsible for the commonest of reflections, it would fall into chaos from one day to the next. And without a doubt all the disorders that this world, which is law, harmony, and order, goes through with perpetual fatigue and toil, – all the disorders derive from the errors that a maturer, stronger, more powerful thought combats and demolishes in order to clarify human consciousness with the light that it needs.

Too philosophical a preamble? But it can be leveraged to demonstrate the practical opportunity of my discourse, which has already announced a pretext that may appear strange and is also quite simple: that in order to speak in a certain reasonable manner about this freedom, which so many mouths are filled with these days, and which also, to be honest, all men have always spoken about, one must resign oneself to practicing philosophy.

The which philosophy, moreover, has its own curious way of attracting and seducing even the least disposed of spirits. A way, which could be called automatic. Enough for it to appear before men for them to follow it. In fact, those who oppose it and do not want anything to do with it, take positions, and follow it like a shadow following a body: they are always on its heels, and laugh and sneer even, but they are always there to hear what it has to say in order to lend it a voice; and to hear what it has to say, to pay attention, to accept the problems that it puts to them, also to look up and down at them at worst in order to try to undermine them, and finally to involve itself too in the philosophical polemic, which is no more no less than philosophy. And in truth those who resist and try to close themselves off and no longer want anything to do with it, what are they doing? Isn't it the case that they have already refused philosophy; but they are contented with taking on a small piece of it in order to cover as best they can those parts of themselves most exposed as the target of criticism. As will happen today, for example, when a liberal grows upset and loses his composure by attacking whoever invites him to put the question in the right context, which can be none other than a philosophical one; but this he cannot do without affirming his ideas; and he will call himself democratic, and he will speak of popular sovereignty, and, even if he has never read a line of Rousseau, he will profess himself his follower and support, with a sympathetic philosophical cultivation, a philosophical system that, as Manzoni says, has its own good name; i.e., it has its place in the history of philosophy, where for so long a time it has been brushed to the side as deemed although not completely erroneous, insufficient and unilateral. The difference, then, can be just this: to make good philosophy, or to make bad philosophy (with or without serious preparation). Not to make any will be the illusion of writers or readers of the *Giornale d'Italia*: but nothing more than an illusion.

Every moderately educated man knows that the story of freedom is the story of tears, blood, and thought: that there has always been freedom and never been freedom; and for that reason people have always fought for it in every field of spiritual activity; and they have never carried away the victory, and never come away fully satisfied, never having quenched the thirst for new battles. Which have been fought and which have always started up again because men have not lived their life instinctively and blindly, in the manner of animals, but have always thought, and from the actual conditions of their existence they have little by little raised themselves in their thinking to a superior ideal of life, and have longed for loftier forms of freedom, which they didn't have, and which were to be acquired. This is the story of humanity: this the story of the single man from his first years to the full development of his personality in society and in the world. Thought always comes first, indicates the goal, then opens the way: action follows. And thought thus is action, and action is thought. So history is mirrored in the progress of thought which from peak to peak raises itself to the summits of the mind, where life tends. And in this mirror, which is the history of philosophy, the millenarian path of man can be seen, and the profound law of the mind that spurs him on can be glimpsed. Enough to look within to realize what man is searching for, and what he is deep down. And there, in that mirror, all the rays of the various forms of activity, with which man manifests his nature and procures the satisfaction of all his most diverse needs, converge. Whence if, in the individual histories corresponding to those varied forms of human activity, we distinguish by necessity moral freedom, religious freedom, economic freedom, political freedom, and diverse political freedoms, all these freedoms are one and only one freedom: the freedom of the mind, the single root of all the most diverse forms of its freedom. And looking into it closely, one sees that this freedom that the mind is so desirous of is not an external good that it had better come into possession of, nor a quality or intimate condition which it might have need of in order to better realize its own nature and explain its own activity; it is its nature itself. The mind is freedom, and freedom is the mind. In other words, if you try to say what is meant by the one or the other of these words, you will find the same meaning.

That all freedoms are different forms of a single freedom is quite easy to understand. In fact, who asks for religious freedom, from whom is it asked? From whoever has the power to withhold it: in other words, the State: and it is not asked for however except through its relationship as a citizen with the supreme powers of the State, which is its political relationship. And the freedom that it asks for is consequently a political freedom, insofar as determinative of that relationship. And why would the citizen ask for all the political freedoms, if it weren't for their deprivation becoming an intolerable limitation of its personality? And why intolerable, if not that the external activity in which everyone's personality lives and is made manifest is not something additional and accessory to the internal personality, which is explained in its mode of thinking and willing; in other words, if it weren't for that so-called external activity being the concrete realization and real manifestation of that intimate will and thought, which is its most profound personality? What prevents a man from thinking one way and acting another if not the law internal to his own thought? And if the freedom relative to the internal determination of the personality is called moral, is it not evident that political freedom is joined to the moral one and is as if the necessary consequence of it and the verification? Men who adapt to social servitude are internally, morally, and intellectually servants; and internal freedom puts pressure on social systems and tends to be realized in always more liberal regimes.

And internally or externally why does man want freedom? Because man, who has a will and is a man therefore, could not want to be deprived of his freedom either: he would not live like a man. Whatever he wants, he must first of all exercise his will. And to will means that he must act and exist in a certain way; to exist in the way that is needed, adapting, as they say, ourselves to the environment, or the environment to ourselves; by establishing a relationship in which we live our life as such from one moment to the next, in perpetual motion, we begin to develop. What is willed is never an abstract thing, but something in relationship to ourself: a modification to the world in which we live, which together with us forms a single system, which corresponds to our existence's specific way of being. To modify it therefore is to modify our existence, which will endure on condition of this modification. So that to want something is always to will to exist, to will one's proper existence; to will oneself. And because one says will, mind you, and not whim, or rather efficacious will and not inert or false will, to will oneself is to produce oneself. Whence a great personality is always the daughter of itself, without parents, without teachers: original, creative. It is always a great will.

Now, great or small, this will is the entire essence of the mind. The material is what is immobile, passive, immutable, always that. The restless mind, absolute mobility, and it is what creates itself: as much for what is called morality, as for what is called intelligence. Since a person cannot be a gentleman unless he wills to be one, thus that lofty intelligence whereby the world of thought is always more embraced, and more permeated and governed, is not attained unless by the effort of someone who wants to understand a great deal and therefore observe a great deal and think and seek and travail in the hard work of pondering. Great or small, I said; because also to stand on one's two feet and lift up one's head and not fall dead to the ground, requires effort, tension, and a secret albeit semi-conscious will, which is in us, and is our entire being, which affirms itself, and knows itself, and always pushes itself more to make itself worthy. From the moment a man first comes into the world, from the moment a consciousness dawns amidst the crepuscular shadows of the beginning, through all the eternal tension of this force of forces that is called the mind, hovering and fluttering over this world, this animating and vivifying force of the universe, behold the will: behold this *sui generis* activity that does not derive from anything else, because it is self-generated and consists precisely in this selfsame generation, in nothing that it can be said to participate in, unless by its own inherent virtue.

Well then: we can think either that something

exists and acts because something else makes it exist and act; and then say that its existence or action is effected by a cause. Or that something exists or acts because it exists or acts on its own initiative; and then we say that its existence and action are free; indeed, that they are the same act of freedom even. All things, as such, are determined as the effects of certain causes. People, no; and what makes them people, the mind, is freedom.

This at least is what we say today; and we retain that there is no mind that is not the child of itself, and that there is not therefore life of the mind if not in freedom. To reach this conviction men have had to think and reflect a great deal, and to make many attempts at framing all reality into one organic concept. But they have always lived willing: they have always willed, once born, to live; and they have run away from horrid death, which is the death of that will and the disappearance of the mind. And because death has always menaced them since the moment they came into the light, and they have seen at every instant the path of life blocked before them, with the inclement weather of the heavens and all the risks of savage nature, and the solitude of the desert and the hardness of the earth greedy for nutriment, and the huge hunger of wild animals and the ruthless prepotency of men stronger than themselves and the maladies and all the horrid lineup of sufferings and terrors, – and what have they done? They have worked, they have fought, they have come up with ways to multiply their strength, to conquer resistance and to combat enemy forces, to knock down obstacles, to smooth out the way before them, to create more favorable conditions in life; but all that while thinking the entire time, and making of their thought the first instrument of every activity of theirs. Is this not the eternal story of men? All their life consequently is an eternal thinking, an indefatigable philosophizing. Since, as the detractors of philosophy might have said: this is not an invention of philosophy professors!

But if we try to collect within a single concise look at the entire history of thought and civilization from this point of view of the concept of freedom, we can say that it can be divided into two large periods, distinct from a different mode of conceiving of freedom. There are in fact two modes of conceiving of it, according to the relationship that man puts between himself and the world. And these two modes characterize respectively ancient thought and modern thought, without however our being able to say neither that in antiquity men lived by this concept that is characteristic of their time, nor that in the modern age every trace of that old concept has been lost. That in fact the modern concept of freedom can be called Christian; and also that there are minds in the modern age highly representative in many respects of the soul of Christianity, which have nevertheless held on firmly to the ancient concept of freedom, which has faded after many centuries already.

Allow me briefly to delineate the spiritual situation referred to by each of the two concepts that I am referring to.

The first was precisely that of the Orientals', but it was not surpassed by the Greeks; even if, while creating science, they put forward the problem of modern civilization which Christianity then had to demonstrate how it could be resolved. The Orientals and the Greeks had no awareness of the potential of man, and they had no faith in the immense strength that is hidden in his thought. They conceived reality as opposed to man and all nature as outside this guest who, with eyes wide open, enters it at birth and looks around and sees himself surrounded on every side, from the day of his birth to that of his death; and he either believes it the instrument of mysterious and transcendent entities, or considers it moving by itself and alive, closed in its fatal law, and he does not believe that anything is expected of him other than to look at it, study it, understand it, and adapt to it. To transform it, to make use of it like an instrument for his own purposes, he does not even suspect that it is possible for him to think such a thing! To live within it, cannot be but to bend and cede to the ineluctable laws that one must recognize. Wisdom, the art of living well, provided that man lives without suffering, without wearing down in vain his own strength against insurmountable obstacles and remaining prostrate and forced to acknowledge the infinite crushing power of this exterminating reality from which there is no possible escape, can be nothing but ascesis, based on the deep conviction of the vanity of every battle that man engages in with the laws of reality: he renounces the world, which is not ours, and which we can never take possession of. Every desire of ours that pushes us towards it, is a cause of suffering. Suffering is deprivation, the suppression of life. To live [well] is to live without suffering, in the free expansion of one's proper being. So you want to be free, and to live without suffering? Extirpate from your heart the root of every desire. It is the Buddhist ideal: ideal evidently negative. Man will be the master of himself, of his own happy life, when he has renounced everything that by nature he is led to seek the source of his happiness from. Everyone man; even the Buddhist monk who, with his begging bowl, seeks something that others can give to him, – unless they renounce the risk of working and struggling with nature, which alone can give man the food he needs. This negative ideal was similar to the ideal of Buddhism in India, as well as of the Cynical philosophy of Greece, and, fundamentally, of Epicureanism itself. And it became popular again in the doctrine of poverty at the very heart of Christianity, principally because of the work of Francesco d'Assisi. A doctrine useful in practice, but theoretically absurd; inasmuch as it is necessary not to be too attached too to the things that one can do without, but rather to seek the essential in oneself; but it is impossible to sequester one's own self absolutely from the rest of the world, to which one is bound not only naturally, but spiritually and morally.

But Greek thought was unable to overcome this negative concept of freedom, because all the philosophy arrived at by that thought was naturalistic, even in Plato, even in Plotinus. True reality for the Greeks is nature: that reality, which the mind finds itself faced with and presupposes as a condition and the basis of its own activity. Which for this reason has no creative virtue. The world is not made, in any way, shape or form, by the mind, and therefore man, like every other natural being, even if privileged by thought, cannot live unless within the limits prescribed to him by the universal order of nature. He is forbidden, so to speak, every originality. He must renounce every desire to create something new beyond what already exists. He must limit himself in his life to his own natural self; to follow, even in himself, nature, and that means not to add anything of himself, which is a product of the will, which is freedom, i.e., a product of himself. The wise man in this particular case must put away his own wisdom: by following nature, not engaging in battles fated for certain defeat. The freedom of the wise man who among the Stoics proudly likes to compare himself to Jove, lord of the world, consists however in the negation of freedom: because it is not obtained except by suppressing the exercise of that activity in which freedom consists. Like the freedom of speech of someone who, unable to speak freely, keeps quiet.

It goes without saying that, while speaking like this, I am not trying to assert that all Oriental or Greek life occurred under this concept of freedom. The Greek democracies were a rather violent assertion of the need ingrained in the human spirit to break the obstacles around it that prevented the expansion of its own being. But the political conflicts that developed, mainly in Athens, after the Persian War, as a result of the effort to build of a structure propitious for this fundamental need of the spirit, were the leaven of philosophy, which from the Sophists forward strove to define the law, the relationship between historical law and natural law and therefore between man and nature, and consequently to find in systematic reflection a justification and a point of support for the instinctive aspirations of the people, so that thought could define and circumscribe and in some fashion assure the right of freedom. But as philosophical reflection this movement never obtained, nor could it obtain, anything but a negative concept, as I mentioned.

But the world is nature? Is it a reality that we find at birth and leave as such at death? With Christianity, this conception was vigorously shaken. At first it was said that there is the flesh and there is the spirit: the kingdom of nature and the kingdom of freedom. Dualism. Then, little by little, one came to understand that this dualism is only apparent; and that in reality all is spirit. And then the modern, positive concept of freedom arose, founded on the intuition of the infinite potential of the spirit, and therefore of man. Modern man knows that this world that he finds at birth, he is born to modify it, while confronting its adverse forces, learning to understand them in order to overcome their resistance as well as their hostility, and subject them to his own will and to make use of them for his own purposes: that is, to spiritualize them. Modern man does not run away from a fight; on the contrary, with an indomitable faith in victory and triumph, he does not know how to live except in this fight, through which he can realize the rule over nature, which is the annulment of nature as such with its heavy materiality and its mechanisms deaf to every voice of the spirit. Such is the life worthy of man, of this thinking being, who with his thought embraces the universe in all its immensity for all time and in all places. Modern man is born with something of an instinctive plan: *aut Caesar aut nihil.*[24] To serve is to die; to live is to dominate, to affirm oneself; and given he has unlimited nature and aspires for that reason to infinity and eternity, he does not stop or turn back before the impediment of fate. He makes everything his own, with his intellect and with his hands, with science and with machines, with love and with force, with laws and with war. And he dominates, and always wants to dominate more, and to make himself the ruler of the world: appropriating it to himself, assimilating it to himself, embracing it, knocking down every barrier between himself and everything else that sooner or later presents itself to him as opposition and inimical. Man, in general, by which I mean all men, friends or enemies, constant collaborators in a common effort for the spiritualization of the world; and each man in particular. Whose life is will, self-affirmation, the establishment of a personality, great or small, but always free; because this is human nature, from the time of its most humble origins.

It is enough to think about what each one of us feels inside and experiences in life when he needs to respond to an appeal that is made to him: to any appeal, which rouses him and invites him to say whether he is there, or who he is. Above all to the appeal that we make to ourselves when we are awake and vigilant over our life and actions. And each person responds to it continually, collecting in his consciousness all that he perceives himself to be, and affirming

[24]*Aut Caesar aut nihil*: Latin for "Caesar or nothing."

his “I.” Hence, he confirms himself in fact by a more or less energetic act, according to the reaction that he is induced to oppose to the world in which he finds himself, but which always involves a certain employment of energy and a certain effort: and therefore an activity, lacking which we will be unable to respond to the call, we will be absent, and we will lose our way in the disordered and incomprehensible multitude of all things, that we are accustomed to distinguishing from ourselves, as deeply diverse from us. In the same way, in the morning, as we are waking up, we need to orient ourselves; and this orientation, possible only slowly sometimes, consists precisely in our waking up: and in order to orient ourselves, we begin to recognize the place where we fell asleep, the objects that were there, all the reality that we left behind in our act of falling asleep in order to dream and wander about freely in the endless fields of subjective imagination. But, on rejoining that reality, we perceive it as *our* reality, we find ourselves in it and through it, with that reality that in the previous experience we were joined to, making it the concrete contents of our consciousness. To reawaken, to find ourselves, and to be therefore alive and present in the world in which we live – is to reignite in oneself, with one’s concrete contents, the consciousness of oneself, or rather that action by which one says: I; and each person substitutes himself for others and for all things and for himself. That “I” which, put forward as such, speaks and acts and makes itself noticed and appreciated for what it is, in other words for what it makes of itself through its own effort; and the world has to reckon with it for that reason; the more it affirms itself and makes itself appreciated, the more effectively it speaks and the more powerfully its acts.

There is no need to be a great man to make the world notice us and take interest in us. It is a question of more and less. Even a baby that does not speak yet, but already begins to stand up on its own two delicate feet, and therefore to have a more distinct consciousness of itself, to have a better look around, and then to explain its own activity in a more informed way; it attracts others' attention to itself even, and displays a dominating will. The parents, or whoever takes care of the child, know this well. It always has something to ask for, an order to give, even if expressed with a cry. It touches everything, takes possession of objects that are within its reach and wants the toy that best corresponds to the game of its lively fantasy. And its joy is in the eagerness with which others guess or satisfy its desire. All of a sudden, the toy that was its exultation, and its world, from which it could not be separated, now bores and bothers it. Its mind can no longer be contained by it: in its infinity it is naturally led to detach itself from the limitations of that particular game. And the toy is broken. The mind triumphs in destruction as in construction, wandering in a world that is suitable to its aspirations. Even the child demonstrates in this way its personality: it proves that it too exists.

And each one of us, withdrawing and regrouping in the shadows of his darkest consciousness, which can be considered the simplest, most primitive, and most elementary form of one's own existence, at that point where life seems to blossom, and beyond which nothing more of us remains, an effort of the will is sensed there however, the striving of a being that wants to exist and does, inasmuch as it wants to exist and cannot be suppressed or suffocated, because even by its cry it makes itself heard and makes itself present and demonstrates that it exists, and with its cry it protests and presses on reality, and fights and avenges itself and establishes in a superior justice the being that it feels it needs to be. This is the world of the mind, or spirit, in which we live, and which we feel vibrating inside us with life and with a powerful rhythm. The world of Christian gospel, which for the longest time pervades all modern civilization, that Western Civilization that has its home in Europe since the Renaissance, from which it spreads out little by little throughout the world.

Christianity, in essence, what did it come to announce to humanity? This: that the world in which we must place that ideal that presses on us mainly to realize, in which we must seek the freedom that is our life, is not that world of nature, where the earth is, from which we expect our daily bread and which it cannot give to us if nourishing rain does not fall; the earth where we are born without merit and without guilt, and where we will die, whether we like it or not: in which we are shackled slaves, from which no science or any ingenious astuteness can ever free us. This is not our world. Our world instead is that which sprouts within us, in the soul remade by the faith in our own strength, God's true grace, which makes us rise above our limited and immediate nature: in the mind, which is no longer a mockery of the senses, something exposed to the mechanism of natural forces, but is the will: that will that we mentioned earlier; that being that makes itself, in freedom; and for that reason reality is not something that already exists, but something that does not yet exist, but must; and because of this, it must be sacrificed and cease to be what it is; and thus everyone must get rid of their egotistical nature and, in the ardent desire of a divine will, rise up to the ideal, which is the love of one's neighbor, unity of feeling, fraternity, the actualization of an immortal spirit, in which each person finds his true life. The world, in a word, of the mind; which men usually do not see or do not recognize, even if they have it close by, even if within themselves, distracted as they are by the sight of things outside themselves. Which, conversely, can attract us only so long as we see them, and it is we who therefore see them resplend with those colors in which we dress them ourselves, and they acquire value in relation to our making use of them or not, and they themselves are grafted on to the trunk of this interior life of ours, which is our work entirely. Luxuriant life, which thousands upon thousands of sensations mix with an equal number of feelings, which are ignited in a fire of passions where infinite thoughts and marvelous phantoms develop and are nourished, and an ideal world of beauty and love and truth and divine things is built, and powerful forces are given off, which fall on the same nature, invest it, spiritualize it, making it participate in the history of the human spirit. Yes, we have need of bread, but the bread that we extract from the hard earth with the sweat of our brow, because we feel that it *must* give us this bread and it will give it to us, if we want it to in this way: for us and for our progeny, whom we *must* feed; for all those who do not have the strength like us to plow the earth and sow it, but who participate and cooperate with us in a shared life, from which we must not alienate ourselves, nor know how to; and they *must* be sustained by us in our labor, which is however not a simple mechanical effort, but a spiritual force belonging to a moral system. The utility is contained in a *duty*, and it is assumed in the superior sphere of that ethical life, which is not, but *must* be. And thus the fruit of this or that tree, which we plant, cultivate, and feel as our own, the property of our person, part of that sphere in which our being expands and establishes itself, can be lacking for unforeseen circumstances; but human life always triumphs, if it turns instead to that tree of good and evil, which is planted in the heart of man; and it never happens that it does not thrive, does not flourish, does not produce fruit, if cultivated by goodwill. If we look for the key to the universal mystery in the abysses of the ocean, we will not find it; and life will always remain in thick darkness; but it will be illuminated immediately by a light at midday if we look for that key where it is, in the inner recesses of our heart, where the secret of life is, where we as men, as mind, as freedom, live in fact, even if incapable of understanding it: the moral life.

If this is the world, you understand that the concept of freedom can no longer be that of old naturalism. If man has the world outside himself, his freedom can only be negative; but if the world that means something to a man, his true world, is not external to himself, but is in his mind instead, like his mind itself, his will, then freedom not only can be positive, but cannot be negative. So not only can he do something, in which to celebrate his own dominating will and to demonstrate his freedom, but he can, and for that reason he must, do everything. His freedom does not consist anymore in withdrawing within himself, sequestering himself from the world, in that it is not possible anymore for him to sequester himself once the world is within him, and is him. In fact, he is freer the more he expands in the world, where his life is, not permeating a preexisting world that is outside himself, but rather creating his world.

Difficult concept of freedom to whoever is immersed in the common way of thinking about things; and who sees this spatial universe in which man is just a small dot, nearly imperceptible; and the earth itself and the planetary system that it is a member of, like a particle of the whole, limited in space and time, so that it will disperse eventually, just as it formed slowly from a nebula in which there were neither animals nor men, nor anything of that which men see around themselves as composing this world. Before and after? Silence. And man can then believe himself in possession of this freedom, which is creation and therefore the boundless potential of an artificer, who has nothing behind him, and nothing before him, that is not his work?

But I will tell you: let us close our eyes and not wander, not even in our imagination, among the forms of this indefinite nature that we will never see unless we ourselves create and explain the painting before us by the laborious process of our own internal activity. Behold in our soul the whispering of a word, in which our feeling, our subjective life, is incarnate; and this word is an image, something alive, that flickers inside us and wanders freely in the sky, where immediately we contemplate it almost like a creature apart, a miracle to us, which we had extracted from our viscera: alive, with a life where, if words are spoken loudly around it and it becomes aware of other souls, it awakens equal admiration like a beautiful and immortal thing; but whether it makes sounds or not, and finds others who admire it or not, it possesses that virtue to awaken in the breast of men and gods the irresistible sensation that is the enjoyment of beauty. So what is this life without time, of infinite value, that gurgles up from the secret fountain of our mind no sooner than a slight throb is felt, and, so to speak, the rhythm of life begins? And what is that feeling of infinite responsibility that is awakened in every consciousness exquisitely tuned to moral justice as soon as a feeling takes shape, in the secrecy of the heart even, which, good or bad, is the principle of a thread that will be interwoven into the entire weft of our future life and therefore into the words that we say and the things that we do, into the weft of someone else's life, into the complex of the moral world, unbreakable, with its inexhaustible consequences, never-fading merit, and the blame that is forever whole and always atoned for? And what is that force whereby, thinking, we gather in our thought the past and future ages, places near and far, things seen and never to be seen, the good and the bad, truth and error, all men and gods, and we judge everything, even place it at the feet of the Almighty, and therefore submit it to the authority of our criterion? Whence this arrogance, which no humility can destroy? And can any one of us continue however to imagine and live a spiritual life of any sort whatsoever without supposing this infinite power within himself, surpassing its every particular limit, beyond birth and death, of oneself and all particular things, and to have faith in this profound reality, pulsating in every movement of his interior life?

Modern man is sustained by this faith, which has in fact overcome all the systems with which he has reiteratively attempted, every time he has lost his way, to wound spiritualism and inject into the human spirit the despair of ever realizing an entirely human world, resplendent with the value of freedom. To say, in this brief hour, what trials this Christian faith, in the power of the spirit and the corresponding positive concept of freedom, has had to go through and overcome, is not possible. But to condense everything into concepts that it is useful above all to clarify, I will note that here too there have been two forms with which the new way of thinking has been compelled to conceive of freedom.

The first form is that *individualistic* one, particular to our Humanism, when this concept of the spiritual potential of man, and therefore of his freedom, was restored to honor with great energy and celebrated by poets and philosophers as the living product of the economic, political, and artistic life in which the Italy of that period marvelously flourished in the world. Form that our Renaissance attempted to overcome with its naturalism, but it reappeared and prevailed through the same anti-historicism that is inherent in each naturalistic institution; and it triumphed in the abstract rationalism of the 17th and 18th centuries, in which in fact the current modern doctrine of liberalism was formulated. In Machiavelli's *The Prince,* the humanistic ideal is reflected, insofar as the principate is the work of the will, that with "*virtù*" (force of will and intelligence or knowledge of men and life) it breaks down every obstacle [in its way] and creates the reality that it yearns for; but this creative will is the will of a particular individual, a great but limited personality (e.g., that of Valentino). And his work, arisen from an arbitrary violence that does not take into account all historical forces, dies with him, as soon as death calls, which it had not planned on. Modern philosophy of the seventeenth and eighteenth centuries is the daughter of Descartes who reconstructs everything with reason. But his is the reason of the particular individual, which burns its bridges with history, and consequently does not attribute any value to the past. Therefore abstract individualism, which Protestantism is a potent ally of with its doctrine of *private examination,* the negation of every objective authority, of tradition and therefore also of history. Man senses his greatness; reclaims his freedom; but he does not know how to be anything else than a particular individual, and he believes that already as such he has that infinite worth, which, according to Christianity, is the spiritual life's concern.

Enormous error. Man as an individual is a man

among men and material things; in space, he is a part of nature. He exists and he does not exist. He exists today, but yesterday he did not exist; nor this very day does he exist anywhere else. And if everything that emanates from him showed traces of traits of him as such, no word, no thought, no action of his would have any value, i.e., he could not pretend to respond to an ideal norm. He would be the effect of certain causes; in any case, that which from time to time could be, under the circumstances, the conditions of fact. And then, why the distinction between true and false, right and wrong? Whence the pretension to be heard in every man who speaks? And how to explain that men understand each other, and that the word of one person means the same thing to everyone else? How to explain that whoever discovers a truth can communicate it to others and can expect, sooner or later, universal consent? What ever would this common terrain be, in which all men, in the historical development of humanity, gather together and interweave their discourses and all their work, if man were nothing more than this particular individual, whose skin cannot be penetrated from the outside, and whose soul, analogically, is a monad without windows?

Rationalism, which was also the Jacobin philosophy of the French Revolution, took its cue from the naturalism of the Renaissance; and despite its exaltation of reason and of the prerogatives of man as a being gifted not only with reason, but also feeling, and in short the active force insofar as his being aware, it made sense of the sensualism and materialism of the 18th century. Italian naturalism, in order to broaden the boundaries of human individuality, had in a certain way spiritualized nature but also naturalized the spirit; animating the former with the sense of man himself, and imbuing the latter with the ample breath and divine ineluctability of the life of nature. But as a result everything that is human and elevates man above natural existence, making his entire life a historical conquest through freedom, became, like everything in nature, an immediate and primitive datum, whose every variety is a historical accident lacking in meaning and value. Man therefore is born with his religion; and his true religion is a *natural religion*. Man is born with his rights; and every true right is a *natural right*. And man, it goes without saying, is born like every being that enters life in order to die; like a particular individual; no more, no less than any other natural being, e.g., an animal. And the ideal of life returns to being the life of nature as a result. Remember Rousseau. Freedom, yes; but of the spirit as it is immediately posited: freedom of the individual, or of the people as a collection of individuals, who get along, renouncing a part of their freedom in order to give rise to a tutelary force of the rest, which they are more concerned with defending. The State, however, is nothing if not the holder of power that the individual confides to it. The individual, in essence, is everything; the State nothing, for the State is the tool that the individual molds and uses as long as it benefits him, but which he breaks as soon as it becomes a nuisance to him. There is no objective necessity, a law, that comes into being through the historical process, absorbing every individual activity; a law, which the individual must kneel down before. History does not create an organism that the individual becomes a part of. Outside the individual, there is nothing that has absolute value. If reason convinces him of the irrationality of history, he will make a *tabula rasa*.

Intimately materialistic doctrine, because the individual, the man who is by nature what he is and in history can do nothing else than rot, is the negation of the essence of the life of the spirit. Man cries when he is born; and his cry, as we have said, is a protest. But this protest is an action that is not at all natural and comparable to any sort of animalistic yelp or some other natural act. Here it is an affirmation of oneself; something that would not be if man were only what nature made him. There is a manifestation of freedom, which is not a given, but a production. But this cry is a protest, because it is heard. There is an adult who perceives it, and feels it resonate in his mind. It is still undeveloped language, and yet significative. It is the soul that does not shut itself in, but expands outwardly. And it can expand, because that which it expresses has its universality, and it demonstrates that the neonatal is not a little plant or a little animal, but a spirit; nothing special, like all other things of nature.

Against this [backdrop of a] mean and petty philosophy, – materialistic at least for its tendencies, which wants to inculcate in men the pretension of an absurd individualistic freedom, and which inspires that classical economy that will become the *force majeure* of a posterior liberalism grounded in individualism and which will even be the first root of anarchism in the nineteenth century, – is, in the first half of the eighteenth century, the great Italian philosopher, an autodidact, who has the strength to go against the current and, with the originality of a genius, lays the foundation for a philosophy that remains with him like a dark night lit up by the sudden and intermittent flashes of large bolts of lightning, but will later become a mode of thinking characteristic of the following century; when history will result in honor, and man will finally open his eyes onto this divine and truly infinite potential that is hidden in his breast. The *New Science* by Giambattista Vico is the profound intuition of this truth: that man, the true man who sings his sorrows and his hopes, and thinks and explains his reasoning, and founds with religion the city, law, and the State, and who will wage war, and who will run and return from barbarism to the *gentilesse* of more refined customs, – he is neither a particular individual, nor a sum of individuals, but always a man, whose tongue and whose hand, as if moving by themselves, are the organs of a *common sense*, of a divine and providential plan, of a great reasoning, which is the substance and the strength of every human mind; whereby each man exists in history, which gives him a language, and a soul such that he might repay it while contributing with the use that he makes of his soul to the increment and development of history itself. History is no longer something arbitrary and accidental. Divine and also human labor binds the individual to his profound nature, where the principle of each greatness of his resides and the source of every right.

With Vico, who will directly or indirectly

have a great influence on the thought of the following century and later, after the Revolution, with the idealistic criticism that reacted to abstract rationalism, sensualism, materialism and economic individualism, in the Socialist, historicist, Romantic movement, the problem of the relationship between the individual and universal reality in general and historical reality and therefore the State in specific, was brought to an end by making the old ingenious and absurd concept of freedom no longer possible. The concept of natural law succumbed to the blows of the historical school of rights and the idealistic philosophy of becoming; and the law was, like every attribute of man or of the spirit, like language, like religion, like customs, a development, a formation without any primitive datum. Socialism, in its various forms, but above all Saint-Simonianism, gave a sense of human solidarity to the economic field as well as the juridical, and to the consequent impossibility of conceiving of the individual as a real subject of activity and rights. The shock given by Napoleon to the national feeling of various peoples gave a fresh start to the liberal movement of sects and thinkers, which resulted in Mazzinianism, on which all the spiritual tendencies of the century converged; and liberalism, because of Mazzini, at least in Italy, was the antithesis of individualism, conceiving of freedom as an attribute of the people more than of the individual, who has no value except insofar as he contributes, even with his self-sacrifice, in death even, to the existence and life of the nation, which is incarnated in the State. The more valuable the individual, the more valuable the State, in whose foundation and development he participates; and just as he does not find the State, he does not find himself either. He must make for himself, he must acquire, his own proper value, which he can only do on one condition: that all his life he devote himself to making the nation into a free State, and the instrument of freedom. For that reason life is a mission. It is, in other words, the realization of an ideal program, just as the life of the spirit must be Christianly understood. A mission, the nation, just like the State, to be realized in a superior reign of justice and human brotherhood; a mission is also the same life of the citizen, who must always be ready for every sacrifice so that his nation might be redeemed in the autonomy of the State; and consecrate his every action, his every word, his every thought, to the triumph of this ideal.

The Italian liberalism of the Risorgimento, even with some trace of the individualism of a distinctly economical character, as in Cavour, is permeated with the Mazzinian spirit. Everything, sooner or later, directly or not, will drink from that fountain; and in the ardor of the enterprise that they had in hand, nobody, Cavour included, ever thought of the natural rights of Italians; they thought of a free Italy, of an independent Italy, united, and of modern, constitutional systems that are naturally strong, but only insofar as they could guarantee its strength, assure its future progress, and admit it into the company of the great nations of Europe. And when it became time to act and make it, this Italy, without further ado or preparations, everyone, Cavour included, not to mention Mazzini, Garibaldi, Ricasoli, Farini, saw salvation in the dictatorship and scorned the partisan babbling of the assemblies, which in '48 and '49 they had given such a bad demonstration of.

In Germany, a doctrine of the State was elaborated, in the development of Romantic philosophy, which in our great Gioberti, the philosopher of our Risorgimento, was found to be strengthened by the Italian tradition of Vico. According to this doctrine, everything that is human is social and historical. In the slow and tragic toil of history, man becomes man; and his freedom, which is his own spiritual nature, cannot be a presupposition, but rather the result of the life he begins to live through the relationships that he gradually integrates and he himself realizes in society. Which, inasmuch as unified under one law and one common power, or rather in one single will, is the State. This however is in no way extrinsic to and superimposed on the individual; it is his concreteness. It is, in other words, that organic system from which everything that is divided and withdrawn falls away and disappears. And if it is true that spiritual reality is a person, self-consciousness, and a will, which flows from a thus-constituted consciousness, and therefore individuality; if it is true therefore that language, religion, custom, morality, art, science, and any spiritual production whatsoever is always a spiritual activity, it is impossible that this activity should derive from an abstract individuality, a primitive element of the State, but from the presupposed State and from the independent State. The human spirit is all that it is, does all that it does, inasmuch as an individuality formed by ideas and functions, positions and criteria, exigencies and aptitudes, in which system consists the State.

Which is no longer to be conceived of materialistically, and by that I mean bureaucratically, as that body of organs which little by little it begins creating in order to fulfill all its duties and reach its goals, but as that will, that personality, which proposes these goals and consequently assigns these duties to itself. And whoever says personality says individuality: Kings, ministers, judges, citizens, all members of the State in their particular individuality, agreeing or inasmuch as they agree in an identical consciousness and in the same will, they realize that personality, they actuate the State. Whoever looks for it above himself, in heaven, on the throne or in ministerial portfolios, will never find it. For that reason today we say: be careful, the State is not *inter homines*, but *in interiore homine*.[25] Which does not mean to say that the State is fragmented and disintegrated into individual personalities, except for those who fall into the trap of materialistic and atomistic conceptions of abstract individualism. But whoever understands this coincidence of the true individual with the State, in whose history is the history of man; whoever realizes the profound universality of this true individual which is the basis on which every one of us, so to speak, operates in his life, the source from which he draws every principle of his proper industriousness; whoever is capable of distinguishing the external aspects of the human individual, whereby he appears as an object among objects, a particular among particulars, limited in space and in time, to be conditioned by nature (and consequently absolutely incapable of freedom), by an inter-

[25] *Inter homines... interiore homine*: Latin for "among men...[but] within man."

nal substance, in which he recognizes himself and affirms himself as a free actor, who is responsible for and wants to be responsible for all that he says or does; he cannot let it escape him that the State being in the individual does not compromise his superiority and authority at all, for which an absolute objectivity is demanded. Not because God is in our hearts does he cease to be the supreme objective reality which every thinking man feels himself indissolubly close to.

But if it is true, as it certainly is, that the individual who does not coincide with the State is not and cannot be free, for his own particularity (which is another way of saying his naturalness), imagine how one might speak today of the rights of the individual against the State, and of the freedom that is due him by the State, or of the law of the latter as a limit and for that reason a negation of individual freedom. Whoever employs this language – which was at one time the language of the theoreticians of natural rights and the resultant social contract – he thinks first of the individual; and the individual as such, in his mode of natural and immediate being, free already, because already a man, already invested with the essence itself of the mind; and then he thinks of the State, which, intervening at a later date, would certainly like to limit the primitive freedom. But, the doctrine of iusnaturalism (and every naturalism), and for that reason contractualism as well, all that fantastical situation of the State when faced with the individual collapsed. And whoever wants to renew today those old ingenuous representations, and make a polemical platform of them in sustainment of liberalism, ignores that that sort of liberalism is dead for at least a century now. And today, after the terrors that socialists and syndicalists aroused in liberals, bringing out those old rags, and hoisting them like banners that can lead to new victories, can be a sign of excessive candor.

Today, any other liberalism than that of the freedom organized within the State is inconceivable; just as any other freedom outside of what is realized in the universal mind is inconceivable: in the mind, that is, whose operation conforms to a moral or esthetic or logical or juridical norm, valid for everyone, and which appears nevertheless exemplary and admirable. Fascism, in its antiliberal polemic, denies the freedom of old individualism; but it is the latest and most mature form of the new concept of freedom, a child of the 19th century. And if fascists say so, it is not just to spite their adversaries who contest them the right to speak in the name of freedom.

It is said: – if the free man's will coincides with that of the State, opposition is not possible; and barring any internal criticism, there is less possibility of any development and perfection, whereby the State can always respond better to the aspirations and needs of the citizen. Who, putting himself in opposition to the State, stimulates it with his resistance and with his criticism, and provokes the movement that is necessary to any spiritual reality. –

Yes, criticism and opposition are necessary, because movement is necessary; and freedom is movement. But this does not imply a conflict between the individual and something outside of him, affronting him from without; but only that internal conflict, which makes every really sensible and intelligent man always dissatisfied with himself and desirous of freeing himself from the inconvenience of this dissatisfaction. Against what external limit does the poet struggle, not satisfied with his work, as he sets about to correct it and elevate it to a superior grade of perfection? And what is the enemy against which the good man arms himself, who makes a scruple of his small error, or the sinner assaulted by the remorse and torment of the unrecognized and trampled on moral beauty? The criticism is internal to that same free conscience in which the State is immanent. And within it is the mainspring of that movement and its progress in freedom.

It is then said: – This statal conception of freedom and the life of the spirit in general fails to appreciate the double bound, internal and external, of the State. Whose sphere, internally, does not exhaust every spiritual activity; and externally excludes evidently what it should not exclude if it truly incarnated that infinite and universal activity of the spirit, which just about every universal value belongs to: in other words, all human life contained in other States. The State is not history. –

Myopic objection. The internal limit cannot be anything other than what the State recognizes for its own ends. When it adopted for example the theory of separatism with respect to the Church, the entirety of legal institutions, through which such separation is achieved, cannot fail to be part of the institutions in which State sovereignty is deployed. If instruction is left to private initiative, it will guarantee these initiatives with rights that would not make sense if they were excluded from that sovereignty. If it consents to forms of association that are not legally recognized, even the position of such social gatherings acquires a certain legal appearance that greatly depends on the power of the State, and the latter can change it. Only revolution interrupts the action of the State and restricts it within certain limits; but revolution, what else is it if not a crisis of the State which is transformed?

And as for international relations, other States are limited by a certain State in the same way that other individuals, it is said, limit our individuality. If we remain closed within this representation of the individual among individuals, our freedom and all our spiritual life, as we have seen, is no longer conceivable. Instead, our true individuality is that which knocks down all the barriers between us and others, and enables us to reach that common ground in which we and others are one single individuality in goodness, in art, and in knowledge. And so it is with the State. Whose sovereignty is recognized by other States, and gives rise to all those agreements that are not the limitation, but rather the expansion of it; or it resorts to war, whose victory or defeat is always a solution realized in a treaty which is, from the start, one common will, and for that reason the reaffirmation of the State's sovereignty, or the absorption of a historically false and circumscribed sovereignty by a superior sovereignty, which is more solid and therefore more responsive to that universal historical reality, which is the touchstone of everything that exists spiritually. War and the history of States in their reciprocal interdependence, far from being the negation, are God's trial and judgment of the absolute sovereignty of the State: i.e., of its universal and infinite value.

In conclusion, o Gentlemen, modern man is at a crossroads: on the one side lies the freedom of egoists, which leads to anarchy and to the ruination of ideals, in which a man can find himself; on the other side, the freedom of men, who over and above the particular "I" [of the individual] feel the potential of the ideal, which is the Fatherland as much as the family, the State, and the law, and it is freedom, not as privilege at birth and the gratuitous gift of gods, but as the conquest of our efforts, from which the family and the State are created, and a higher law, in which resides the honor of the world and the reward of our work. On the one hand, the right of whoever has nothing to give to the world; on the other, the duty of whoever has nothing to ask from it. But modern man, o Gentlemen, has chosen his life for a long time now.

IV. Fascism in Culture[26]

Gentlemen,

I am sorry to stand before you and speak to you after the assembly has already heard so many discourses and has shown some signs that it has had enough. I would renounce it if I did not feel it as a precise duty, the necessity to speak several words that are on my mind here and now.

The Hon. Panunzio just now said to us: We fascists have need of a defined doctrine; well, it is up to us who are gathered here as representatives of fascist culture at least to express a wish: that the Party formulate its doctrine.

No, my friend Panunzio. The very fact of this gathering that so many of the men here have participated in, who with work and thought have represented a not negligible part in Italy's recent history; the fact of this great gathering in which, with diverse voices even, one common soul has manifested itself, a vibrant soul of one same feeling, totally outstretched toward the same ideal, the soul of fascism, can demonstrate that the Fascist Party has a vast ideal content of its own, without the need to define its doctrine and to fix its syllabus.

Great spiritual movements resort to the definitions of a syllabus when their original inspirations have lost their strength, – those that this morning

[26]Original footnote: Closing discourse given on March 30, 1925 at the Congress of Fascist Culture in Bologna.

Marinetti called artistic inspirations, i.e., creative and really inventive ideas, from which such movements historically drew their first and most important impetus. But today we are at the beginning, and we must feel this obscure need that presses on our hearts, with joy, with a new life: this need that is our inspiration, this impulse that governs us and transports us.

Many times our Leader, with profound intuition of fascist psychology, has told us this truth: that we all obey a sort of mystical feeling. In the mystical state of the soul, clear and distinct ideas are not formed, concepts are not defined, yearnings of faith cannot be expressed in precise propositions and well-constructed reasonings; but precisely in the mystical moment, when the soul is more wrapped up in the penumbra of a world that is born, or that is announced, and presses on us with all its prepotent and irresistible strength of creation and instills in us a new, no longer experimental energy, it is precisely at that moment that the creative faith geminates in the heart of men; the faith that animates us, o fascists, the faith that has given us so much joy and so many satisfactions, but which has even sustained us on days of suffering, when malicious seductions tempted our soul, and we resisted because of this faith, which was not a reasoned doctrine, but was our own very feeling and our being.

I had proposed to myself to speak at this convention of fascist intellectuals about this character of fascism, which no fascist of the intellectual credo has need anymore to be made aware of. Seeing that Professor Piccoli, whom you heard speaking against intellectualism earlier today, is perfectly right. And all intellectuals are naturally taken by this malady of the spirit that is intellectualism; for which reason, a man gradually forgets to participate in life himself even, always and in all ways, with its joys, with its sorrows, and with all its responsibilities, and ends up believing himself to be a simple spectator, positioned for that reason beyond good and evil. Malady, which the human soul has been and is exposed to in every era and in every nation; but which (let's not forget it!) has been lurking for centuries within the soul of Italians, and has corroded and devastated the roots of every generous activity, of every proposition and magnanimous hardihood. Well then, I said that even fascists now want, with their initiatives of culture and with this same conference, to highlight and promote the work of culture and to show how they value them with respect to national goals, and to commit themselves to a new program in favor of Italian culture. All that to me, a man of study and schooling, cannot fail to give great pleasure. That the fascists should interest themselves in the problems of art and science, and their conditions, and the diffusion of sane culture among the people and the spiritual formation of the Italian ruling class, all that is optimal, and demonstrates the strong and sound moral temperament of the fascist movement, and is a happy augury of the civilization that it will provide to our country. We have with satisfaction and pride applauded the reports that have been made by representatives of the various fascist centers, especially in Milan and Bologna, around the fervid, genial, fecund activity already put forward by them. We have listened with interest and profit to the communications and important proposals about the ideas of capital importance that fascist consciousness feels the need to advance as intransgressible postulates at the head of doctrines fundamental to science and life, and about practical problems essential for various orders of study and for those who cultivate them. And we can rejoice at the demonstration given at this first Congress, practically improvised even, of the elevated way in which, in general, the problems of Italian culture are felt by men who participate in this great effort of national renewal, which is fascism. But here we are also many of us professors, many who have more studied than lived life; here and there one has been able to discover some unconscious and certainly involuntary movement of coquetry revealing signs of a psychology against which there is a need to keep oneself on guard, as if to say almost: – Behold, even we, barbarians, we busy ourselves and know how to busy ourselves with culture and science. Would that our adversaries might be persuaded that we are not less than them even in this! – And someone, it seemed to me, was so gratified to find himself among *intellectuals*.

Now, we need to be clear. Fascism is a war on intellectualism. The fascist spirit is will, it is not intellect: and I hope I will not be misunderstood. Fascist intellectuals must not be *intellectuals*. Fascism fights, and has to fight, unremittingly and ruthlessly, not intelligence, but the intellectualism that is, as I have said, the malady of intelligence: not deriving from the abuse of intelligence, which is never employed enough, but from the insufficient use of it, whereby one can incur and persist in the false belief that one can withdraw from life and, idling, tinker with systems of empty ideas, blind to the tragedy of men who work and love and suffer and die; whereas the use of intelligence is also, for those who understand it, drama, it is the fight of man with mystery, it is the effort of dominion over nature, it is the intensification of life. Even intelligence is for that reason will. And fascism at least feels that, and will scorn culture as an ornament or decoration of the brain, but longs for the culture whereby the spirit arms itself and fortifies itself in order always to conquer new battles. And this can be, this must be our barbarism. Barbarism even of intellectuals! Against science; and above all against philosophy; but, to be clear, against the science and the philosophy of decadents, of the spineless, of people who always stand at the window and are content with criticizing, almost as if it were none of their business! Although, I want to mention it here between parentheses, one of the great merits of fascism is this: to oblige gradually all those who were once standing at the window to descend into the street, if only to wage fascism against fascism. And when all Italians will have descended into the street and think and reflect without feeling any more temptation to return to the window, Italians will begin to be that great people whom they must be.

So let us be careful not to mistake what must be our culture for what it was once intended to be, as it was longed for in the 18th century, in the Age of Enlightenment, when the concept of instructing the people began to affirm itself in all its historical significance. Today we have perhaps oscillated between two concepts: between what I would call unqualified culture, equal for all, which is what it is in itself, something that contains its value in itself like metal currency, which can pass from one hand to another, without losing its value and without acquiring any; the quasi material contents of intelligence, transmissible from one brain to another and communicable to both a small and a large number of men who feel the need for it and can make use of it; and what can be called fascist culture which, because of its spirit, its fundamental note, its significance, its value, its possibility to serve a life plan, is diverse from every other culture. In one discourse there was mention of an instrument that needs to be mastered; that needs to be put into the hands of the greatest possible number of our followers, so that from the worker enrolled in our labor unions to the legislator and the government official who need to fulfill our Party's program, there are men technically prepared to understand, to study, to resolve problems, and to hold the banner of the fasces high in every field of human activity, where intelligence alone if illuminated can give proof of one's mettle. But as for the other concept of culture that Arpinati seemed to have in mind when, with his beautiful and bold faith, he told us that he will transform this Institute of fascist culture of his into a real and proper university for fascist studies. Bravo, Arpinati! We need not be so preoccupied with the culture of fascism, as with the fascism of culture. For the former, there are already many universities in Italy; too many even! For the latter, one new free university, with only one faculty, will not be too many; it will be the center and the focus of the new spirit that must inform itself and gradually renew Italian culture.

Yes, there is an objective science, which is almost a technique of human intelligence: a unique instrument that one person will use for one particular purpose, someone else for another. But already the Catholics have felt that this technique is not enough; they have understood that this instrument is an abstraction; who will brandish it? What will be his purpose? Beyond the inanimate instrument, there is the living man, with his interests, his passions, small and great, particular and universal; and there is also this man's science, because this man thinks, is aware of himself, his action, the ends to which he tends, the means he will adopt. And the science of this man who directs his steps toward goals that are always a choice? In this choice, not everyone is in agreement; each person has his belief. And at the universities, however secular they may claim or wish to be, there is not only instrumental science, but also the science of man: from abstract science one proceeds to concrete science, in which men compare their faiths, their interests, and contrast their passions. There are moral and political sciences, in the broader sense, into which man puts his complete self and searches for it, with all his faith, with all his soul (*applause*).

For this reason Catholics, because of the passionate feeling they have for their indispensable faith, have wanted their university. And we fascists, who do not want an agnostic State, and consequently want the State to be an educator and a teacher, we who are accused by liberals of fighting against freedom, we can boast of this act of liberalism, which none of the past governments, vaunted as liberal, ever had the courage to do, to have laid the foundation of a new public scholastic right, making the Catholic university of Milan possible; because we believed that a confessional university, like this free institution, should confer those same purposes of culture that the State pursues in other ways and in other forms at its universities.

Now, as with the Catholics, so with the fascists, it is good for them to found their own university: a fascist university, not because it is erected on this magnificent site which the Hon. Arpinati endowed the fascist institute of culture in Bologna with; nor because only duly-registered professors and auto-candidates will be called on to teach at one of the seats of Montecitorio or Palazzo Madama in reward for their constant service to the Party; but because within it another atmosphere will be breathed: another science will be taught there. Not that that science will be bent to purposes foreign to its very nature, so as to denature it, alter it, falsify it, as some timorous soul might begin immediately to fear. It will be openly, loudly professed there as the science that it is, in every soul that accepts the truth of fascism; and around the nucleus of its faith it orders and organizes its entire personality, its ideas and its memories together with all the data of its culture, as both the one and the other are colored by its ideas, because they are judged, framed, reduced to a system and thus identified with the content of its real and active personality. Science, which should not be a roughcast collection of knowledge thrown there, into an instructed mind, but which does not mold a man's consciousness, and therefore the man, his character; but rather that which is the true and serious science, when it exists: science made man, a person (*verbum caro*); and it is not, to be clear, a generic and abstract man that is made, but a real, concrete man, that this time is a fascist, as at other times it can be, and is, an antifascist. If someone persists in asking for a science that leaves man and his faith out of the equation, in an absolute manner, and his profound convictions by which he lives and which he cannot and must never renounce, then tell him that he either does not understand or is a hypocrite. May it prosper then in Bologna, the free fascist university, with a single faculty, of political and social sciences; and may it be the breeding ground of the ruling class which we have need of; and may it be the principle here of a new national culture, so that every movement of ideas is extended by the law of its own nature, and little by little invests all the thought of a nation and is reflected in all parts of society (*applause*).

I am sure that the illustrious man who has taken my place as the president of this assembly, the magnificent Rector of the glorious University of Bologna, whose singular titles of nobility in the history of Italy and all Europe will certainly not be held in little esteem by the fascists, restorers and vindicators of every Italian glory, nor that the ideas proclaimed so unexpectedly here today will cast a shadow on his University. Nor will those same ideas cast a shadow on the illustrious colleagues of the Faculty of Law, next to whom, I do not wish to say in front of whom, the new faculty of political science will be erected. They know that the State universities are neither *de facto* nor *de jure* fascist. Fascists teach there and antifascists teach there; just as Catholics teach there, and Jews teach there. Thus is it, thus must it be. They will be able to see it in a sympathetic light, even if politically in disagreement, this free, special school of higher education, which will not be a copy, and will not confer any title that can make it actually appear to be in competition with the juridical faculty of the State university. Indeed, dissenters will see it, I believe, more sympathetically, those who prefer to appear solicitous of every form of freedom; because an institution like the one announced today will be a new application of the principle of freedom, which has been introduced into the juridical system of the Italian university.

Let us found, o fascists, our free university; but let us be careful not to imagine it as our refuge, the catacombs almost in which we are to be shut in with our faith, disliked by the profane and suspected by one does not know what multitude of infidels disposed to persecute us. Our party is not a sect, nor a little church. Our party wants to be (it is a plan, not a pretext, o you who contradict us; it is a hope that infuses confidence into our bosom, not an insolent and untruthful affirmation!) – it wants to be the Italian people. Fascists are perhaps the minority; but we aspire to be the future Italy. It is an article of faith. So we do not intend to found a university of the party, sectarian, that sets itself apart from the free, national movement of culture, that leaves it to the State to watch over, to favor, to promote, and to provide the means necessary to scientific research as the essential activity for the economic and moral interests of the nation. We cannot found a free school with the same intentions as the Catholics. They will never admit, for the idea they have of the State, that to this are to be attributed those cultural and ethical ends that they recognize only in the family and in the Church – i.e., in the individual and in his conscience essentially; – and therefore they will never believe that the State has the right to open it, to maintain and to govern universities and schools of every grade. For them, the true legitimate university will always be that of the Sacred Heart or those other analogous ones that may appear in the future; and Catholic universities ought, in their opinion, over time and by God's grace, to replace the lay universities of the State.

We fascists have another concept of the State. This morning, Professor Arias in his lucid communication drew our attention to the absurd theories and practical damages of the agnostic State's typically liberal doctrines in economics. [According to which] in order to respect the free play of individual and private economic forces, the State should ignore the general interest of the nation, which realizes its consciousness in the State, senses its own interest in this consciousness and acquires the strength to assert it, thus sustaining and directing all individual initiatives which are undoubtedly the single source from which every truly productive economic activity springs.

But we – and here is a very strong point, Hon. Panunzio, which our fascist faith firmly holds us to – we do not know how to conceive of the State as an inanimate and indifferent vessel that contains individuals within itself without knowing it. We leave this container, and all its contents, to liberal gentlemen. Seeing as we do not know of any individuals who are held together in that way by a force that is external to their individuality, and we would not know what to do with them. If this is what liberalism must be, we are decidedly antiliberal (*applause*). We know no other individual than the one who speaks a language and thinks a thought and wants a will and lives a life finally, who has a history, wherein he is held fast in his heart and united with his people, who has his memories and his hopes, and his one consciousness, and his one interest, his one will, one and only one life; and he realizes it in all his thoughts and in the innermost palpitating secrets of his consciousness, as in his words and in his actions, in peace and in war, meditating and working, praying, loving, hating, combatting. In this common life or will that is the profound will of every more or less aware, more or less energetic and productive individual, which, for us, is the State; not something materially existent, but a living idea, which is realized and constitutes our duty, which we cannot shrink from: the immortal Fatherland, which is our life and is our death! (*Applause.*) In this sense and for these reasons we are elated in the idea of the State, which is not a Government, but tends to be a Government, organism, unity, person, consciousness, will. And for that reason we want in this consciousness, one consciousness for everyone, whatever has value for us and constitutes the substance and the reward of our life: and first and foremost the brightness of thought whereby everything is illuminated and grows in our spirit and in the life in which our spirit is manifested and lives. And we aspire to a completely united and close-knit nation, through its education and all the arguments by which it will procure an advancement in its interior development, in the system of life that the State organizes and guarantees. Therefore, fascist universities will need finally to be universities of the State. This is the ideal. But today at the universities of the State, many old men teach, to whom the nation owes a great deal: so many of them, who formed their mind and their spirit when the spark of new faith had not yet been lit in the heart of Italians, young Italians and Italians of the war years; and we don't understand each other, and we look at them with suspicion, and they at us with a smile on their face, with a closed soul. Well then, this is the Italian university for the most part: this is the old Italy, which we cannot cancel; which, instead, we ought to respect even. For the new Italy, we will work. It does not exist, we must create it. It will be the Italy of the young who begin to be educated, and who for that reason ask us for a special university. One day, they will have this Italy, which resplends at the top of our thoughts. And then all the universities will be open to the new life, and everyone will work for its increment, for its fortune, and for its glory (*applause*). Then there will no longer be any need of free fascist universities!

But let us return to the main topic of this discourse, from which moreover only in appearance have I distanced myself; because the new university would respond precisely to the need indicated by me, to the greater need that we in this Congress wish to affirm: which is this, not to introduce culture into fascism, but rather fascism into culture, and to create and to diffuse this new culture which is permeated with the spirit that unites us here; with the spirit, I say, that will have to unite all Italians.

To introduce our spirit of fascism into culture, as into all parts of life; it is easy to say, and easy perhaps also to understand; but how difficult to remember when it must be remembered, i.e., at all moments in our conduct, even in our thoughts!

Fascism, o Gentlemen, has this special characteristic among all forms of political thought: that it is not merely a doctrine or a tendency to resolve the entirety of actual political and contingent, present and future problems in a certain way. Fascism, let us be quite clear about it, is not merely politics or a political party. All political parties have a specific teaching that members of the party themselves must be mindful of when they carry out a specific political function, but which, so as not to cause undue and damaging confusion among the different things [in life] that every sensible man must, however, take care to keep distinct, they must put their politics to the side when they fall in love, when they educate their children, when they turn their mind to God, when they go to school, when they practice the arts, or science, or philosophy. Whoever enters a church, or does not enter a church, and is surprised in the midst of the tumult of action and daily passion by the wearisomeness and dissatisfaction of every particular thing that our active mind latches on to in life; he reflects inwardly and transcends the infinite relationships wherein however he is bound by all mundane things; and he lifts himself up with a single thought of the infinite that is at the base of his spiritual life, – he certainly cannot feel any longer in his heart the goad of his political passion. Or when a man finds some peace amidst life's struggle, in the daily hustle and bustle of the world that he participates in, assuming his post and struggling now and then to hold on to it, and from his pacified mind, in an infinitely vast self-consciousness, a splendid form of beauty arises in which he sees the eternal image of his life reflected, and he snuggles up in happy admiration, – he is no longer thinking about his political party, nor does he find adversaries in the heaven of his art when others, at the invitation of his song, draw near. This is what everyone thinks about politics with respect to other forms of spiritual life; and this is why those who do not understand us and who mistake us for a political party, just like other political parties, are frightened when they hear us say, for example, that we want to introduce the fascist soul into education.

But fascism, let us say it very loudly, in the hope that they might feel it and at least suspect it as something new to study and to understand; fascism is politics, but it is also something more than politics. Something then that for Italians ought not to prove to be an unheard-of novelty. Some good Mazzinians have come here, who with great intent strive to maintain in Rome a Mazzinian university of their own; and they have asked our Congress to express a vote for the establishment, if not of a regular university, at least of a chair dedicated to the expounding of Mazzinian thought, as was once proposed for the establishment of a chair for Dante studies in Rome. We listened sympathetically to their proposal, although it does not seem to me that it will be accepted; because all these specialities introduce pedantic fetishisms into the mind, which every intelligent man must avoid; because great men also belong to history, in which alone they are understood, and from which they must not be detached however; and above all because Mazzini's spirit deserves this respect, of not being lowered, it too, to the *matter* of teaching, to being contained within the confines of his books in order to be commented on; whereas his spirit, like every immortal spirit, wanders freely and pervades, like his place in history, even the life forms that Mazzini could not contemplate because they have appeared, or come to maturity, after him. We will not found the Mazzinian chair; but as fascists we will remember, we must remember, Giuseppe Mazzini, as our precursor, as one of our fathers. And every Italian who is capable of reading his writings, his essays and fragments with a pure heart, but completely animated by a spirit that untiringly vibrates; every Italian who contemplates his life, who enters the heart that endured the Roman heroism of the defense the Roman Republic, will never say that Mazzini was a politician; instead, he will refuse to ascribe to him the many traits that compose the shrewd, prudent, and effective politician; but he will also feel that there was something more than a doctrine or a political intelligence in that great soul of his. There was something that closely relates to politics, but politics it is not, whereby the great Genovese could infuse into the breast of Italians an unknown strength, a powerful force, a religious will of being, of being finally, and not in words, but actually, with the spirit disposed to die rather than to submit to the shame of renunciation; of being the Italian People, whom poets and writers for centuries told us existed, but nobody, descending in arms this side of the Alps, could find. What was this man's secret, which exercised such fascination on contemporary generations? His action always failed; his thought is full of contradictions and too often echos the common motives of his era; but at the base of his thought and action was a great faith focused on the political Risorgimento of the Italian nation, and infused with an unadulterated inspiration of religiosity. His people are one end of an indissoluble binomial: *God and people*: his people are bound in his soul to that absolute, which cannot be escaped; whereby politics becomes, as he said, mission, or religious life. Hence we fascists, turning back through the history of this Italy, which is our ardent passion, as we look for our model, – we feel that we encounter, in the austere figure of Giuseppe Mazzini, the purest and most luminous form of our faith and our ideal (*applause*). He was to evoke, from the bosom of Italians, that Giovine Italia that has risen up again with fascism and around us celebrates eternal youth, the spring of life, flowering with faith and hope (*applause*).

To him, without new chairs and without new academies, to him, o fascists, let us turn every day to be inspired, to renovate ourselves, to lift ourselves up, and to conceive of life in the Mazzinian fashion.

Here is the point. I was saying several weeks ago in

Florence to my listeners: look Mazzini in the face. All his portraits – and there are some very beautiful ones among them – represent him with a melancholically severe face, like someone who lives in a world that is hoped for, but does not exist. One would say about that forehead, about those lips, that mirth never broke out into a laugh. His pensive face reminds us of the saints, who seriously, profoundly feel as though they are in the presence of God at every moment; at every moment they feel the tremendous responsibility of what they do, say, or think. Well then, I say, fascists like Mazzini do not laugh. They do not laugh that laugh that signifies taking things lightly, as Italians have, alas, for so many centuries, who are extremely intelligent but without the ardor for religious things; wise, but of that famous kind of wisdom whose principal teaching was the motto: saying is one thing, doing another. No, the fascist youth who in '19 and '20, in the explosive years of the new faith, consecrated this faith in Italians' hearts with a martyrdom, giving us the first unforgettable examples of how one can practice politics and defend, against a larger number and against brute force, the beauty of a political ideal that has a self-awareness and a history, a right and a future, – these youth of ours did not know that saying is one thing, doing another. They gave their life, not led to this step by a common law of the State, but by free sacrifice to the ideal, which was felt superior to any reality. And around us, in the middle of much weakness and vulgarity, in the middle of the many who follow and also obey, but who do not know why they march and where they are going, do we not see it thousands and thousands of times, in which the soul of those martyrs is reflected, and which assures us that a new Italy really has risen: the Italy foretold by Mazzini in which there is no longer any separation between *thought and action*, and life is modeled on the ideal, with the individual's absolute devotion to that superior reality wherein he finds his worth?

That person is not a fascist today who does not feel in his soul, when speaking to himself, by himself, this unconditional devotion to everything that transcends his particular personality, and from which he draws his own proper worth: and thus, politically, in relation to the State. But he will never be as devoted to the State as he ought to be, whoever does not have such feeling and moral disposition tightly bound in his soul, deeply, in such a way as to always hear the voice inexorably calling him to the sacrifice of his individual comforts or interests. We heard this morning a most effective discourse on foreign politics by Forges Davanzati.[27] He earned our unanimous applause by affirming energetically the concept of the State as power. Yes, the State is absolute power, which is realized not by presuming itself but demonstrating itself as such, externally and internally, which are merely the obverse and reverse sides of the same coin. And power supposes a will, which is fused and united, and is as if the strong will of self-awareness. Which implies that citizens do not see the State above themselves, in the same way as that old worn-out and flabby liberalism, which needs to be made anew today. A State that is above, and therefore external to its

[27]Forges Davanzati: Roberto Forges Davanzati (AD 1880-1936), an Italian politician and journalist. Originally a socialist, he later became a national syndicalist and then a nationalist.

citizens, is not power, because citizens then become so many forces that limit the force of the State, confront it, and take away its absoluteness, that infinity which is the particular power of the State. In which it is moreover required that the State's will and the individual's will coincide, and the citizen might feel his fatherland, which the State is the concrete and active form of, like its highest reality which he must continually adapt to in order to live the ideal life which he feels the need for, and to which at every moment he is ready to sacrifice himself for things both big and small (which are more important than the big).

This is – is it not? – what everyone goes around habitually saying and repeating. But, with respect to habits, when it is a question of our moral life, one needs to be on one's guard, o friends. Let us examine our consciences every evening; let us put a hand over our breast, followers and leaders, soldiers and citizens, deputies and ministers, however many we are, let us be proud of our membership, and let us go preaching the fascist renewal. Can we say, to each other's face, seriously, that this profession of faith of ours is the norm that always inspires our behavior? Can we say that we have always remembered to do what was said, to have always said no to our self-interest when it was in opposition to that of the fatherland, to have never, ever given in to the enticements of our egotistical instinct, to have omitted nothing, in order dignantly to hold on to the position we wanted to hold on to? Remember! We're almost there. Valentino Piccoli[28] informed you here today that there

[28]Valentino Piccioli: (AD 1892-1938), an Italian man of letters and critic, the director of several national daily newspapers in the first

is a difference between a notion known and understood, learnt and remembered, and a conviction that is our business and therefore the norm of our life. To remember an idea that we are used to hearing spoken or that we are used to speaking ourselves is easy to do if this idea is just a poor notion lodged for good in our memory; but to remember it as an active principle of our behavior, this is the difficulty, which I have permitted myself, at the conclusion of this our Congress, to bring all your passionate attention to. Think about the difference there would be between the indifferent historical knowledge of the fact that such-and-such a woman was our mother, just as such-and-such another woman gave birth to a Tom, or a Dick, or a Harry, and the intimate and dear and sacred knowledge and ever-vivid and present memory that we have in effect of our mother, whom we see, when we reflect on our life together, in the most tender and sweet years of our life, together, with our brothers, living one life, with one spirit; which is the same spirit that we live with today, and will always live with, and in which that voice that now is spent still echoes and will always echo, and which unlocked all our feelings and awakened love in us, and gave us our language, and made us men, and infused faith and the courage for life in us; and it still echoes, immortal, the secret inspiration of our heart, irresistible (*applause*). Whoever hears that voice, will he be able to say: "Yes, this is beautiful, this would be the right thing to do, if only..."? Does it have to do then with ideas that have not yet left the mind and are unable to be expressed clearly? Or does it not have to do rather with ideas

---

half of the 20th century.

that were made feeling and that fused with our self-same being, which cannot be suppressed without our losing our way and becoming unrecognizable to ourselves? Well, when I ask you whether we can say we have always been mindful of our duty, of our honored uniform of pure fascists, I intend by this a second kind of memory, which requires an absolute intransigence directed not only toward others, but also and primarily toward ourselves.

Now, I believe we are all fascists, and we can acknowledge it frankly amongst ourselves. And if we are not all fascists, it does not matter, we must acknowledge it: our intransigence is verbal at times. We do not always do what we say; we do not always practice that absolute devotion to the ideal that we preach. Not always does it burn and shine, that religious flame in which we proposed to purify young Italy, in order to create a great, strong Italy collected in the strength of a clear and energetic consciousness of its spiritual mission in the world. We must acknowledge it loudly because only this sincere and humble acknowledgement can give merit to the faith that we champion. Otherwise it will devolve into rhetorical verbalism and shameful hypocrisy.

May this Congress wherein fascists assemble more prepared and disposed to reflect on their proper faith and duty, – may it close with this noble act of humility, recognizing that our idea is too lofty because it might presume that we embody it and worthily represent it. Let us renew in ourselves, today and always, – we who must have an acuter sense of the greatness of the idea that we are the bearers of, – the persuasion of antiquity which held *nihil actum, si quid superesset agendum*.[29] Let us not boast, let us not counterpose our person to that of our adversaries; we still have much work to do, much dross in our souls to burn away, many internal battles to overcome, much as yet to learn in order to say sincerely that we conceive of life according to Mazzini's vision: to conceive of life and to live it in a fascist manner. To say it and to feel it will not be our weakness, it will be our strength. Our adversaries will respect us more; and what counts more, we will respect ourselves more, because to feel one's proper defects is the first step toward freeing oneself of them and acquiring the strength necessary to the task.

So indeed life should be taken seriously, not deluding ourselves in the blessed and very vain illusion of being already at peace with one's conscience. No, this simple and even great resolution – which is our motto – of taking life seriously, feeling the responsibility of every one of our even small acts, even this resolution must be taken seriously. I won't say another word. Whoever has followed me thus far, whoever is prepared to understand me, will have understood. I can only tell you this: be vigilant. Be vigilant over others and over yourselves.

And to you, men of study, I say: be vigilant, at the lectern when you are amongst the young, and when you write, when you think. Be fascists even then, but

[29] *Nihil actum... agendum*: Latin for "nothing is done, if anything remains to be done." Marcus Annaeus Lucanus (Lucan), *Pharsalia*, II, 657.

on one condition: that you take what you do seriously; in yourself and in all your activities. Since only in this way does one escape the habit of frivolity which is the enemy of fascism, and is permeated with that religious spirit, with which only then is it possible to practice true fascist politics. I will explain. Everything is interrelated in the physical world, just as in the moral world; and frivolity fundamentally results by seeing everything that our spirit turns to, in thought or action, as isolated and standing alone, and by not seeing consequently the thousands of connections by which that thing is essentially conjoined with every other thing, in such a way that it is transformed into an abstraction considered conceivable or manageable on its own. So the action fails because actually it was performed while closing one's eyes to the world in which one acts, the accounts don't balance, and the most exquisitely rational logic makes us spin cobwebs that are destined to break on the first attempt to seize them with something possessing the slightest hint of reality. The intelligent man, the discerning man, the man who in any case comes to some conclusions, is he who possesses the synthetic and organic vision of the diverse aspects whereby reality in its entirety, here and there, today and tomorrow, is represented to the thought, and comes to be realized. But the deeply intelligent man is he who does not consider this completely diverse world, which in space and in time stirs around him, and which is always an organism of parts that are appealed to in succession and form a system that must be learnt and understood in its entirety, as outside himself and indifferent; but he understands it and treats it as intimately bound to his same person; and not like the house that he inhabits and can abandon, but rather like his own inseparable body: like that body that he must use in order to live and to achieve his destiny, in which his heart beats, his blood pulsates, life seethes, which he enjoys and appreciates, sees and hears, and senses in general, and which consequently explains his entire being in joy and sorrow. You can conceive of the world in one way or another; but one lives seriously through that very human reflection that is a religious reflection; when one knows, indeed when one feels, that we are not guests in this world, and that the world is not outside of us, and as there is no feeling that crosses even fleetingly the secret of the soul, that does not light up in our eye and in our face, there is no word that is pronounced in the silence of our heart which does not affect, through our being which is modified by it, the universe, both moral and material, in the system of its infinite connections, in which we too are also involved, and to which we bring therefore our internal modifications. For this reason, the religious man examines himself, listens to himself, watches over himself, and always fears to be in sin, even in thought, in the presence of his God, who searches him internally with eyes that are never tired and never closed. Yes, this is our duty, o fascists: never to close our eyes, we neither. Never to compromise, as I have said, but first of all with ourselves. And for this reason always to reflect and to think; and to put into practice the conclusions that are arrived at, without unnecessary dilations, without hesitations; resolutely to wish with that energy that distinguishes the man who has a character from the man who does not. And we must give a character to Italians. It is something that they have had need of in the past; and it is something that will create that national greatness in the future, which is our plan.

This is what I mean by taking life seriously; this for me is fascism pure and simple. This must be the fundamental note of all fascist life; and this also must be the fundamental note of culture, which depends on fascists to promote.

Gentlemen,

You have justly applauded those who spoke to you today in the name of art, and whoever said to you that fascism also is art, because it too is the original movement of the spirit and is not deduction, but creation; it puts its trust, even while in action, in a genial inspiration, rather than in a conclusion of well-constructed reasonings. Yes, by all means, fascism for its spontaneity, for its originality, is art. But I would like to fill out this definition. The artist is, in fact, by himself, the spirit that looks for and finds his freedom outside the real world where there is fatigue and sorrow, where there is the harsh law that limits the individual, and where a force weighs on man, which finally is superior to any natural or human force, and is called God or Fate, which no will, no science can overcome. And for this reason, art exalts us and gives us almost a taste of the nectar of the Gods, the taste of absolute freedom, which is celestial beatitude; but that is not enough for us. From the stupendous dream into which it draws us, life calls us back to the diverse reality where our limits are, where our needs are which must be satisfied, which must be fulfilled. And while the dream of art lasts, the poet, trusting in the splendid creatures of his fantasy, finishes by taking hold of them, which are external to him and which live their own life, which has a law, were it only beauty, which imposes itself on him and makes him feel his deficiency and the imperfections he needs to overcome and the infinite melancholy of unachieved and unachievable perfection. Even the artist however bends to the sense of duty, and groans sometimes under the law, like the saint who trembles at the sight of God and implores grace. Since life is art, but it is also religion. It is the exaltation of our creative virtue, but it is also a sense of our limits and of the existence of something that we ourselves are not and that does not depend on us, and it besieges us and pressures us from within, and presses on us, and asks us for an account of what we are doing and what we are. A mystery? It appears so; but one must needs look at it and live by it and with it, feeling its presence. Living as best one can on one condition: with the faith that this which overcomes us and limits us is not a gate that locks us up in our petty nature, but is rather an infinite reserve of energy, whereby it is given to us and it will always be given to us [the opportunity] to attain the strength of conquering our nature, of elevating ourselves higher, of living finally a spiritual life. This is the great strength of religion; and yet fascism has instinctively gone against religion, whose negligence was in the past conjoined with all the other signs of the decadence of old Italy. The interpretation of the religious politics of fascism put into circulation by the usual green serpents, by which I mean the usual clever and shrewd, old-style politicians, is another proof of their absolute incapacity to understand fascism. Fascism, o Gentlemen, is itself a religion. And for that reason it has been able to reconsecrate war, and the victory formerly vituperatively despised, in the heart of Italians; for that reason it has made martyrdom for the ideal of the Fatherland loved again; for that reason it stands at attention, while its inept and pusillanimous adversaries hurl insults at it, invincible. (*Unanimous, prolonged applause*.)

Part the Second: Fascism and Liberalism

I. My Liberalism[30]

There is a liberalism that is convenient to its adversaries, and which is often heard in fact invoked by everyone, although most are reluctant to adhere to it on their own. And it is the materialistic liberalism of the 18th century, born in England in the century preceding it, but having become in the 17th century the credo of the Revolution.[31] Which had, in order to overthrow the historical State, no other force to use than the individual lined up against that same State, because it saw in the State nothing but an enemy and an obstacle to its aspirations. This is, fundamentally, classical liberalism, wherein the State presupposes freedom and cannot respect it without limiting itself and being subject to a tendency toward a limited political form, equivalent to the negation of the same State.

But there is another liberalism, born in the 19th century in the full maturity of the same thought of the Revolution, through that criticism of materialism that in all the countries of Europe in various modes led to the reaffirmation of spiritual values. And it is the only liberalism that can logically be conceived of, because the only coherent one capable of supporting a truly liberal conception of life. Honestly, a liberalism without a State is a liberalism without freedom. A State that presupposes freedom denies it precisely by the

[30]Original footnote: Published in the *Nuova Politica liberale*, a. I, first installment, January 1923. October 28, 1923.

[31]The Revolution: presumably in reference to the events in England that led to the execution of King Charles I in 1649, or to the Glorious Revolution of 1688.

very fact that it presupposes it, there being no freedom outside the life of the spirit which, in contradistinction to natural things, is not presupposed, but created, mastered, developed. One becomes free, one is not naturally free. And the State is liberal, in fact and not in word, if it promotes the development of freedom by considering it as the ideal to be realized, and not as a natural right to be guaranteed.

My liberalism – it goes without saying – is not the first: it is not the doctrine that denies, but that vigorously affirms the State as an ethical reality. Which is, itself, to be realized, and is realized by achieving freedom, which is as much to say every man's humanity, the positive energy of the individual. And precisely for that reason the State, as I understand it, is an ethical reality. It does not do away with individual conscience and will – which is a totally spiritual reality – at the base of an edifice that it can rest on mechanically; rather it assumes them as a world to be realized, and in whose development and progress it properly consists.

This liberal State, moreover, does not absorb the individual into itself and does not cancel him, as the pavid liberal of individualism fears, in his suspicion of seeing liberal doctrine turned into socialistic statolatry. Socialism, yes, falls into the same materialistic error as the antihistorical and Jacobin liberalism of the 18th century, inasmuch as it presupposed the individual and denied the State, and it presupposes the State, even as the static ideal, realizable once and for all, and must for that reason lead necessarily to the negation of the individual and the freedom that is all one with the concrete, historical, and therefore individual development of the spirit.

But new liberalism, or the doctrine of the ethical State, is not considered from the viewpoint of old liberalism, which knew the State only as opposed to the individual and to whomever the individual is opposed with the conviction of a dilemma: *mors tua vita mea,*[32] or vice versa. So the State became conceived of materialistically as equal to the individual. And yet the ethical State is not anything materially representable or objectively definable in contrast to the citizen, in whose consciousness it must live. It is not external to the individual; rather it is the very essence of his individuality. Which manifests itself precisely as will, which wants to be universal, without any limits or obstacles that he must overcome: will which is law. And the State, what else is it if not the reconciliation and unity of will and law? Will is will when it is law, just as law is law only insofar as it is will. So the individual carries out his own nature to the same extent as he becomes the State, and he feels deep within his same consciousness the incessant pulsing of a universal ethical reality, which transcends the confines of his particular abstract personality, and which, as it draws him toward death in the supreme danger of the fatherland, almost as if finding his true self while losing his illusory being, in this way it makes him recognize moment by moment the powerful force of a law, which his own inferior instinct and every natural passion bends before.

The politics of this liberalism is certainly not

[32]*Mors tua vita mea*: Latin for "your death my life."

that great party or lottery which the politics of vulgar democracy is, all prudence or candor. Neither the prudence of serpents nor the innocence of doves[33] will ever be enough to make one feel the massive reality of that ethical State, which requires minds disposed to conceiving of life in an austere way, under the law of sacrifice and the subordination of every private interest to a superior ideal. But political life is by definition the life of abnegation and disinterest, and the religion of the fatherland; it is the flame that consumes within a man the dross of his base egoism, and purifies it in the cult of an idea. Cavour, our great liberal, always lived however in the same moral atmosphere as Mazzini, animated by a like faith in the reality of a fatherland that was to be created and of an Italy to be evoked by the same spirit of Italians or by the political reality of Europe, moved by a like spirit eager almost for the holocaust of one's own person.

For this reason, I am firmly convinced of the supreme necessity of a strong State, as the duty and right of the citizen, and of an iron discipline, which would be a strict school of political wills and characters. For this reason, I am firmly convinced of the need to rouse and develop an energetic sense of religiousness and morality in politics, and to maintain, on the other hand, a sense of measure and political determination, in other words a historical and social concreteness in the ethico-religious development of the individual. This is the gist of my liberalism.

---

[33]Serpents... doves: See Matthew 10:16.

II. The March on Rome[34]

In the march on Rome, the entire Italian ideological movement of the first twenty years of our century overflowed: the reaction against ideologies that in Italy had prevailed in the last five lustra of the preceding century and that constituted the democratic, socialist (at least in the spurious form that Marxism had assumed in Latin countries), positivist, enlightened, or pseudo-rationalist conception of society, life, and the world. What were the elements of this reaction? The idealistic philosophy that uncovered and annihilated the hidden materialism in all those ideologies; the resurgence of religious feeling; the syndicalism of Sorel with his moral and mystical tendencies; war.

War was the crucible in which were fused the spiritual forces that came to be formed in the ferment of youthful spirits, among the philosophical or religious, literary or social, passions and discussions. They were fused and they were shaped into a concrete spiritual life, which is always action, will, a creative potential of new forms. The war, for educated Italian youth, for those who had some problem and some internal torment, and who were actually the soul of the war, was felt and lived through like a great fatal experiment of the Italian people: a sort of divine judgment, in which this people which had never fought, altogether, a national war, had to put itself to the test for life or death. Mysticism, which the fact of war by itself would not explain without those antecedents

[34]Original footnote: Published in the *Idee nationale* on October 28, 1923, and in the *Nuova Politica Liberale* of December 1923.

that darkly brooded in souls.

After the war, fascism appeared to explode all of a sudden like a violent cry of youth; and at first in fact it had the impetus and the impetuousness of a youthful soul. But this violence, which was necessarily illegal and no less necessarily however led to the revolution, was also the very shape of the new way of thinking, which could no longer be an abstract idea, in that it was the precise equivalent of the constructive activity of a new moral life. The new philosophy in fact no longer recognized ideas that as such were not will, action; no longer understood how it could distinguish between theory and practice. And it had taught that the man who actually thinks, deeply, feeling the truth of his thought, and living it, cannot help outflowing into reality and giving a hand to shape that world in which the truth of his thought is realized and demonstrated.

In this respect fascism is a spiritual attitude of the highest moral value and of a singular historical significance. In this respect, all peoples watch Italy with vivid interest, even if in some of them there arises and insinuates itself the hint of a discomfort that a fascist Italy can give! But fascism for Italy is the new strength of its redemption: the strength that must redeem it from centenary, rather millenary servitude, which until just yesterday oppressed it. This servitude (who does not know about it?) at times and for a long time now was political slavery and a national incapacity to develop into a State; but it was substantially and always an internal servitude, deriving from a false belief that thought is one thing and action another, and that speaking is one thing and doing another; and that consequently one can pay tribute to the ideal with a cult of noble thoughts and beautiful words but without committing oneself to the fight that the ideal might achieve with sacrifice, even amidst tears and blood. Fascism – that pure fascism of youth who feel it like a religion, ready to give their life for it even – is the greatest victory that Italians have brought against their greatest enemy: rhetoric.

– *October 28, 1923.*

III. The Italian Liberal Tradition

Today one talks a lot, too much even, about liberalism, the liberal State, the liberal party, the origins and liberal traditions of the Italian State; and there is no lack of those who are ready to seize on this or that scrap of the flag; which a very vague, confused, and superficial historical and political culture sees fantastically fluttering over our recent history.

What is more, for those who do not go beyond such a culture, it is impossible not to distinguish two more or less very different periods in these liberal traditions. The first is that of the varied and complex liberal movement that preceded '48 with its demand for reform and constitutional franchise; and then after '48, leveraging the only surviving constitutional Italian State, it promoted and worked for the political unification of all provinces by means of the revolution and plebiscites. And this first period has a predominantly political significance, even if indeterminate and rather negative (against the regime of absolute power, against foreign dominion, and against the correlated division of the Italian people into many States).

The second period, sufficiently prominent in historical character, has instead a predominantly social and economical significance because, as liberal, it was designated as the politico-capitalistic regime against which the socialist party was arrayed. A very generic and largely comprehensive significance, it too; which moreover, in daily polemics, one thinks very little about and wants to think very little about, because the adversaries of fascism are not ignorant, and they do not fail to appreciate, in general, that the promoters of economic liberalism found greater satisfaction in fascism than all the liberal governments that preceded it in the management of the Italian State. And if it is true that, in this respect, the fascist conception of society cannot be contained by the schemas of the old liberal economy, it is certain that the antifascist polemic cannot be waged today in this arena in the name of liberal principles.

The polemic wants to be essentially political. And the adversaries of fascism intend to appeal to the old liberalism of the origins, to that of Cavour and his continuers, to the liberalism of the great traditions of the Risorgimento; to that liberalism in other words that together with Cavour, historically, welcomes into its fold not only Gioberti, but also Mazzini and Crispi and even Orsini; not only Ricasoli and D'Azeglio, but also Guerrazzi and Brofferio; not only Farini and Minghetti, but also Rattazzi and Valerio; not only Casati, but also Cattaneo and Ferrari; and in short political men of diverse temperament and aspect; right, center, left, and extreme. And if there is, out of all of them, an authentic liberal of Cavour's same genius and character, he is not a unilinear doctrinaire or all of one piece, from whom formulas and theorems can be taken on loan, adapted for all times and all situations; the very thing that would have made of Cavour a politician by the dozen, rather than the statesman whom everyone admires! A statesman who adored, yes, the Constitution, but without the fetishism that today big liberals of the last hour warm up to cold, who always have his name on their lips; because it is his article of May 27, 1848, in which he resolutely championed for the system of popular elections for the constitution of the Senate; in fact, it is that other document of March 10, 1848, of the day after, so to speak, the promulgation of the Statute, in which he declared that in his first article the Statute was not conformant with his desires, and he expressed his conviction that that article would in practice soon be reduced to "a homage to the Catholic religion." And in which he likewise noted that the Statute having been defined a "fundamental and irrevocable law of the monarchy" did not preclude "the path to any future progress" and did not establish "an absolute system of immobility contrary to common sense and to the needs of modern society"; he added that it is absurd "to pretend that the legislator had wanted to constrain himself and the nation never again to bring about the smallest change for the minimum improvement in a political law"; and that "this would be tantamount to wanting to make constituent power disappear from the heart of society; it would be to deprive it of the indispensable power of modifying its own political forms, according to new social exigencies." And he concluded that "a nation cannot divest itself of the faculty of changing its own political laws by legal means; it cannot, in the least, by any means, abdicate constituent power; this is placed, in absolute monarchies, in the legitimate sovereign; in constitutional monarchies, the parliament; in other words, the king and the two houses are fully vested with it."[35] And when it was necessary in the highest interests of the Fatherland, he did not hesitate, no, not even Cavour, during the difficult days following Orsini's attempt,[36] to restrict the freedom of the press by a law that was able to pass at that time with a vote of 100 to 42 in the Lower House, and unanimously in the Senate! Which was certainly a concession that Cavour had to make to his fundamental theoretical convictions; but it was precisely to his advantage by demonstrating the elasticity that is indispensable to peoples as well as to governments in the understanding and application of principles.

With specific regard to the freedom of the press, he himself, in a discourse he gave on February 5, 1852, had warned: "There was someone who employed this generic phrase: 'The principles are violated.' – Now, o gentlemen, to be completely frank, I will tell you that great phrases, great maxims, have many times led the State to ruin. I profess to respecting great principles, and I believe that they must never be violated; but one needs to distinguish between principles and their applications; and in their application there is a particular need to consider both times and circumstances."[37] And I wager that if Cavour today could raise his head up out of the sepulcher, and hear his disinterested and naïve conjurors, the first

[35]Original footnote: *Scritti*, Zanichelli, I, 95, 32, 34-5.

[36]Orsini: Felice Orsini (AD 1819-1858), an Italian writer and revolutionary who organized an attempt on French emperor Napoleon III's life.

[37]Original footnote: *Discoursi parlamentari*, IV, 347.

thing he would feel the need to inform us about is this: that the statesman does not have rules without exception, nor rigid maxims by which he can be ruled; and that the difficulty of his labor lies precisely in that. This is the first thing. And the second? The profound and accomplished historians of Cavourian liberalism who hold court in the newspapers of Italy and all its throng of followers would not have believed me if I said it. And there is no need to say it here.

Unfortunately, Cavour is dead for more than sixty years now; and we must however get along by ourselves with the fate of the country, if nothing else by striving to interpret what his thoughts would have been under the changed circumstances: just as all his successors from Ricasoli forward have done. Not all of whom resemble him, to be honest, I don't mean in intelligence or spirit, but in main ideas, criteria, orientation; and primarily in their manner of conceiving of the State; however, one may say what one wishes against the ideas in general, but there is no statesman who does not have a concept of State all his own; concept that expresses not so much what he says, so much as what he does. Yes, and to begin with Ricasoli, what an abyss between the authoritarian and religiously severe and inflexible dictator of Tuscany and the educated Torinese gentleman in the English fashion, all spirit and brio, although, undoubtedly, he too had the temperament of a dictator with an iron will! Everyone, from Ricasoli forward, has had his education and his temperament; and has found a new Italy, with ever new problems. It was not possible that from Cavour or other great men anything other than inspirations could be drawn. Everyone has had to fend for himself.

Then March 18, 1876 came along: historical date, in which a new page in history seemed about to begin for Italy. And it began in fact. The passing of the government from Right to Left, from moderates to progressives, appeared a step down and a regression to the men who had guided Italy during the time of its political constitution, legislative unification, and financial consolidation; and it certainly marked the beginning of a decline of political custom and administrative methods, and set in motion the parliamentary degeneration of our constitutional system. But to historians it appears also like progress, in that it opened the way to a form of politics that the great revolution, recently accomplished, had neglected: politics, which had to rally the great masses around the government, and make them participate and be interested in the life of a State that had arisen almost unbeknownst to them because of a minority of the middle classes and the upper classes. Italian democracy from Depretis to Giolitti has fulfilled this historical function, which is not reasonable or possible to ignore, but by this time it must be considered exhausted.

And now we need to go back to the principles. This is what fascism has wanted to do. To go back, it is understood, not to repeat, which would not be possible, but to restore that internal energy of the State, which is necessary to its revival. Seeing that, in part, fascism is liberalism: at least the liberalism of men who sincerely believed in freedom, and had however an austere concept of it. When in my letter of May 31 of '23, I declared to the Prime Minster, the Hon. Mussolini, that "liberalism, as I understand it and as the men of the glorious Right of the Risorgimento understood it, the liberalism of freedom in the laws and consequently in the strong State and in the State conceived of as an ethical reality," I didn't believe it was represented in Italy by the liberals, who were more or less openly against it, but it was precisely from them [the liberals] that a general outcry arose among the learned members of the liberal party of the time, as if I had misconstrued the meaning of this word. "Of course," observes Croce,[38] "in every political regime, even in the most purportedly despotic one, there is freedom," but the affirmation "becomes fallacious inasmuch as it exhibits a generality with the appearance of conveying something specific and particular, while condemning other parties as liberal or illiberal." But...

First of all, it is not a generality that the freedom of true liberalism is freedom within the law (and not outside the law, and consequently against the law, as the individualist conceives of it in the manner of old liberalism);

Secondly, it is not a generality that the freedom of a sincere liberal is the freedom that is realized and can only be realized in the strong State (and therefore it is not the freedom of all liberals today, who have banded together in order to bring down, with their combined strength, a government that aims at, to begin with, establishing the authority of the State in its fullness);

[38]Original footnote: In *Critica*, May 1924, p. 148.

Thirdly, all the less do I believe the third of the differential characteristics indicated by me to be a generality, that true freedom can only exist in the State that is understood and realized as ethical.

In fact, Croce himself, who professes to be a liberal in his own way, does not wish to understand this conception of the State as a concrete moral reality and prefers to make it an abstract economical organization, and he fights against that doctrine, which I hold essential to the liberal concept of the State. He fights against it like a kind of "governmental conception" of morality.

On these three points, and I will be the first to admit it, Cavour may have wavered. But the entire party of the Right, which inherited its political program from him and was delving deeper into its postulates, which were to be its essence, held firm to these principles, which fascism appeals to, and which the same Croce maintains (apart from some difficulties that his philosophy created for him) with all the ardor of his spirit in the best of Italian traditions. And these three points, – let it be said with tolerance for those who, through the opportunity for cowardly or shrewd politicking, love to call themselves liberals and not fascists, – are the substance, I don't say of liberal doctrine in general (empty form, in which each can put so many things! according to his taste), but of the historical Italian liberal consciousness. They were the concepts around which one fought in 1876 in Parliament when, the Right having fallen, the two political conceptions, both old and new, found themselves face to face. And the newspapers of the time were filled with polemics similar to those that one delights in today, if there are even people today still whose stomach holds up to the daily prose of so many experts of public law who snap at fascism's heels.

The occasion arose during the debate for the laws on railroad agreements in which the former minster of public works, Silvio Spaventa, on June 24, made the following declaration of faith, which reads like something from our own days:

> *I do not wish at this time to make a theory of the State. For me, the State has had diverse forms and purposes in history. Take the warrior State [for example]; take with the hieratic State; take the commercial State; take the* Rechtsstaat,[39] *as the Germans say, the State of law, which the English government is a type of. Then take the modern State, the State we call the civil State.*
>
> *Under all these diverse forms, I conceive of the State in this guise. It is, to me, the guiding conscience whereby a nation knows how to be managed in its operations, society feels secure in its institutions, citizens see themselves safeguarded in their property and in their persons. In the State, then, there is justice, defense, leadership. This leadership sometimes makes a warrior*

[39] *Rechtsstaat*: German for "rule of law" or "state of law."

> *State out of the State; sometimes it makes a State that has for its object more the future salvation of souls than their satisfaction and perfection in this world, as in a hieratic State; sometimes it makes out of the State a State of commercial activity, like the Hanseatic League, like the East India Company; sometimes it makes out of the State what the modern State is today: a State that leads people in the direction of culture, a State that not only restricts itself to distributing justice and defending society, but wants to lead it by the means that conduce to the loftiest ends of humanity.*[40]

Even Marco Minghetti, entering into the discussion the day after, observed:[41]

> *Yesterday, the Hon. Barazzuoli cited the Italian school to me. Frankly, I took him at his word. From Genovesi, from Verri, from Romagnosi to Pellegrino Rossi, to Cavour, in which of these great thinkers does he find the negation of the State? Where did he read that the office of the State must limit itself to the defense of rights and the maintenance of justice, and that in*

---

[40]Original footnote: S. Spaventa, *The Politics of the Right*, edited by B. Croce, Bari, Laterza, 1910, pp. 266-7.

[41]Original footnote: *Parliamentary Discourses*, VII, 260.

> *doing so its work is complete, is accomplished? He will read in those writings that on the one hand one must leave to private citizens, to Associations, the maximum possible freedom; but that on the other hand it is the State's duty to vary according to the times, to make up for what private citizens and associations lack, which is a function of progress, of leadership, as the most excellent Hon. Spaventa said, inasmuch as, in a free State, the most active forces of the country are united, and only there are the general interests of the entire nation dealt with.*

What is included in this leadership of the State? That depends, according to Spaventa, on the changing needs and diverse situations in which the State finds itself. So the sphere of its activity cannot be closed within fixed limits: "Today the State takes over the railroads, tomorrow it releases them and takes over something else." So that Spaventa, who was a strenuous proponent in '76 of the transfer of the railroads to the State, was quite aware that this was a contingent problem susceptible only to an equally contingent solution. What can be said about it in general, he added, is that "the leadership that the State imparts to Society is in the direction of culture."

"The modern State," Spaventa resumed:

> *... is born from the so-called State of law, in other words from that State in which all citizens feel and recognize*

> *themselves equal before the law. This equality is, it can be said, the fruit of the history of Europe since the French Revolution. From this feeling of equality arises a terrible exigence in the consciousness of the multitude, for whom it is not enough to be equal before the law, but who intend to rise up, who intend to have a share in the goods of life, which in past centuries were reserved only for the few. And the civility of peoples consists precisely in this. A people cannot be said to be civil who are merely educated; just as one does not call a people civil who only enjoy themselves. Civilization is the unity of culture and well-being. A people cannot be called civil where only a few are educated and find enjoyment; that people is truly civil wherein the greatest number of them are educated and find enjoyment.*[42]

At this point the parliamentary Records indicate [the following]:

"Approbation on the Right – Loud comments on the Left." Whence the exclamation of the orator: "I am surprised to hear this noise coming from representatives of Italian democracy!" It is understood, in fact, that since then these gentlemen had bought for themselves the privilege of defending the people! Re-

[42]Original footnote: Op. cit., pp. 227-8, V. also: S. Spaventa, *Parliamentary Discourses*, Rome, 1913, pp. 419-20.

sponding then to one of the greater objections of his adversaries, Spaventa with great force asserted:

> *As for the authority and strength of the State then, even here I have reflected many times on the accusations and complaints, which are caused by this excessive strength and authority; and I asked myself: but what are we exactly? We were born yesterday, we are still children; are we really a strong State? We have succeeded in the reunification of Italy; do you believe that this unity is strong enough already to resist the clashes of centuries?*

Voices from the left responded: *Yes, yes*. And Spaventa for that reason continued:

> *I am pleased to hear it; this is my belief, but the work that we have done is only fifteen years old. Machiavelli said that new States that are weak will die. Now the strength and the real authority of the States consists, today more than ever, in really and efficaciously representing the common interests; in directing, as I said, society in its progress, not for this or that class, for this or that man, so much as for everyone.*
>
> *"You are worshippers of the State?" Yes, I am a worshipper of the State.*

> *When we live in an epoch where everything is destroyed, little or nothing is being built, the faith in something, which is not only our miserable egoism, – this faith I believe is necessary and salutary for my country.*[43]

On this topic of the "worship of the State," the polemic of the House and then of the press flared up. It was the concept of the strong State, insofar as ethical, the director of civil society. Many liberals, coming from Catholicism, could not grasp it. But that was however the political testament of the Right, of which Spaventa remained the most authoritative representative to the last, placed for that reason as leader of the Roman Constitutional Association in 1879, where he gave his great speech: *The Politics and Administration of the Right and the Work of the Left.*

Among his friends in 1876 who were sitting in the House was the philosopher Francesco Fiorentino, who passionately sided with the ideas of the Right. Who, when the House dissolved, wanted to give a historically and logically reasoned form to the concept of the State that Spaventa had so vigorously affirmed; and in two successive issues of the *Neapolitan Journal of Philosophy and Letters, Moral and Political Sciences* (where Antonio Salandra was also waging his first battles at that time) he wrote two letters to the same Spaventa on the *Modern State*, rapid, vivacious, very lucid, as he knew how to do. I thought it was appropriate to pull these letters out of oblivion,

---

[43]Original footnote: *Politics of the Right*, p. 233; *Discourses*, p. 423.

not because there is much to learn from them (some things I myself would not subscribe to, and I am not in agreement with that more exactly elaborated and more particularly spiritual idea, which today can be obtained from the essence of the State); but because I think that many people today will be interested to read them and that they might serve as very significant historical documents of what is effectively the thought of Italian liberals, whose tradition today is exalted.

– Rome, October 6, 1924.

IV. Against Certain Anonymous Critics[44]

Dear Director,

Thank you for having republished in *Idea Nazionale* that preface of mine to Fiorentino's pamphlet on the *Modern State*. All the more so as I see that it has gotten on the nerves of the big "liberals," guarantors of great traditions, who hold sway over the famous, previously supportive press. But now I do not want to, and cannot, polemicize with the *Giornale d'Italia,* where, as you have no doubt seen, an elegant writer, "One who remembers" (and who appears instead to have an empty memory, in addition to the loyal spirit of anonymous writers like that "Old pedagogue" of another evening newspaper, who believes himself capable of inflicting on me his eternal and intelligent pedagoguery because he does not sign [his pieces] with the name and cognomen of Professor Enrico Carrara), makes reference to that same volume of Spaventa's which I had employed and cited; and he believes, good man that he is, to disrespect me and contradict my thesis with two other citations, which confirm in fact what I was saying about the concept that Spaventa, along with all the liberals of the old Right, had of the strong State.

But, as for the *Giornale d'Italia*, which is pleased to use towards me those fashions and that

[44]Original footnote: Letter published in the *Idea Nazionale* of October 16, 1925.

tone, which that new director with his exquisite provincial taste has made fashionable and now prints that I have failed as "a reckless minister of instruction," and that "many years and hard work will be needed to repair the problems I have left," – how to take it seriously if it is the same newspaper that wants support by the government of instruction and exalts my friend, the Hon. Casati, who continues my work with the same criteria and the same methodology, and was just recently lauded in Milan by the Prime Minster as the "most gentilian follower of Gentile"?

I will content myself with informing that good man who remembers, or does not remember, these three things:

1. that I have too much respect for history to want to give the fascist membership card to Spaventa or to any other politicians from before the war; and that for me, if substantive content of authentic liberalism of the old Right can be found within fascism, not all of fascism can be looked for in that doctrine, because fascism aims at new problems that no one could propose before the war and before syndicalism.

2. that when I call fascists more liberal than liberals (the liberals of Livorno, who shouted down my egregious friend, the Hon. Codacci-Pisanelli, and who now protest with marvelous naïvety that they were and are and will always be in agreement!) I make it a question of principles, on the same terrain as adversaries who theorize, for their part, to no end;

and I do not wish to judge single acts of government, in which I have no reason to exclude any error *a priori* because I have never believed in the infallibility of anyone; but I retain that, to set the record straight, one would see that the responsibility for some errors is the fault of the opposition more than that of the Government; the opposition, which sells its very soul to undermine the strength and authority of the Government in every way possible;

3. that when our adversaries reproach fascism for its violence, they do not make the necessary examination of conscience to see whether their polemic of bad faith is not violence, or gratuitous insults, unproved and unprovable judgments, and calumnies audaciously and insistently repeated with the manifest purpose of exercising an undue pressure on public opinion.

And I will stop there.

– Rome, October 15, 1924.

V. Everyone at His Post[45]

Dear Spampanato,

I applaud your courageous initiative and I wish you readers of good faith for the new review, so that your sincere and ardent faith is merited in the new life, which many now have attempted in a number of different ways to suffocate. And I am pleased that your review is based out of Naples, where a revival of healthy political energies is discerned by many indications, but where there is still much work to do to ensure that it does not lack the necessary stimulus for concrete and efficacious action. Interest has grown, is manifested in the discussions and in the same tone of certain polemics, often acerbic beyond measure, but significative of a state of mind which could translate into an effective force, just as useful to the public good as simple negative criticism, however passionate it may be, is unproductive for the most part, if not damaging.

As for this interest, which tends to be diffused ever more broadly, it is fitting to take advantage of that clarification that everyone invokes, but which most are limited, unfortunately, merely to invoke.

Since the worst enemy of Italians, whatever party they belong to, whatever business they are involved in, is themselves, in their mind. And it is in their nature to theorize, to intellectualize, to write lit-

[45]Original footnote: From the first issue of the fascist review of Naples, *La Montagna* (Dec. 15, 1924), edited by the attorney Bruno Spampanato.

erature or abstract philosophy, losing sight of life and live action, in which all struggles are resolved and in which in fact the substance of human life consists.

Today there is a lot of talk about the crisis of fascism. Well then, if we leave aside resolute and irreducible adversaries, who have their good or their bad reasons for desirously hastening the catastrophe, one cannot fail to recognize the innocence of many who stand there watching in expectation that the crisis will be resolved, if it can be resolved; and that it will be resolved within that closed circle in which they collocate the fascist phenomenon (as they call it), object of pure observation almost, which contains in itself all the particular conditions, the particular means of being, and the particular law.

Many people suffer for certain characteristics of the phenomenon; and they deplore, with more or less distress, the prevailment of that or this tendency, in the same way as a farmer who arises at morning and looks at the sky, and who is afflicted by the imminent storm, which he cannot ward off despite its threat to destroy his crops. To me it happens every day to hear people who have their political opinions, and who ought to feel the moral obligation to serve them, who repeat: – *Certainly, a fascism like this, who would not want it? But the fascists!...* – And they wait for the fascists (those same fascists!) to take the road to Damascus finally;[46] or for these ideas, which they too believe are fine and worthy of triumph, to turn back and hide so as no longer to trouble good

[46]To take the road to Damascus: in reference to St. Paul and his conversion; see Acts 9:1-9.

Italians, who have a great need for calm and tranquility, and who, preparing themselves thus far docilely for the difficult experiment, – come on, it cannot be denied that they have given every desirable proof of good will.

But here is the rub, dear Spampanato, and it is cured with iron and fire. Whoever wants fascism and does not want fascists (in other words, certain fascists) has the sacrosanct duty not to stand at the window, but to go down into the street: what I mean is, to become a fascist, and to act within the fascist party. And it does not help to say that those who are within, have the duty, no less sacrosanct, to stay there. Since, if they do not exit, it means one of two things: either they lied to themselves and to the country when they embraced the program; or now they betray themselves and the country, turning to fight that program out of the hatred or irritation for the men who execute it, and whom they are to replace.

So, two distinct points to be kept equally in mind. One is to clarify, yes, the idea, and to demonstrate why turning back is impossible. The other is to require that everyone take his place and that he hold on to it faithfully.

I am sure that you will work for one or the other of these points with all your power.

– Rome, December 4, 1924.

VI. The Religious Character of the Present Political Fight[47]

I think that it would be very useful for an understanding of the present Italian political situation, – dominated, as everyone will want to acknowledge, by fascism, whatever his personal opinions, – if I were to address several aspects of it which have been talked about too much of late. Since the study of said aspects, controversial and fiercely debated from opposite points of view, can however fill newspaper columns and always make them more annoying and intolerable, but does not appear very beneficial for clarifying people's ideas, converting their spirits, swelling the ranks of this or that party, or finally facilitating any sort of solution to the political problem that we have before us.

I mention one example: that of freedom, which can be discussed forever until one finds oneself in the realm of principles, which are always very difficult to define, because it is a difficult undertaking ultimately to isolate them from all the consequences, applications, and concrete contingencies for which they are immediately invoked, and which in fact give rise to and nourish real interest so that people's dispositions are actually attracted to the principles them-

[47]Original footnote: in the review, *Educazione politica*, March 1925.

selves. They are however pulled here and there by the strength of passions that are rebellious to every purely theoretical and fundamental consideration. And so the strangest experts of political philosophy improvise, whereby whoever reasons the most and makes a duty of proceeding methodically and rigorously gets the worst of it. Whereas on closer inspection it is observed that those who in theory are among their adversaries are actually, without realizing it, entirely in agreement even with the indeterminateness and logical incorrectness of the concepts they employ; and that the divergence lies more in the appreciation of the *circumstances* in which the principles must be applied, or the *limits*, which everyone agrees are necessary, but which it is difficult then to identity in a way than no one criticizes. No matter what the treaties of constitutional law and fundamental charters say with their more or less abstract formulas, those limits depend from time to time on the judgment that is gradually to be formed and imposed on the ends to be reached through political freedoms, let alone the means more adapted with each case to the reaching of those ends. Since, evidently, political freedoms are simple instruments; that, as such, they cannot have any other value than what is conferred on them by the ends to which they are useful. And whoever exalts freedom (without qualification) when it has simply to do with guarantees that the State can and ought to give to the individual, confuses very disparate things and knows not what he says. So that to hear some people flocking today in great numbers before the goddess Liberty, in protest against the fascist tyranny or for I don't know what melancholic nostalgia of the times, improbable by now, of the social dissolution of the State which followed immediately upon its victory and which fascism broke, one has a measure of the intelligence, indeed of the political temperament, of certain people.

So let us leave aside, at least for the time being, these all too trite and too little instructive arguments and let us see whether we cannot draw some lesson from other types of considerations, which appear more remote than the more current political interests do.

This then, for me, is the purely *religious* character of the fascist spirit which is profoundly suggestive and therefore capable of becoming particularly useful for the practical orientation of all those who live the political life with seriousness and sincerity. B. Mussolini has many times expressed, with the energy that is characteristic of his intuitive thinking, the mystical side of fascism as a system of religious belief offered with heart and soul to the nation; wishing in a special way to point out the absoluteness of this ideal, not of the historical formation to be preserved or perpetuated, but rather of the moral conception of the future of the people to which the individual belongs, and in which concept he is exalted, as an individual subordinate to a higher law, ready to immolate himself for it, since everything of value that he can attribute to and acquire for himself depends on it. And there is no doubt that one of the most powerful motives, indeed the most powerful motive for the fascination exerted by Mussolini on the young, on the masses, and on everyone, derives from this chord which he knows how to make vibrate loudly in souls, and which vibrates primarily in him every time he abandons himself to the inspiration central to his thought, and becomes truly eloquent. Whoever has heard him speak, irrespective of polemics and argumentation, knows the truth of this observation which is the statement of a fact experienced by everyone. On this point Mussolini's temperament coincides with that of Mazzini, and in the fascist youth who run to join the fasci and above all the militia, he inspires a religious feeling similar to that which animated the followers of Giovine Italia, which was the most potent leaven of the Italian revolution for independence and unification.

It is pointless to look for differences and reasons for differences between the fascist conception of the nation and the Mazzinian one. Without a doubt the Mazzinian concept has become much more concrete in fascism and much more tightly bound to the historical development of many other concepts that the concept of nation is connected to, not to mention that it has benefited from all the clarifications that the political philosophy of the nineteenth century has brought to bear on relationships between the nation and the State, and between the State and the individual citizen. But what is meant to be observed here is that just as the motto of Giovine Italia, "God and People," made the imperative and absolute value of ideal rights or of the exigencies of the people dependent on a religious concept, or, rather, on seeing the living revelation of God in the people, so the fascist concept of the nation State or of the Fatherland superior to all classes, groups, and individuals, who presuppose the

State and who live in its sphere and are therefore conditioned by it, is not a utilitarian concept, as if the means justified the ends, but is precisely the concept of an absolute something, which is an end in itself, and for that reason divine.

Given the greater concreteness of the fascist ideal, it was no longer possible for fascism to bind its conception of the State to that vague rationalistic, religious doctrine that Mazzini, under the influence of Saint-Simonianism, tended to reduce the religion of the new Italy to, which he too so vigorously desired permeated and governed by religious feeling. Fascism does not fall back onto the practical uncertainties of Mazzinianism with respect to Catholicism, wanting to exert influence on a people who, when it tried to reform its Catholicism, never knew how to stop, like other nations, at the midpoint of an evangelical doctrine subtracted from its historical development and fixed at best in a form of accommodating theology [lying somewhere] between mysticism and rationalism, but passed directly and resolutely to the negation of every supernaturalism and superintelligibilism to wander freely in the field of pure philosophy. Fascism which understands the necessity of the religious life of the spirit, outside of which there is nothing but the materialism of liberalistic individualism or social democracy, understands consequently how to graft itself on to the ancient but also always alive and powerful trunk of Italian historical religiosity, which as a result of the graft will come alive again and sprout new buds and turn green again with new leaves. Anyone who has said that the political conception of fascism does not go beyond the classical, ancient type of liberalism should try to make sense of the ecclesiastical politics of fascism – but seriously, and without the short-sighted disregard and insipid guffaws of the most superficial and unintelligent sort who pretend to be clever. Since it is not understood by insisting to look for the key to it in the personal psychology of a Tom or a Dick [or a Harry], but only in the logic and in the general and indisputable character of the movement. Nor is it necessary to point out that any explanation of this brand of politics is devoid of value on the basis of the general attribution of a pretended conservative or reactionary tendency for fascist politics. Attribution destitute of any basis, against which the concerns of conservatives, and other evidently and boldly revolutionary characters, or, if one will, innovators of the social politics of fascism, would be enough. And the fact of fascism's audacities, which to some have seemed really temerarious, would also be enough in some of its more passionate reforms, promoted with great energy by an absolutely antithetical spirit, in every way, by every criteria of ordinary conservatism.

But independently of the heroic spirit of martyrdom, which nobody will want to deny to that psychology that gave the fascist movement its first impulse and therefore its primitive and characteristic character, apart from the more solid and justifiable interpretation of the political direction practically adopted by fascism in religious matters, I believe I need to draw the reader's attention to one of the more expressive signs of this character of fascism, which corresponds to a fact that more seriously troubles the Italian conscience of today.

The fact is this: that in Italy today, because of fascism, what appeared to be until yesterday the most solid personal ties of friendship or family are now broken; and people whom only yesterday were sought out, and who nourished the most unlimited esteem and greatest attachment for one another, if they meet again today after many months of not seeing each other because of their different political opinions, not only do they not run up to each other as before, but they do not even greet, in fact they turn their backs on each other, contemptuously and resentfully. And this does not happen only among participants in militant politics, whereby the impassioned and bitter struggle of opposite parties can array even friends against one another, and cause them to see an enemy in an adversary. He enters into a rage, and arms himself against an intimate friend and collaborator of many years in common affairs of the greatest interest and personal and moral value, someone who until yesterday kept himself at a distance from the arena of conflict, and was happy for example to close himself off in his studies, claiming that one can do well at one thing only in life, and that if there are those who must and can serve the country in the assemblies and in the conflict of parties, there are on the other hand those who are born to serve it living hidden like the sage Epicurus, completely absorbed in the eternal struggle of the mind. Indeed, the closer the friendship and the higher the esteem in the past, the more ardent the despite, the ire, the aversion today, and the more acute the need to lacerate and bite.

To me who writes, it has happened and happens. And has offered material for reflection, but not surprisingly, and not also too very regretfully, if I have to tell the truth. Not because it can be pleasing to anyone, and all the less so to me, to see a friend who distances himself; or because I am disposed to refuge myself in that miserable stronghold of intellectual egoism which, strong in the motto *amicus Plato sed magis amica veritas*,[48] whets and tempts idiots, incapable of any criticism, to enjoy their truth, which can never be such, and never for that reason effectively consoling, as every truth is, if it does not take into account another person's truth. No. My regret has not been great because, sincerely, the ideal of a comfortable life, living in the affection of truly affectionate friends and the applause of listeners and spectators satisfied in their inclinations, has never been my ideal; and I have always found pleasure rather in the bitter taste of being beholden to nobody and to giving testimony in this way, not to facile expressions, but rather, with the sacrifice of dear things, to those ideas which seemed worthy to me of fighting for and living for.

No great regret, then. But also no great surprise, even though too many people around me have been surprised: – How is it that Tom or Dick is no longer your friend? But how is that possible? – To me, in truth, reading the Gospel, from which I have learnt a lot of things, those divine words by Jesus have always made a vivid impression on me: – *Non veni pacem mittere, sed gladium. Veni enim separare*

[48]*Amicus Plato...*: Latin for "Plato is a friend, but truth is a better friend." Originally attributed by Ammonius, in his *Life of Aristotle,* to Plato, but with respect to Socrates (*amicus Socrates, sed...*). Often attributed to Aristotle in his *Ethics*.

hominem adversus patrem suum et filiam adversus matrem suam.[49] – Or as it is referred to elsewhere: *Ignem veni mittere in terram. Putatis quia pacem veni dare in terram? Non, dico vobis, sed separationem: erunt enim ex hoc quinque in domo una divisi, tres in duos et duo in tres dividentur.*[50] – Sword, fire: anything but peace! War in families: two against three, and three against two: the father against the son, and the son against the father. Thus one is worthy of Christ: let each person accepts his cross and follow it. *Qui invenit animam suam, perdet illam: et qui perdiderit animam suam propter me, inveniet eam.* This the divine pact, and the eternal story of all religions, which have ignited in human hearts the greatest flames of love, but also the vastest fires of hatred. All history groans because of it. And for this reason those tender philosophers of the Enlightenment, so very light, but so philanthropic, whose oracles the Masons still read today with infinite reverence, got upset with positive religions, in other words with religion in general; which latter, according to a penetrating image by a German philosopher, stands in relation to individual religions as fruit does to cherries, pears, melons, etc. So either one eats one of these species of fruit, or one renounces fruit altogether. Or one accepts a religion, or one turns one's back on religion or, as people like to say today, in order to attenuate and diminish this hard matter even more, on religiosity.

Even fascism, then, as every faith with a reli-

[49]*Non veni...suam*: Matthew 10:34-35 (Vulgate).

[50]*Ignem veni... dividentur*: Luke 12:49, 51-53 (Vulgate).

gious character *venit gladium mittere et ignem*.[51]

No, someone will say. It is a moral question that divides and exasperates souls. – It is an error: the so-called moral question is only one of the elements that enter into the formation of this psychology, which I refer to, and which I consider inexplicable without the fundamental religious note. The same moral question is kept awake and exasperated by this passion, which stirs at the bottom of natures, and which is the source from which spouts that intolerance, that intransigence, that violence and that quasi simplification of argumentation, with which from one side and the other the matter is debated implacably, in perhaps absolutely inappropriate terms, which in any case do not admit of a solution. Seeing as it is superfluous to point out that this religious tonality of fascist psychology has generated the same tonality in antifascist psychology; since that separation, which Jesus spoke about, is born of that struggle whereby a new spirit stands up and fights against an old one. Which, in this case, one feels squarely struck by fascism, and nearly at the root of his very existence.

If one looks not at the surface, where every moment the vulgar observer believes he sees the task of fascism finished or, as he says, consumed, but deep down where, surprise after surprise, one certifies that there is a solid, iron core, which does not succeed in breaking or dissolving – the question today is precisely this. That there are in opposition two complete conceptions of life, radically opposed, neither of which

[51] *Venit gladium...*: Latin for "came to cast sword and fire." With a reference, again, to Matthew 10:34.

understands the other; neither of which succeeds in finding a common point of contact with the other, so as to enter into a initial relationship with it of resolutive conciliation. In a first instance, this opposition was not felt so clearly or so strongly. Rather, this or that form of conservative liberalism appeared to find the energetic expression of its own tendencies in the new movement. But, little by little, the iron logic of fascism began to reveal itself and impose itself on the intellect and on the will of fascists and others; and therefore the separation became ever more accentuated; fascism became always more tightly closed, and isolating, in order to strengthen its content and its combative force and moral expansion. The many attempts at that "normalization" which, fundamentally, had to be the conciliation of souls, and in other words that peace, which even Christ despised, are all fatally flawed.

Today one wants to lose his soul, in order to find it again; and arrangements for the sake of quiet living are no longer possible. There will still be thousands upon thousands of fascists ignorant of that and extremely disposed to any arrangement; but this means nothing; because – well do they know, the great judges of our present history – fascists don't make fascism, but fascism makes fascists, hoisting the flag, which draws a crowd; in the middle of which there is someone who thinks and someone who does not think, someone who understands and someone who does not understand, someone who has a heart and someone who does not have one, someone who is worthy and someone who is unworthy; but nevertheless they are all drawn, each according to his own way of feeling, by that flag, and they march. The flag is raised high by its own strength, by the virtue that exalts it, so that it can communicate with individuals, but not receive from them; held up by an idea, which has its own logic, which nobody can twist and deviate from its infallible goal. Today, on the one hand, there is fascism which is the recognition of a law, which presently the single individual must be subordinate to; on the other hand, liberalism (even socialists now want to be liberals!) which sees nothing else than the single individual. *Mors tua, vita mea*. One needs to see this quite clearly, and act in consequence.

VII. The Liberalism of B. Croce[52]

1.

The Roman journal that for several months now has arrogated to itself the magnanimous defense of I do not know what liberalism (certainly not that of Sonnino, whom the same journal wanted to be the interpreter of in the past, and whose thinking now and again it assumes nonetheless the attitude of being the continuer of) did a nice thing recently by publishing a small article by Benedetto Croce, containing the eulogy of liberalism as "the party of culture," as "the ideality that demands experience and meditation, historical sense and the sense of complex and complicated things, and in short mental and moral finesse," and as "the party that goes forward into the future," etc., etc. Political article in short, inspired by those sentiments that are diffuse in many souls that passionately participate in Italy in the present political battle and desperately yearn for an irrevocable past or a future that with each passing day grows more distant and disappears into vagueness, into incertitude, into impossibility. One can really feel the heart of a man beating there, who from the serene temples of his studies faces that tumult of life, where opposed and intransigent principles more bitterly fight for the conquest of the State, which is life itself in the concrete compages of all its interests; and he is attracted by the spectacle

[52]Original footnote: In *The Epoch* of March 21, 1925, and in *Political Education,* a III, fasc. 2.

because he is disturbed in his studies, once again, and taken away from the tranquil peace, from the divine freedom of abstract intellectual occupations, which in every period have so greatly benefited from the apolitical individualism of democratic and liberalistic societies. In this way, the scholar's passion becomes a political passion; it becomes an annoyance with disorderly and violent passions, which break out in society during periods of intense politic crisis and tenacious efforts at revival. And from the philosopher and the historian, behold, the expression not of a meditated and rigorous, universal and superior thought appears, but a judgment by a party man, even though propped up by that type of argumentation which the philosopher and the historian are accustomed to use: concepts, definitions, historical citations.

I have already seen several journals express surprise at this eulogy of liberalism in the mouth of Croce; of a democratic liberalism that is in stark contrast to all the political ideas of Hegelian and Vician inspiration expressed by Croce on other occasions. But the topic would seem deserving of closer inspection; and in spite of his annoyance with fascism, by which Croce lends a hand today to liberal Italians of different stripes, many of whom he has always superciliously and justly scorned and will always scorn the intolerable company of, one would find that all the philosophical education and constant and profounder inspiration of Croce's thought makes him a genuine fascist without the black shirt. I am sincerely sorry at this time to say something that might displease him: but no matter how much we love Croce and feel him standing in person beside us, and within us, we cannot resign ourselves to abandoning him to the past, where sometimes he would love, by certain predilections for nostalgic and erudite longing, and even vibrating with internal commotion and elegant estheticism, to refuge himself in contempt of things and of men who are annoying, which unfortunately besiege us in the present; we have no choice but to refer younger generations, those who have yet to learn how to understand life in the new way, to his books.

It is pointless to pause and discuss this eulogy of liberalism as Croce's personal position; it is not Croce the man's, with his work habits, his personal tastes, his likes and dislikes, but Croce the thinker's. That story that he rebukes the nationalists with for not knowing, and that he knew himself extremely well, he did not ask to speak about it, as he could have done. When he said that "our Risorgimento was liberal," he carelessly repeated an assertion that was often seen in the *Giornale d'Italia*. But he knows very well that if by liberalism one means what the fascists mean today when they fight against them, and what the same liberals mean today when they oppose fascism, the Italian Risorgimento was not liberal; because the marrow of it was Mazzinianism, in other words radical criticism and the antithesis of this liberalism. Silvio Spaventa and the deputies of May 15, violators of the constitution, were revolutionaries, they were not liberals in the manner of Borzino. Ricasoli and Farini, without whose magnanimous resolve Cavour would have failed, were dictators, like Garibaldi; and they remembered constitutional liberty only when it suited them. And Cavour, extremely liberal, when it suited him, also protested about the freedom of the press, against the great principles that always ruined nations: and he always governed that House that bowed before him, like a boss. And Massimo d'Azeglio after Novara did not hesitate to turn around and dissolve the House a second time in order to save the country "from internal enemies." And nobody in conclusion ever had a scruple putting the country before the idol of freedom – which Croce knows how formal and extrinsic and inexistent it is – idolized by liberals. And so? So the story of Croce the "liberal" is not the story of the historical Croce.

Nor is the philosophy. Are *sophisms and verbal quibbles* the fascist constructions of the strong State and the ethical State? To me they appear rather like sophisms and verbal quibbles, the attempts that Croce made to demonstrate it: as when he called it a *tautological proposition* when someone wants the synthesis of freedom and the law, because the law is intrinsic to the same freedom; or when polemically he came out and said that *the State is a simple abstraction and general representation* (what he himself denies, discoursing now about liberalism and calling it "adverse to the communistic ideal of the abolition of the State"; inconceivable adverseness, as if it were a matter of a simple abstraction).

But let's leave history and philosophy to the side. The secret attraction for fascism is detected in this same eulogy of liberalism, where he accuses nationalism of being mere literature (beautiful or ugly literature) rather than politics, while he admits that nationalism "with the experience and above all with the assistance of fascism" has made much progress in the terrain of reality. This opposition of literature and politics is exquisitely fascist. Other parties, one knows, have always spoken about it. But in politics, there are no inventions or discoveries. For the most part, the novelty consists in doing what others are contented to say: and that is no small thing. And faced with Italian liberalism, as a man of Croce's temperament can understand it, placing a hand over his breast, he will recognize, and already implicitly recognizes, that fascism, in this respect, has titles and advantages of the first order.

Now, just to spite us, he sees in fascism the antithesis of socialism (which is inexact); and in antithesis to the extreme democracy of the latter, he baptizes it *authoritarianism and reactionaryism*. And he warns the nationalists that "authoritarian regimes last only in peoples in decline, but for those on the move and in ascent they have no durability," and so forth in this manner. But the double baptism cannot hold great importance for Croce who cannot see anything concrete and real behind either name; the political reality being really much more complex and complicated than the two abstract concepts of authority and reaction. And now, reaction! If reaction to individualistic democratism is meant, which the same Croce has criticized so many times, is it even possible that he should want a non-reactionary liberalism?

No, this is not the thought of Benedetto Croce, extremely Vician in every fiber of his thought. They are [those of] the democracies of "fully expounded reason," in other words the times of liberalism, and of men of a more refined and elegant culture and sensibilities, as Croce polemically imagines his liberals here, rich in experience and accustomed to contemplation, the times of the decadence of nations; which rise again, returning instead to their origins, to the fierceness of primitive barbarism.[53] Which was also the thought – not always well explained, to be honest, nor certainly possessed – of Croce's other master and inspirer, Francesco de Sanctis, author of the discourse *Science and Life*, and writings on Zola, and the promoter, as minister of instruction, of gymnastics, when the good De Meis began to suspect that the "Professor," in order to remake the character and fiber of Italians, wanted to have them regress to the level of animals.

I would rather that young fascists read De Sanctis, the great critic, but also an even greater educator: De Sanctis, exalted by Croce. For example, he said:

> *Science is synonymous with life, all of it? It can stop the course of corruption and dissolution, renew the blood, remake the character? I hear it said: nations rise because of knowledge. Can knowledge make this miracle happen? Well, if we look at ancient history, it does not appear so. Greek knowledge could not postpone the dissolution of the Greek people, nor purify the corruption of the Latin world. The intellectual renaissance in Italy was at the*

[53]Original footnote: Croce wiggles out of it here, as his nature leads him, with a joke. See *Critica*, 1925, p. 190.

> *same time the beginning of its decline. The greater the culture, and the more disgraceful the fall. In the face of these facts, Vico is better understood. Intellect appears last in life, and the more one knows, the more one acts like an adult, and the more the feeling and imagination is exhausted, two forces from which great initiatives and great enthusiasms derive. Science is the product of mature age, and does not have the strength to remake the course of the years, to restore youth. Maturity is certainly the most splendid time in life, not the beginning, but the fruit, and the noble crown of history, which is the stimulation and beginning of a new history... Science grows at the expense of life. The more it gives to thought, the more it takes from action.*[54]

This is Croce's entire philosophy *in a nutshell*, in which this antithesis between thought and action can be said to be unbending. The great liberal De Sanctis. But with respect to political freedom he himself says that it is an *instrument of work*; and that in order to use it one needed to make men free; in order to form them, he himself pointed out the way *in the restoration of the limits of freedom*. One needs to reread the discourse *Science and Life*.

---

[54]From *La Scienza e la Vita* (*Science and Life*), a speech that De Sanctis gave at the University of Naples on November 16, 1872 and which was later published by Morano.

But Croce does not have this need, who made of De Sanctis and Vico his lifeblood; and consequently he was sympathetic to Marxism (which is pure antiliberalism) and he has fiercely combatted the so-called Masonic mentality, which is the democratic mentality of liberals fought by us fascists; he sensed the religious, austere, and profoundly moral elements contained in the spirit of Sorelian syndicalism, and he had Sorel's book on violence translated, whose ideas play a large part also in the genesis of the fascist character.

Croce is right there; and youth still feel and will always feel that one needs to go and look for him there. This his eulogy of liberalism could be said to be written in order to confound the ideas. Croce, the philosopher of distinctions, to indulge in the not disinterested confusionism of the liberal guerrilla warfare against fascism, the liberalism of chatterboxes who, to listen to them, have all been liberals without qualification, all of one cloth! This is not Croce, the master of new generations. It is fashionable, he said,

> *to vituperate the Italian life of the decades preceding the war, talking about them like a period of laxity and cowardice. But those who, like me, had grown up in those decades of free competition, and who had educated others with the energy of thought and with the practice of discussing and convincing, will not consent to that light judgment, to that easy condemnation, to that unworthy vituperation;*

> *and will caution others to look closely and recognize, that everything we have that is still good was produced or prepared in that time of freedom, whether it be disordered in appearance and sometimes in fact or not.*

Does Croce mean to say that he himself was formed in that period? We all know instead that he and others with him developed in opposition to the mental and moral trends and habits of that period, turning to the men who in that period, not unreasonably, were forgotten or disregarded. This is a true story.

2.

Dear Director,[55]

What would you have me say in response to Croce's letter to the *Giornale d'Italia* of yesterday evening. Croce discusses neither the arguments nor the facts adopted by me in order to demonstrate these two points, which in turn I hold to be absolutely incontestable:

1) that the liberalism of the Italian Risorgimento is not at all the liberalism that today is fighting against fascism and which Croce himself has decided to defend, aligning himself with a group that, in the past – apart from that incident in his life which was his participation in the last ministry of Giolitti – was certainly not his own; and that could be defined, to be

[55]Original footnote: In the March 25, 1925 issue of *Epoca*,

certain that we are talking about the same thing, as the liberalism of the *Giornale d'Italia*;

2) that all the substance of his thought is, *in spite of himself*, exquisitely fascist, if by fascism we mean that kernel of ideas from which the political movement that goes by that name derives its origin and inspiration.

To say, as Croce says, that these two points are based on a politico-philosophical hybridism that would allow for unjustified logical passages and inexact historical affirmations, etc., etc., is to make rash statements that have never been demonstrated, nor can be demonstrated. Indeed, insofar as the supposed hybridism is concerned, they have already been repeatedly proven false with reasonings that nobody has so much as weakened, and that the entire history of philosophy and politics has instead confirmed for all those who are not prisoners of the noted Crocian distinctions. They are contradicted in fact by the same Croce when he enters into the political polemic armed and cataphracted with the most glittering arms fabricated in his celebrated philosophical forge.

Nor can Croce himself hope to be taken at his word in these summary sentences of his regarding my mode of philosophizing and treating history, when it is noted and arch-noted in Italy, in the world even, that until yesterday, and for more than a quarter of a century, he was of the opposite opinion, and of a completely different sincerity and seriousness than that pack of dogs who are now at my heels in many newspapers, and that he was also (and is!) of the opposite opinion. Now I know why, because Fascism is involved; and someone, because of it, does violence to philosophy and history: but who?

Here's who. Croce says he is embarrassed by the well-known, very accurate assessment that the recent scholastic reform had a fascist character to it: Why? Because the State examination was included in a government program for the first time by the Hon. Giolitti; and the first minister of instruction who turned it into a legislative bill was none other than Croce himself. And it appears to him an argument against those who said that the school reform was the fascist government's most fascist reform. But to me it appears like another argument in favor of my thesis of the fascist Croce without a black shirt!

I allow myself this observation: that if liberalism is what I say it is, the aforementioned liberalism of the *Giornale d'Italia*, the liberal party today fights against the scholastic reform; but above all that politics are not what one says one will do, but what one does; and that Giolitti actually announced the proposal to introduce the State examination (and Croce will recall that, while we had found in fascism the political force to realize what we were hoping to do, despite our anti-Giolittism we were bound at that time to the minster of instruction, because of the State examination); but Giolitti didn't do anything then; or could not do anything, which amounts to the same thing, given that each government is the exponent of a political situation. And to do something, we needed the austere, religious even, will of renewal, which manifested itself and imposed itself on Italy by the movement inspired and directed by Benito Mussolini.

To deny this is absurd. Of course, not all fascists are fascists. That is nothing new. It has always been like this. For this reason life is a struggle and a gradual and exhausting development. Croce himself taught as much, together with all the other things that young fascists today turn to him for, and salute him as their spiritual father, even if, like so many others, he will not recognize his children. History will remember us.

Not certain newspapers however.

Speaking of which: yesterday evening on the tramway I saw a melancholic passenger half asleep over his evening newspaper, which had on the first page, in large letters, across two or three columns I don't know what lucubration on *Giambattista Vico the fascist*. But why doesn't that worthy student of Vico not submit his articles to the review that is suitable today for that material, my *Giornale critico della filosofia italiana?*

Cordially yours.

VIII. Against the Agnosticism of Education[56]

Dear Sacconi,

I too, and for some time now, am against the political agnosticism of education, just as I am against every other agnosticism. I hate the citing of one's own work, pointless moreover; but I would like to call attention to the fact that even in this area I did not wait for the march on Rome to think what I think. A not completely pointless remark perhaps for those opponents of good faith of mine, who wrote so many precise and meditated things about my convictions.

Education cannot be agnostic in either religion, or philosophy, because it cannot be agnostic in morality. And for that reason it cannot be agnostic in politics either. Agnosticism is the suspension of judgment and the consequent renunciation to commit oneself by action for one party or another. It is the separation of personality from life. The which can be lofty and generous as much as one wants and inspired by the broadest possible conceptions, but with one condition: that it unfold according to specific parties and social currents. It is a cultivation of spectator souls more or less indifferent to life itself, and deprived thereby of a sense of responsibility – which everyone

[56]Original footnote: In the journal *La Corporazione della Scuola*, edited by the prof. Acuzio Sacconi, Rome, a. I, n. I, May 10, 1925.

ought to have – of the moral reality in which one finds oneself living, and whose course one participates in and contributes to, even if one's attitude be inert and negative. Now, it is evident that a school that begins down this path, instead of fulfilling its essential office as the instrument and constructive activity of moral life, becomes instead the fatal organ of the disintegration and demolition of all fundamental energies of the spiritual life of the people.

For this reason, we fight against the laicism of the so-called neutral education, which, fortunately, nobody sees the need to speak about anymore for several years now. Good sign, and it proves that some progress has also been made in spite of ignorance, prejudices, and the ill will that are still at play. It was once a dogma that a child's conscience needed to be respected and not burdened with religious teaching and the premature inculcation of a faith that only later, freely, with eyes open and after mature reasoning it would have to choose for itself. It could appear like a common ruse to remand something until the end of time that absolutely had to be repudiated and exterminated. And instead, at least for some people, it was an ingenuousness, a result of the real and authentic ignorance of the life of the spirit. Which is always free, always mature, always rational, and yet never free, never mature, never rational. And in this state of being and not being lies its strength.

For this reason, we fight and we ought to fight that other sort of laicism that wants the banishment of politics from education: from education as a relationship between teacher and students, and from education as a consciousness of the teacher and the ideal of life that it ought to make its own. Of course, politics divides, and education must unite; and it unites while nourishing that common humanity by which men understand each other and collaborate at the spiritual edifice, in which civil society comes to be realized. Education makes brothers of men who are not only of the same time, but of all times, making us relive the same life of our fathers and appreciate the value of everything that beautifully, greatly, and worthily, and truly was the joy of their spirit; and not only those of one place or one people, but of all places and all peoples, beside whom one has thought, and thinks, together with us, and has labored, and labors, with us at the common work of humanity. All this is very true. Every time we return in our minds, from the most violent passions of the political fight, which over the course of the years pulls us and wraps us in its coils, digging the deepest divisions between our dispositions, – to the happy years of youth spent at school, when our present adversaries were our companions, when we worked together with thought and spirit at the art that equally belongs to everyone, at the knowledge that is the universal and immortal work of every time and place, – a wave of tenderness invades our heart which is similar to what accompanies it in our earliest memories, when gathered daily around the same hearth was, in unified feeling, the family that is alas now dispersed.

But childhood, as beautiful as it may be, also needs to pass: the family grows and must grow and separate; and woe to the child raised as if he had to spend the rest of his life always under the eyes of his mother and was never allowed to go beyond the threshold of his parents' home. School cannot participate in the daily struggle of life, which is a life of ever occurring contrasts. But school must prepare for this life; and at first the child and later also the youth must be habituated to lend an ear to the sounds that, outside the walls where he is raised, are emitted by the life that waits for him with its problems, with its diverse and divergent interests, destined also to be reconciled; he must be trained in the study of those problems and how to have a tenacious will to resolve them. He must for that reason begin to acquire a taste for it, to welcome and foster in his mind a seed of some sort, which can in due time establish hearty roots, germinate, and live vigorously in a person who has character, and who matters.

Dante himself must be read with a soul that is not deprived of any temperament or faith because otherwise his soul, so strongly tempered and shaken by his faith, would strike us as incomprehensible. As a whole man, he can speak only to other whole men and men like him engaged in all the problems that comprise the seriousness of life.

Thus education cannot be limited to grammar, mathematics, or other matter that is merely the ornament and decoration of the intellect. This intellect can be formed only by forming the personality. Understanding everything therefore, and loving everything, insofar as to understand is to love. But love must always originate from a center and return to it: a center that is a point of view, a faith, a column on which the consciousness rests securely. And the teacher that models education in his image must naturally bring to it a soul that is open to all the voices in life; but a soul that is a soul, with an orientation all its own, with a direction all its own, the center of its world, which is its ultimate criterion for every judgment and every action in the fulfillment of its most delicate office.

Therefore, today we want a national, Italian school governed by a vigorous concept of not so much the rights but rather the duties of the Italian people, and in other words of every Italian. Concept not narrow-mindedly and foolishly *chauvinistic*, but intransigent nevertheless, and religious. And this is politics, but sacred politics; whose apostates we understand as not so much champions of the largesse of ideas and freedom of spirit, but miserable and vulgar profaners of the temple, which it is up to us jealously to guard.

Freedom? Yes, it is the goddess of the temple that we are speaking about: but freedom, as you know, is not the natural prerogative of anyone, but rather an ideal to be realized, a duty to be fulfilled, the highest conquest that man can aspire to through abnegation of himself and self-sacrifice.

IX. The Fascist Reviews[57]

Dear Arpinati,

I send you my warmest wishes for the *Vita Nova*, which I learn with pleasure intends to live up to its fine name, ceasing to be a variety review, as if there weren't enough of them already, and some of which have done well for themselves given the scope that such reviews propose: a scope that has its merit certainly, but is inadequate to that mode of living (and by that I mean life) in which even Mussolini just recently placed the essence of Fascism.

Our way is the serious (I say *religious*) way of conceiving of life and living it. A way that, among other things, no longer allows us to be content with a passably delightful, perhaps even instructive, review that is rich in news and curiosities capable of stimulating even the most difficult and refined tastes among us, if together with delight, instruction, and interest, and through more varied material, a man does not see himself nor feel his passion: a vigorous and intense passion, capable of investing all his life and ruling over his entire mind with that constant and vehement unity that is one of the most notable characteristics of the religious spirit.

This is the fascist way of living.

And to this way of living our periodicals must also conform if we want to be fascist in all things, as

[57]Original footnote: Letter to the Hon. Leandro Arpinati, in the *Vita nova* review of Bologna, August 1925.

we must be if we are to deserve that name. In our periodicals, we cannot settle for simple, pleasant literature, or abstract or idle works of popular appeal, or dilettante travel logs through the attractive aspects of the vast world of things or ideas. All the less permissible is it to abandon ourselves to that more or less skeptical humor, which too many Italians have always found pleasure in, and which now spreads, with I do not know how much benefit to the Italian character, around fascism amidst the colorless mass of men who surround us, as spectators, incapable of discerning what fascism means in essence, what its potential is.

With respect to which, I would incidentally like to observe here that in the fascist camp there is little attempt to vie with our adversaries in this genre of light literature; almost as if to snatch the latest weapon out of their hands. But it would not be suitable to give another thought to this weapon, reminding oneself what the humoristic small papers of the time printed in the best period of the national Risorgimento against the more renowned men who led the movement: innocent and malicious jokes of every sort, which made contemporaries roll on the floor laughing, and which history has forgotten. It is a most unbecoming competition for us.

But I say that it cannot fail to demonstrate the inferiority of fascists, for one obvious reason: which is this, that laughter is the work of Mephistopheles, and whoever has a faith knows no other smile than that of bitter sarcasm; which makes bad blood and cannot please whoever does not relish the strong taste.

Recently, I have had several occasions to touch on this *morality* of laughter. And I am not surprised that nobody from the other side of the aisle has understood me, because whoever understands this morality already would, for that reason alone, be induced to move on from there. But fascists must have a clear idea of this concept: that there is nothing to laugh about in this world. Which does not mean (for the love of god!) that there is no more room except for stupid curmudgeonry. A man who no longer knows how to laugh would no longer be a man. It means simply – and it goes without saying – that one must not insist on this negative and, I was about to say, laxative area of the spiritual life, because a man must pick himself up again and collect himself quickly in order to return to his work and to his construction.

Fascists then have nothing to envy others in this art, which is an inferior art and particular to a society in decline and to spineless men who, when faced with life, do not feel that *res sua agitur*;[58] and in whose eyes there is proof of the torment, but they present the image of fools or drunks who laugh obscenely about their own domestic misadventures.

And to return to the argument, the duty of fascists is that of bringing the attention back to the central problems, both from the practical point of view and from the speculative point of view, because these two views are fundamentally united. Not to mix art or science with politics and philosophy, as some would attempt, who do not wish to understand; but rather to

[58] *Res sua agitur*: Latin for "it concerns them."

integrate into the heart and soul, and therefore into the life and all its manifestations, that which is one part only of our interests or our interior world with all the rest; because every part depends on what is the foundation and the ultimate goal of all our being and our entire conduct: on that profound and unique principle that gives the tone to our person. Style is the man; but action is also the man; even the action that we perform by writing and speaking, even in a review.

Faith, mind you, is, on the one hand, a political faith, inasmuch as to live, as everyone sees, is to live politically. And whoever wants to stand aloof and wash his hands like Pilate, has also, in his way, his political attitude, and commits, if nothing else, his sins of omission. He too assumes his responsibility. In fact he too participates in history, if merely by doing nothing. But faith then is, above all, philosophical. It is well known that even the polemics against philosophy (even that of the Prime Minister in his last discourse, the signification of which moreover escaped only whoever was content to let it escape) is against a certain philosophy: and for that reason it itself is a form of philosophy. So, let us make sure we understand each other. It is up to fascism today to lead its polemic, and therefore to be aware of its own proper philosophy. Its polemic is against intellectualistic, theoretical, theologizing philosophy, which wants to leave the world of men and their suffering in order to find refuge in the heaven of contemplatives and the blessed: it wants to detach thought from life and make a kind of external criticism of it, volatile, floating above the world, in which every man has the duty of feeling himself an adherent and collaborator even in the secret of his heart and in his mind.

The *Vita Nova*, therefore, will be in this sense a review of faith, with a dominant inspiration which is the faith of today's Italians; and which is already that of the best; but which has to be developed and promoted with sincere effort, severe if needed, incessant, tenaciously self-critical. This, at least for me, is the task of the fascist review. Cordial regards.

– *Rome, July 19, 1925.*

X. From Liberalism to Fascism[59]

I am pleased that Licitra collected these writings, already published in a review managed by him and mutual friends, in one small volume. I am pleased because in this way several clear documents of an event are made available to everyone, an event that has been much discussed in the recent Italian political arena, and into which discussion I myself have entered, but which possesses in fact an impersonal and objective significance; and which could be useful if examined closely and carefully. The title itself of the book, *From Liberalism to Fascism*, indicates the event I wish to refer to. And the book opens with a chapter entitled "The New Liberal Politics," which in the November issue of '22 was written as a proem to the above-indicated review and was promised in fact, the following January, for the first fascicle of this review which was also entitled "The New Liberal Politics." It continues then with a series of writings that adhere to the politics of the Hon. Mussolini and fascism, and illustrates and defends his program. A special chapter draws its argument from my act of joining the National Fascist Party, when I declared, – amidst protests from liberals still wet behind the ears and new to their political beliefs (many of whom have subsequently undergone much fatigue defending and preserving them from confusion with fascism or an-

[59]Original footnote: Preface to the small volume by Carmelo Licitra, by the same title (Rome, De Alberti, 1925).

tifascism) – that the Hon. Mussolini in my eyes embodied the liberalism that I had always understood to a "T." The book can still serve then whoever seriously wants to study the question of the correlations between fascism and liberalism, beyond the political motives whereby liberals (national liberals excepted) see the negation of liberalism in fascism; it is a polemic in which, as happens in polemics, distinctions are suppressed, which, from a historical point of view, or rather for anyone who does not want merely to repress a hostility, but rather to become precisely aware of how things stand, it is imperative not to ignore.

The truth, in my opinion, is this: that the liberalism of liberals today who fight against fascism in the area of ideas is indeed the extreme opposite of fascism. But such liberals as these always forget to demonstrate that their liberalism is liberalism; that is, that freedom cannot be understood any other way than how they understand it – in other words… they do not understand it. And there is no need to say, with regard to the liberalism of these whiny opponents, closed in by four formulas that are the empty commonplaces of every sincerely-contemplated thought, that fascists are right when they make liberalism the target of their most ruthless blows. No opposition of principles was ever more radical or more rigid. But when we still did not know the spirit of fascism intimately, and we had not seen it in action as we have seen it since, now that it is in control of the government, and above all we did not know the person who is the soul of fascism, and in whose heart resides the secret of its strength, its methods, and its fortunes because, at least for me, before October 29, 1922, I had never met Mussolini, and I must confess that I had not followed his personal work so very closely as to be able to have an opinion of it; so when we were liberals and we did not yet believe that we were qualified to call ourselves fascists, we felt the need nevertheless to speak about "new liberal politics," as much to say that we had no intention of wandering about confusedly among the dreary mass of vague liberals. And when, by invitation of the Roman section of the Liberal Association, I held a conference on the doctrine of liberalism at the Roman College, – I cannot remember now whether it was in 1920 or '21, – I illustrated in broad strokes the great diversity between the two modes of conceiving political freedom, condemning that classical, iusnaturalistic, and contracturalistic one, of individualists, and demonstrating the inconsistency and by-now anachronistic character of it. And I restated those concepts of mine in a brief declaration inserted into the first fascicle of "New Liberal Politics" under the title of *My Liberalism*.[60]

And I could have said "our." In fact, my friends at the review were of the same mind: extremely cultivated youth, whom I had known, veterans of the war where they had done their duty and bore the signs of it in their person. They continued to wear their military uniform, and carried a flame in their heart, which shined through their ardent, anxious eyes, such as I had never seen before at my school. They had lived the anguishing hours of the war intensely, the exasperated passion of the fatherland and

[60]Original footnote: see which (above).

the moral greatness dreamt by it. And they had returned after victory with the certitude of being about to see it become great immediately, this austere and renovated Fatherland, purified by tragic effort, and already underway, bravely, magnanimously, in the direction of the ideal for which they had been for so many days, so many nights, exposed to death, ready for the sacrifice. But they were disappointed: the people were exhausted and prone to every cowardice in order to grasp at the life of pleasures again; the same combatants having no other care almost than to pocket a reward for the duty they had performed, all the same, and to squander the moral beauty and value of it thereby; and to darken every idea, to cede every loyalty to the overwhelming force of blind egoisms, all the more violent the longer and more harshly checked and suppressed they were. So they had sought refuge in education, not in order to find there a degree for the career they had to assume albeit belatedly, but something that might illuminate their mind, and confirm them in the faith, which they didn't know how to renounce and didn't want to; because with it and for it they had appeared reborn, whereby it would not have been possible for them to return to the mean and utilitarian customs of the period before the war. They were seeking the light; and every day I had the joy of seeing their faces light up with the smile of internal forces that were reviving and a spirit that was growing reassured. There was still something awkward and laborious in their words, as in the discourse of someone who sees things by starts and flashes, which suddenly light up and grow dim again, but tenaciously he forces himself to take advantage of every flare up to fix his attention always more closely and then to turn it within, always deeper, in order to understand and to be understood. They were young men who formerly did not want a certain amount of knowledge, although to acquire it they showed themselves avid and they studied in every way to procure it for themselves: but they sought in knowledge and in the very way of acquiring it something that satisfied the need they had from the war, to live in a superior moral world. A world which, to live within it, one needs also to conceive of it; and to conceive of it so solidly that it does not vanish and dissipate at the first gust of material life, given that men are by nature inclined to live materialistically. A moral world in which there is room for the Fatherland which demands the sacrifice of life and promises no other reward than itself; and there is room equally for everything that men would not have had if they did not force themselves, those who feel a profound and irrepressible need for it, by every fatigue and by every pain, to make it happen.

Among these young men was Licitra: the most pensive and pallid, a combination of timidity and certainty. He tormented himself trying to express his thoughts, which were all tied up. He and his friends, after graduating, having begun to teach, did not know how to lose themselves, as most do, in education and in abstract studies. And they always came to visit me, to ask about founding a review, but a review of life, a political review, which would not have served others all that much, so much as ourselves, to dedicate ourselves to it every day a little bit more in order to solve our problems. Because I had told them that problems and solutions, if they are problems that have an importance and if they are then seriously resolved, cannot be circumscribed within the ambit of an abstract theoretical doctrine, but bind a man in the world, and are practical attitudes and actions, which are intertwined and make a system with all others' actions and with the entire life of the world. We agreed that they would begin the review on their own, since I had too many commitments personally, and also I wanted to give them more freedom. And the review had been established a long time before one could have anticipated the march on Rome: an excellent printer had already been settled on, willing to run the serious risk of a costly publication of young writers because he too was a man of faith; and it was already baptized with the name, already mentioned, which was the result of our studies and our convictions.

Was and is. Seeing that if my adversaries want to contest me the right of calling myself a liberal now, I am not too worked up about it; habituated as I am to seeing myself denied the right of calling myself a spiritualist by those who speak about philosophy and who believe they understand it; and thus to feel myself contested the right to speak about God or about the immortality of the soul, by those who say they also know exactly how one must think in these matters. When one speaks about things that are somewhat difficult, it is not easy to find oneself in agreement with many. And I have, I do not know if it is the disgrace or the fortune of being accustomed to speak, even in politics, about things that are not within everyone's grasp, persuaded that if they were within everyone's grasp, there would be no point in speaking about them! And I have to chuckle when I hear myself being given a lesson on the authentic meaning of liberal doctrine by such people as have never lifted a finger to realize what freedom is, and who ignore in fact that this concept has a history and a development, which it is impossible not to be aware of.

In this little volume by Licitra, they could begin to reflect and contemplate on so many things, which they take for granted, without knowing it, but which they never studied; thus to begin to understand how someone today might believe he has the need to militate among fascists in order to stay faithful to his liberal principles. They might see how much seriousness one must have in order to speak about freedom, which they always have on the tip of their tongue; as if it were pointless to conceive of it, as they imagine, almost as if it were a natural attribute of the individual. As if the nineteenth century had never occurred, which begins with Romanticism and the historical school, continues with the idealism of the ethical State and the idea of State, as our Gioberti said, or mission, as Mazzini said, and then with socialism which systematically destroyed every form of abstract individualism and led to nationalistic and syndicalist doctrines which for opposite reasons were the negation of individuality as political or social value. They could see that the idea of freedom is in fact tied to the historical development of constitutional forms; but precisely because it is tied to this development, it isn't embodied in a limited and absolute form, which is no longer susceptible to ulterior modifications corresponding to the development of the social economy and to the progress of the civil consciousness of the people. But above all they could be induced to consider with a bit of attention the problem of the relationship of individual consciousness and the law and the power of the State.

Today a certain old and facile satire of the idea of the State as an ethical substance, which was once held as the highest form of liberal laical consciousness and is now at the foundation of the fascist conception of the State, comes back into fashion. But today the satire demonstrates no less a minor dose of incomprehension than what old critics, for the most part Catholic, demonstrated; and it is somewhat conjoined with that blessed sufficiency of journalistic dissertators, who triumph today in the prolix, quotidian exercise of our adversaries: the ingenuous sufficiency of those who believe themselves licensed to say any nonsense whatsoever in the columns of the dailies, because secure from any possible efficacious control. But in the printed paper, which we allude to, there is nothing to worry about. One knows that too many have been, and will always be, those who do not know and who do not know that they do not know; and woe to whoever might wish to convert them one by one!

To liberals ignorant of freedom, I would like to give this little warning instead: that what today they call "liberal rebirth" could be the clear demonstration of a very naïve illusion. Is Liberalism being reborn? If so, it was dead. In fact, the greater part of these gentlemen were forgotten decades ago: and the majority called themselves democrats of various stripes, precisely because liberalism as a living party and the designation of a current of militant politics – no longer had a reason to exist. Is it being reborn now? Why? Because there are certain people, many or few, who want to stand under a common denominator, held together not by a positive or real interest, and not therefore by a common base of ideas that they concordantly profess, but by one negative interest. Their sole interest is that of opposing fascism, and seeing themselves free of it, because it does not appear disposed to make sense and go away on its own, or to let itself be domesticated and reduced to a party like any other. Their liberalism is simply anti-fascism. It has no content what has no words, biases, motivations of passionate or personal character. And if this is the "rebirth" that is extolled, is there any danger that nothing has been reborn at all?

As far as I'm concerned, liberalism is not being reborn, because it was not dead. Like every idea, it has transformed in life, which is never lived in vain, and in which nothing however remains unchanged. It has transformed, and now it calls itself, and must call itself, *fascism*: the most coherent, the most historically mature and perfect conception of the State as freedom. A conception that is both theory and practice, as is every serious theory that matures in the heads of men who are not mere professors.

– July 1925

XI. Cavour's Liberalism[61]

The writings of Camillo Cavour, scattered throughout various journals and reviews, together with some of his most notable parliamentary discourses, were for the first time collected in a volume in 1855, edited by Luigi Chiala;[62] Chiala prefaced the volume with a biography of Cavour, but he did not put his name to it. Cavour, Prime Minister and Minister of Foreign Affairs at that time, was one of the most important figures on the European political scene; and for his ingeniously inventive, bold, fruitful international action, he attracted universal attention to himself. For this reason, that volume was considered suitable for an edition for foreigners, with frontispiece in French.

It had become very rare for many years until, in 1892, Domenico Zanichelli, with his two volumes of *The Writings of the Count of Cavour Newly Collected and Published,*[63] began a "Library of political writers" that the publisher Zanichelli of Bologna was

---

[61]Original footnote: Preface to the volume C. Cavour: *Political Writings, Newly Collected and Published by G. G.*, of imminent publication by the "Anonymous Roman Publisher."

[62]Original footnote: *Politico-Economical Works* by the Count Camillo Benso di Cavour, prime minister, etc., Cuneo, Galimberti publisher-bookseller, 1855 (pp C-707 in octavo). The two copies, with frontispieces in Italian and French respectively, possessed by the Libraries of the Lower House and Senate, bear just after the Biography the hand-written signature of L. Chiala.

[63]Original footnote: About these writings, v. P. Matter, Cavour, Paris, Alcan, 1922-25, I, chap. 8, and A. J. Whyte, *The Early Life and Letters of Cavour*, Oxford, 1925, p. 386 ff.

to undertake; but it didn't go beyond those two volumes. The *Writings* were forewarded this time by a long introduction, more prolix than useful, and accompanied by many notes with generous references to the events and acts that the individual writings refer to. This collection, in any case, was quite a bit more abundant and also more accurate than the one from 1855; which the new publisher, moreover, never mentions and, judging by some omissions of his own, was perhaps not aware of. But contrary to what its title might suggest, it too is incomplete and omits Cavour's very important articles on economic science and on Malthusianism which Chiala however had extracted from the *Il Risorgimento* of 1849-50, in addition to many other writings, major and minor, that lay forgotten in the same *Il Risorgimento*, and are now reprinted for the first time in the present volume. It also ignores several writings on agriculture, statistics, and economy, anterior to '48 and included in various foreign reviews. This second collection is also out of print for many years now. Although many people cite and mention Cavour's thoughts and sayings, I don't know how many are directly familiar with his writings. Until a few months ago, nobody had thought about a republication of a selection of his *Parliamentary Discourses*, these also being for the longest time very hard to find, outside of libraries;[64] and one always hopes for a beginning to that collection of Epistles of his, which awaits a Regal Commission, because the collection by Chiala, even though precious, has many gaps in it and is lacking in every respect.

[64]Original footnote: See *Selected Discourses* edited by MASSIMO LELJ, Milan, Bottega di Poesia, 1925.

In the present volume is included all the journalistic activity of Cavour the writer of the *Il Risorgimento*, from when the journal first began publishing to when Cavour, nominated prime minister, believed he had to detach himself from it. And already his collaboration after '48 was always more infrequent the more involved he became in parliamentary activity.

It is not the intention here to recall the history of the journal that at the end of '47 Cavour and Balbo founded in order to maintain a proper balance between the extreme parties that were preparing to fight on the terrain of the new institutions expected in Piedmont. The prophetic name of this journal, *Il Risorgimento*, obliged it to represent the pure spirit, which was historically destined to prevail and triumph, of the national movement that then had some of its greatest voices in the Piedmontese writers (Gioberti, Balbo, Azeglio). It may be that it succeeded, thanks first of all to Cavour, who took over the management of it and had soon filled it with his exuberant personality. Because before '48, he was more of a scholar and a freelance journalist, writing, by the urging of friends (because he didn't feel the calling to be a writer), several essays, for foreign reviews for the most part. Later, he will become the powerful orator and, from the parliamentary tribunal, he will champion and defend his ideas. In '48, Cavour is a journalist. Even in this field he has difficulties to overcome. But they are an incentive rather than an obstacle to his youthful will to make progress, to make himself heard, and to act in the vast field that finally opens up before him. It had been his dream, when in Paris and London he had envied the fate of men of genius and the powerful, who were able to dominate public opinion and by their own strength climb to those positions from which one can have an influence on the destinies of one's country.

Curious difficulties, those encountered by this great journalist! One of his collaborators, a consummate journalist and effortless writer, much later recalled, smiling, those labors of Cavour. One needs to hear these remembrances by Giuseppe Torelli:[65]

> *The Editorial Department of* Il Risorgimento *was composed of the Count of Cavour, Michelangelo Castelli, the Professor Francesco Ferrara, Pier Carlo Boggio, and the author of these Remembrances; they were the main writers: later added to that list was their companion Filippo Cordova. Contributing tirelessly with their attentive work was G. B. Bico, the lawyer Re, and a translator from German. They went forward united in good and friendly accord: there wasn't really what you could call a director, and the political direction was dictated more by the communality of opinions than by a special agenda.*
>
> *The Count of Cavour was the main inspirer, but he wrote little: nor could he be called tireless in the giving of inspiration: he was however taken by sud-*

[65]Original footnote: *Political Remembrances*, Milan, Carrara, 1873, pp. 197-200.

den impulses from time to time, which made him a most active and useful collaborator. The most important political questions went to him who had the greatest skill [in dealing with them], but he enjoyed economic topics more: he treated both with a sure and steady hand, with the abundance of ideas that he had greatly studied and greatly learnt. Not being very familiar with the Italian language, it happened sometimes that the clunky form of his writings did not correspond with their metaphysical value. In those cases he left the form to us, entrusting us with the care of it, if we judged it suffering. Between content and form, the Count of Cavour did not even bother to choose: in his head the concept formed rapidly, complete and clean like a syllogism, and naturally he had to express it in the language (French) that his brain had been educated to think in: in that case the form was worthy of the content. The mental dynamic required to express the same idea in a language that he had not conceived it in was annoying and difficult for him...

And yet in the first Italian writings by the Count of Cavour there was little to change: either by sagacity of instinct, or through the power of com-

> *prehension, without knowing Italian he wrote sometimes with such manner and taste that, after having fixed several material flaws, and tempered the vocabulary that he lacked, the end result was that he had written better than all of us.*

The same Torelli adds:

> *There had been frequent discussions with him about the question of form, which at first he had considered a mechanical affair, the craft of a turner, and his worship for the content became less exclusive... and it did not take long for Cavour to become habile and dextrous in the craft of the turner, and with marvelous rapidity he learnt the language of the nation that he was called on to serve.*

In this volume then the reader will find all that Cavour wrote in *Il Risorgimento*: brief notes and articles and sometimes series of articles, which together make for real and proper studies. And in addition to the writings intended for the newspaper, there is a speech that he was to give before the House but didn't have the opportunity to do so, and which is not found in the collection of his parliamentary speeches. It was also not included in *Il Risorgimento*. Very few articles are unsigned; but some are certain to be Cavour's, because they are referenced in others that bear his signature; and in all of them his hand is easily recognizable, as is that sincere style of his, more of an orator than that of a writer. Among the unsigned articles, the one on *Revolutionary Means* against Brofferio, for several uncertainties in form, could lead a person to have some doubt about its authorship. But it was already reprinted and attributed to Cavour, not only by Zanichelli, but previously by Chiala, who must have had access to the author's writing through his volume. The polemical article against Gioberti (pp. 250 ff.) is signed by the "Direction" of the journal; and the way in which he speaks in his letter to the vice president of the Giobertian National Political Circle[66] leads him to believe it is Cavour's. Moreover, if that article was not written by Cavour, it was inspired by him and without a doubt it reflects his ideas point for point.

Not included in our collection are the first writings by Cavour, of economical character, almost all of them published in French, and which are not newspaper articles, but more or less ample and elaborate studies, which could be included in another volume when the time is right; but which do not have the political or historical interest of these brief essays from *Il Risorgimento*, with which in December 1847 Cavour resolutely entered into the glorious ring of his political activity. The which documents, intimately bound as they are to the history of '48, the richest year of experience of our Risorgimento in its various happenings, hour of generous hopes and confident enthusiasms, hour of bitter delusions and discouraging bitterness, present in everyone's memory, – they have no need for many illustrations. Elements of history

[66]Original footnote: Cf. *Political Writings*, p. 256.

themselves, they deserve to illuminate in a bright light the origins of the movement, which the same Cavour moved forward to the great goal, desired by him since his earliest years, of the fatherland unified in a modern State supported by free institutions. So we have imposed the utmost parsimony in the notes, reducing them to the strictest necessity, in order not to overload with heavy comments the agile and quick prose of the author, and removing every idle digression around those ideas that are the only matter important to the reader of this volume; clear and bright ideas through events that are reflected in Cavour's intelligence. Since the events themselves are well-known; and if they were not, an exact and full explanation of them could be found in these articles, which a journalist, none other than the selfsame Cavour, commented on or contributed to [in other articles] over time. But what he thought about them cannot be precisely and completely found elsewhere: and that thought, over and above its historical value relative to the period in which it was formed, has an even greater one, which is collected in this volume in all its manifestations, even the least of them; because this is the thought of Camillo Cavour, the greatest architect of the Italian nation, which is to say the greatest political thinker Italy has had, if by political thinker we do not mean the producer of more or less abstract philosophemes, but the promoter of the concrete, historical, actual, and active consciousness of a people. And the concepts of such a thinker never have a simple, transient historical value, but are filled with ideal and immortal truths, which in every time and in every place men will have the interest to meditate on. They are not only informative documents, they are also formative. They do not tell us merely how he thought, but how to think.

And that is said, of course, without the fetishisms that today have become fashionable for contingent political reasons, which are obeyed not as a result of an in-depth study made of Cavour's writings and work (which continues to be studied more by foreigners than by Italians), but rather because one studies less, and the name of the great Cavour is exploited for base motives or in the interest of current politics.

The time of fetishisms is passed; consequently, it now becomes possible for us to make a correct assessment of our greatest men of the Risorgimento, their having come down to us wrapped in a halo of unlimited exaltation, with which moreover the most humiliating denegations and the most radical disavowals are contrasted. Seeing as there is never a great man who is not found faced with some negative spirit incapable of rendering him justice. For Cavour, it is enough to think of Brofferio, Guerrazzi, Tommaseo, Mazzini himself, Garibaldi himself. Like Cavour, even Mazzini, even Garibaldi, even Gioberti were for a long time the objects of fetishism by admiring fanatics, whose irrational attitude was enough to make their great names raise suspicions in and be rejected by many minds, which had become fed up with both exalters and exalted. Of course, the Mazzinians and the Giobertians were the main culprits of the general indifference into which until only recently Mazzini's and Gioberti's writings had fallen and remained; around which so much annoying clamor was raised by those who were the least capable of removing the dross from the live kernel of thought of those two writers and masters. And just as in Mazzini and Gioberti, so too in Cavour today we can distinguish between what is alive with him and what is dead, what is not his but of his time and of the current of ideas that he adhered to, and what he put of himself into the action whereby he mastered the forces he was able to employ for his lofty goals.

Today he is exalted as the father of Italian liberalism; and certainly nobody before him, or at least nobody around him in the middle of the last century, in Italy, felt the truth of that liberalism as much as he did, which at the end of the XVIIth century had matured in England. Where it had put down solid roots in public institutions consequent to three movements, of which one, specific to that country: the constitutional revolution; another, which passed into England from Germany: the Protestant reform; and the third, which derived from the Italian Renaissance: the naturalistic conception of man and the world around him. Cavour had studied that form of liberalism in the books by economists, which he was a passionate scholar of; but above all in the life of the countries regulated by liberty, in Geneva, in France, and in England; while he remained, however, unfamiliar with two areas of studies, which had slowly corroded the bases of that abstract liberalism and made the need for a profounder means of conceiving freedom felt, even if the tendency and I would say the almost realistic instinct of his spirit, which was exquisitely tempered by direct observation and meditation of life, had not let the fundamental defect of the naturalistic, abstract concept of freedom escape him. These two areas of study were [, first,] that of the philosophical systems in Italy and in Germany that had formed in opposition to the Anglo-French rationalism theorizing about the purported natural rights of the individual; and [, second,] that which the socialist movement in Germany and in France was giving rise to. Which Cavour most acutely saw the negative side of and, if one may also say so, the fundamental error of – as is demonstrated by the writings in this volume, which he attributed in *Il Risorgimento* to the French socialist experiments attempted after the February Revolution;[67] but he did not recognize the real reason that socialism during the nineteenth century sought to assert itself against the absurd individualism championed to the extreme by utopian dreamers of the freedom of the individual before the State, unsuitable from an economic point of view.

Cavour, what is more, despite all his liberalism, does not forgive it the "monopolists of freedom".[68] He is the ardent supporter of the individual rights of education, conscience, the press, etc. But when the reason of State requires some limitations to one of these freedoms, and the opposition's mouth is filled with the great principles that are about to be tampered with, he protests that these great principles

[67]February Revolution: the first of two revolutions that took place in Russia in 1917, the first of which leading to the second, known as the October, or Bolshevik Revolution.

[68]Original footnote: *Political Writings*, p. 305.

have often brought States to ruin.[69] And he does not let himself be taken in by words; and not only does he fight against Brofferio in Parliament, but he resolutely rallies against the democratism of Valerio, even though [it be] reinforced by the authority of Gioberti (whom initially he had always called, with high veneration, the "great Gioberti"), when to be a democrat must mean to deprive the State of strength. And yet he, the ancient Jacobin (as they depicted him at least, beginning with King Carlo Alberto, those who, tied to the past, distrusted the young patrician's liberal ways) – he who, at the end of '47 and the beginning of '48, when what form of constitution to ask the sovereign for was being discussed in Piedmont and he went from the side of the more moderates like Cesare Balbo to the side of those who were riskier like Brofferio, confessed to his close friends that, for his own part, he was leaning more toward the more democratic solution; he who, the Statute having just been promulgated, when the State had to be launched to be reset and strengthened and consolidated on new bases, and it was extremely dangerous suddenly to question those bases and to consider them provisional, he did not hesitate to agree with his more advanced critics in asking that absolute freedom of religion be openly introduced as soon as possible, while recognizing that it was more than anything a question of formality; he who, as soon as an eventual revision of the Statute was talked about, on the occasion of the union with Lombardy, was quick to applaud the idea and to propose an enlargement of constitutional franchises in the very democratic sense, fighting against the royal

[69]Original footnote: *Parliamentary Discourses*, vol. IV, p. 347.

nomination of senators, and asking for an upper house that was also elected; he always professed himself a supporter of the *juste milieu* and was one of the founders of the *moderate* party, notwithstanding the alliance that caused so much grief to men of the Right; and he resolutely fought against universal suffrage, which is the essential corollary of the democratic theory, considering it postulated by "extreme factions" and declaring it incompatible not only with the actual conditions of European society (suitable only for "a republic already educated for freedom for centuries") but also incompatible "with the constitutional monarchical system."[70] In his proclamation, or as it was called more modestly back then, in his circular to the voters of the Vercelli district (April 13, 1848), he declared in a formal and solemn way to have always wanted "with tenacious intent, a united and free Italy, and our country in full possession of a sincere constitutional system, in which the throne rested on the firm and broad base of popular freedoms"; to love constitutional monarchy as "the only one capable under the present conditions of European society, and in Italy in particular, to reconcile order with freedom, stability necessary to the development of economic interests with the moral and political improvements that satisfy the just and growing demands of the people; because monarchy is the only system of government in which the progressive movement that pushes Christian civilization to better destinies can be maintained within the established limits of reason."

Freedom, but joined with order; all the just de-

[70]Original footnote: *Political Writings*, p. 71.

mands of the people, or rather all the liberal aspirations, but contained within the limits of reason. The *order* is the effective force of the law itself and of the State; to secure which the intervention and government of reason is needed. The writings collected by me echo from beginning to end with these two fundamental notes of Cavour's spirit, both equally strong. And the impetus of feeling, of faith, of instinct of the ideal jumps out now and then with vehement ardor; but it is immediately curbed and as if overpowered by the force of vigilant reason, skilled in knowledge and reflection, straight, staunch, extremely lucid. Cavour, who irritated his adversaries in Parliament sometimes with his smile, with his often sarcastic wit, and above all with the rigid coldness of his ratiocinations, was also a sentimentalist, ready to become impassioned by his dearest ideas, to believe, to let himself be carried away by his faith. Whoever pours over these writings of his, and even more whoever reads his youthful diary and his letters, easily feels in the often eloquent and moving expression of this man, – who also has so acute an eye for the observation of social, economic, or political events, and who presents with so great a mathematical rigor all his rapid arguments, – an impassioned soul, fervent with faith, who, for that reason, often tries to set his gaze on the future and to see there the interior idol of his mind as already real; and he easily comes out with reliable assertions, of a certainty that are not the result of the observations of fact, nor of strictly scientific predictions. When, for example, in January of 1848, he rebukes Mr. Guizot for wanting to propitiate Austria with his equivocal action towards Italy and for wishing to "slacken the pace," in the end he warns him that it will not be possible. It will not be possible, he affirms, because "the work of the Italian Risorgimento is succeeding, and will succeed by an irrevocable decree of Providence, because of the work of the reforming princes, of the risen people."[71] The people had risen, and the princes had begun the reforms: but was that enough to guarantee the unfailing Risorgimento? Cavour started off with the irrevocable decree of Providence, because he drew the strongest motives for his certainty from a deep and obscure faith.

Thus the way in which he speaks about the progress of humanity (which was spoken about quite a bit in the French literature familiar to him) or about the effects that are expected without a shadow of a doubt from freedom (from free [public] education, free trade, etc.), it demonstrates that here his spirit is moved by a postulate, which has more of the character of an impassioned faith than a scientific conviction. And in truth, the studies on which he had cultivated his intelligence, of classic economics, starting with a naturalistic and optimistic intuition of the human spirit – economically subject to true, natural, and for that reason ineluctable laws which are always beneficial – suppose an obscure, religious intuition that sees the world governed by providential laws, superior to the human will.

Without this faith, which was also the faith in a united and free Italy (according to the cited phrase in the circular to the voters of '48), Cavour would not have had those happy audacities, which so many

[71]Original footnote: *Political Writings*, p. 23.

times dismayed his adversaries or rivals, and which led him, step by step, from the sudden request for the Statute, when not even Valerio nor Brofferio were thinking about it, to the war in the Crimea, and to the war of 1859. He himself once said that he was living in a portentous period; and that history was always a great improvisor.[72] A philosophically certain and irreproachable proposition, but in Cavour's mouth it is a personal truth; given that he was the author, for the most part, of the history of that portentous period, he had to feel within himself that every resolutive thought was not born in him as the result of well-deduced reasonings, but by a quasi sudden illumination, or to be clearer, an original synthesis, made possible by the robust temperament of that character of his, animated by a faith no less ardent than Mazzini's. In a solemn moment (March 23, 1848) he wrote an article shrill like a battle cry:

> *The supreme hour for the Sardinian Monarchy has sounded, the hour of strong deliberations, the hour on which depend the fates of empires, the destinies of peoples.*
>
> *In view of the events of Lombardy and Vienna, hesitation, doubt, delays are impossible; they would be the most fatal politics.*
>
> *We men of cool thoughts, used to listening more to the dictates of reason than the impulses of the heart, after*

[72]Original footnote: *Political Writings*, p. 79.

> *having attentively weighed every word of ours, we must in all conscience declare it: one way alone is open to the nation, to the Government, to the King: War! Immediate war, war without delays!*

Dictates of reason? Yes, even in this article Cavour reasons, and he endeavors to demonstrate, that every suitable consideration is for war, and that the international risks that cowardly people feared did not exist; even though the demonstration as far as England was concerned was not that certain. But one voice, more vigorous [than others], imposes itself on all the dictates of reason: "In the present contingencies, there is only one form of politics: not the politics of the Luigi Filippis and Guizots, but the politics of the Fredericks, the Napoleons, and the Carlo Emanuels. Great politics, those of bold resolutions."[73] Without these resolutions, in fact, history would not be that great improviser that it is. Men who always reason do not make history.

But it is also the hour of reason. And one of Cavour's great strengths lay also in reason. Here, for example, is an article in which he argues against the facile illusions and delusions of whoever had hoped for assistance from Switzerland in the first war of independence, as and because Switzerland could not abandon its neutrality. One means alone perhaps could have induced the Diet to change its counsel: the promise of ceding Valtellina to the Helvetic Confed-

[73]Original footnote: *Op. cit.*, p. 107.

eration. It is Cavour himself who says so; and his thought makes one's mind run to the future meeting at Plombières[74] and to the cession of that Savoy that various articles in this volume propose to demonstrate as intimately bound to Piedmont! And what does Cavour say about such a resolution in '48?

> *A like means was not in the Government's power to employ. And even if it could have disposed of such an important province, we do not doubt that it would have indignantly refused to acquire assistance on account of the loss of a stretch of Italian land. The purpose of the war undertaken by Carlo Alberto is to reunite the scattered members of our nation into one single family. The sacrifice of one portion of it would be sacrilege, which would dishonor the great sanctity of our cause.*[75]

Was Garibaldi right then in '60 when he rebelled against the Plombières agreements? No, he was wrong; and he was wrong to think that his feelings or "impulses of the heart" were not shared by Cavour. But he is someone who knew how to listen to his heart at times, and at other times the voice of reason; and consequently how to innovate and to create (improvise) in history, but on the basis of which only ef-

[74]Meeting at Plombières: Cavour and French Emperor Napoleon III met secretly in Plombières, July 20-21, 1858 to discuss a restructuring of the Italian peninsula.

[75]Original footnote: *Political Writings*, p. 158.

fective and productive historical action is possible: on the basis of reality, which utopia is unable to take into account.

Cavour was an idealist, like other architects of the Risorgimento; but he was not a utopist. And for that reason, thought, as the systematization of concepts, is inferior in him to the historical worth of a man. Whose greatness (that is, true thought) can only be measured by his praxis. Which is not as liberal as one might expect from Cavour's profession of faith in matters of principle. And this is the key to the problem, how with principles so very debatable, although so energetically professed, he had been able to realize the marvels of the improvisatorial history which is his.

The principles are highly debatable. The conception of freedom, placed at the foundation of his constitutional system and therefore of his politics, is, as he theoretically conceives it, it must be said, false. The freedom that he talks about is the freedom of citizens *uti singuli*: that is, a freedom that would be a given: something materialistically and dogmatically supposed as an attribute of the particular individual; even though at one time, in order to refute the logical consequence of principles that he himself had embraced, the theory of universal suffrage, he declares himself "decidedly opposed to that fallacious doctrine which proclaimed the right to participate in the government of society a *natural right*" and judges such a doctrine the "consequence of one of the most dangerous sophisms of modern times."[76] Only from that

[76]Original footnote: *Political Writings*, p. 72.

point of view can one speak about the freedom of instruction in the absolute way in which Cavour[77] always spoke about it, about freedom of the press, and about other individual rights in that acceptation in which he intended them, at least theoretically, as guaranteed by the Statute. And above all only from such a strictly individualistic point of view could he claim, as he always claimed, by inspiration of Protestant or rather individualistic origin, with great force of conviction, religious liberty; and he sustained consequently that famous separatistic theory of the "free Church in a free State."

Now this entire conception of freedom was already intrinsically outdated at the time of Cavour. It was outdated by the doctrines that had demonstrated that the individual does not exist outside of history, or rather as a member of society; indeed, of a historically determined society; and he cannot have rights unless they are in function of this spiritual organism that he participates in. The State, Gioberti also said, is not individual will (nor the effect of a combination of individual wills), but an idea, a reason: which he does not immediately participate in, except by means of reflection. It is not however the individual who creates the State; but, if anything, the State that creates the individual. Hence Gioberti fought tooth and nail against free public education, requested in '50 and in '51 in Piedmont by the Church, which Cavour and his friends, like Berti and Farini, became the natural allies of. For them, in fact, as for the "Catholics," the Church came first, and then the State (for Cavour the

[77]Original footnote: Cf. my preface in the vol. B. SPAVENTA, *The Freedom of Instruction*, Florence, Vallecchi, 1921.

individual came first, in whom however faith was included as a strictly intimate and incommunicable activity); for Gioberti, instead, the State came first, and then the individual.

And the entire Roman question, which anguishingly tormented the last years of Cavour's life, was formulated on a logical exigency of this conception of freedom of his and, hence, of his position of the State toward the Church. And it was a contradictory formulation; one that, after Cavour, Ricasoli remained entangled in, and all other successors after him, until that solution that was arrived at, through the iron logic of things, on September 20, 1870.[78] The contradiction arose from the concept of the Church's freedom before the State, not as freedom that the State in its unlimited and original sovereignty confers and guarantees to it, but as freedom that the Church is originally vested with, and which limits and conditions the sovereignty of the State. Any accord between two mutually independent and autonomous powers can be nothing more than the effect of a coincidence of will. Thus the desire and always vain hope entertained by mutual agreements for a peaceful solution; but also the firm plan for the absolute secularization of the State and for the acquisition of Rome, the capital. That is, all the negotiations were conducted with this implicit, even too manifest, understanding: that the other power sooner or later, by reason or by force, would have to cede (which is moreover the eternal game of international law, whereby in the vicissitude of peace and war the State demonstrates its

[78]September 20, 1870: the Capture of Rome, last step in the unification of Italy, or the Risorgimento.

power and proves therefore its reality!). So the Church is effectively not free, nor on a par or on the same level with the State: but only in possession of the quantity of freedom that can be recognized or attributed to it by the State in its necessary development. Not peaceful negotiations, but struggle and war, in that this alone is the means of living allowed to the State by its intrinsic nature. And (is there any need to say it?) Cavour, convinced champion of the freedom of the Church, acted in fact as if he were convinced of the exact opposite: that is, that only the State is or can be free, and that from the State, as from a single source, emanates and has always emanated every right, and for that reason every definitive form, of freedom.

And in fact he always acted with a deep, albeit unexpressed and unaware, feeling, or at least not raised to the consciousness of an explicitly expressed theory: with a deep feeling for the supreme value of the work that he had in hand: the new Italian State to be constructed. Value, to which all others in his nature were subordinated, whether he admitted it or not, so that there was nothing more sacred than this ideal of the Fatherland, which shined in his mind; nothing, if push came to shove, that was not to be sacrificed to this sublime Fatherland, which was his burning passion and the very reason for him for living. Monarchy, parliament, church, religion, yes, all highly respectable things, and which he made the object of a sincere worship in his heart; but over and above everything else, that Fatherland, not as an idea that could remain as such and always be equally fine, but like a power to be installed, like a new kingdom to be stood up in the world, that it might count for something, and that it might prove that there was a free people, the master of its own destiny, capable of operating on its own account in the history of modern peoples. For this Fatherland of his, he was ready to lose his soul, as happens to all great statists and founders of nations; on its altar he would not have hesitated for a single instant to burn all his feelings, all his interests, all his favorite ideas, even the Statute, if necessary, even religion, if it was shown to him as incompatible with the State, wherein the Fatherland was to be embodied. When a Hegelian philosopher against Treitschke,[79] the author of one of the most intelligent essays on Cavour, wrote a book to combat the Cavourian formula "free Church in a free State," sustaining that in that way one would empty the State of every ethical and religious content, it could appear that he was right (although that philosopher was wrong in another way, proposing the inversion of the formula). But in reality that formula contained a rather more substantial truth than what Cavour believed he was expressing, by proclaiming the one freedom that the Church can have, not so much separated from the State and encamped in a sphere external to the action of the State as it establishes every right and every freedom, but rather contained within it, on a par with all other institutions and spiritual activities that the State must guarantee the freedom of, within the State. Which was the norm not of the thought that Cavour theorized, but of the praxis by which he gripped the fate of the Italian people in his

[79]Treitschke: Heinrich von Treitschke (AD 1834-1896), a German historian and philosopher.

fist with powerful vigor.

These remarks can be useful to the understanding, in their proper significance, of the writings contained in this volume, all anterior, as mentioned, to Cavour's actions as a man of government.

– *July 1925.*

Part the Third: Constitutional Reforms

I. Constitutional Reforms and Fascism[80]

Gentlemen,

[80]Original footnote: This discourse was given on October 28, 1924, to inaugurate the work of the Committee of Fifteen and published the day after in the *National Idea*. Being republished now (in the *New Liberal Politics* of December 1924) at a distance of two months, a response might be in order to those who in the meantime have written or spoken against the undertaking (unable to do otherwise) of the Committee of Fifteen. But I have a well-founded suspicion that they had not read this discourse, or had not read it attentively; and for this reason they jumped to precipitous objections, which I had anticipated and confuted. And in both hypotheses I do not believe that I can do any more than I have done: that is, to consent to the request of friends at the *New Liberal Politics* to reprint my discourse.

I limit myself only to the addition of two words for those orators who busied themselves with this problem of constitutional reforms in the House, and they expressed the doubt, or denied it outright, that this problem of reforms should be imposed on Parliament by a profound movement of the people; and they contested once again that one could speak of revolution as fascists do. It is a historical question of great importance, the which is not resolved by restricting oneself only to defining what happened on one certain day, that of October 28, 1922. The French Revolution is not about the taking of the Bastille. And I would ask these illustrious gentlemen to take a look around, and to reflect and consider with all the seriousness that the subject demands, whether the revolution is not underway, is at the beginning in fact, uncertain of itself as yet, of its ends, and of its possible outcomes; and for that reason it is even more dangerous. To close one's eyes for a moment can be comfortable; but it is not useful. I believe that everyone feels that it is not very easy to exit from the present troubles that invest all Italian life (and not only Italian life). It is everyone's anguish. It is very easy, on the other hand, to speak about normalization, and

Some of the arguments that the P.N.F.[81] has given us the honor of proposing for our study, those that the Hon. Mussolini's message mainly refer to, have to do with the very constitution of the State. And in fact they have attracted, as you know, the public's most vivid attention. To some actually it appeared that they entailed I do not know what threats to those foundations upon which, in virtue of plebiscites, the Italian people have risen to a national life; I do not know what dark threats to that sacred tree, in whose shade all Italians of our time were born and have lived, and want to live and die. You know with what industry the press of the opposition has sought to instill alarm into the mind of citizens against the announced intention of the Fascist party to revise the Constitution. It is believed or pretended to be believed that it is aiming to cut off at its roots the freedom that our fathers fought for at the expense of sacrifices, whose remembrance was and always will be exalted with a religious spirit, which is in truth the greatest title of nobility of the Italian people for the stupendous demonstrations of civil virtue that they gave for the admiration of the world. But I confess that, amidst the excited polemicization of so many experts of jurisprudence and ardent zealots of the nation's ideal patrimony, for my own part I have not always been able to distinguish between a good faith

always to whine that not much is being done here or there or nothing is done to restore the absolute rule of law. But by now one should understand that the problem is much more serious than these whining critics make of it, and that the malady is deep and has need of a radical cure. (*Note from December 1924*).

[81]P.N.F.: the National Fascist Party (*Partito Nazionale Fascista*, in Italian).

and a bad one in the ingenuous superstition for sacred names and the malicious machinations of the political intriguer accustomed to sniggering in his heart about those names, and already used by long habit to applauding all the more skeptical, cynical, and audacious underminers of the greatest institutions of the Fatherland.

But even if there were one person alone who with a pure heart was trepidatious for the intangible legacy of our glorious past (let us say it very clearly), we could not set about our work today without concerning ourselves about it. That if a hypothesis, however, appeared before us, and on account of it the suspicion that our work, instead of edifying, as is our clear intention and firm hope, served to destroy, we, in our conscience as citizens who place the Fatherland above all factions, we who can smile at the too little disinterested judgments of our adversaries and disdain the spiteful campaigns of certain newspapers, we would immediately abandon the work thus far begun. That hypothesis must be dispelled, certainly not by those who already judge us, because it suits them, even before their catching a glimpse of our conclusions, but by ourselves, convinced that the institutions as laws cannot set down roots and survive if they do not correspond to the needs, to the ideas, to the feelings of the people to whom they are given; that every arbitrary innovation, though rational in a Jacobin way, is neither efficacious nor lasting; that the history of a people does not develop by extrinsic and mechanical additions of elements that are the fruit of abstract excogitations, but rather by internal and spontaneous development, like a living plant that draws its vital sap from an underground root system; and that, finally, no revolution was ever fecund if it was not limited in its institutions to giving form and strength of law to the advances already really or virtually made in the life and spirit of the nation.

Gentlemen, when, on the day after the March on Rome, Benito Mussolini brought back to His Majesty the King, on the Quirinal, the Italy of Vittorio Veneto, that Italy which for a moment seemed to be eclipsed and to disappear from the sky and from our Italian bosoms, he understood how to bind in an indissoluble knot the future of the Fatherland to the past: the future that had emerged, or been revived, by the faith of youth who saw their Italy resplend with universal glory in the war, an Italy proud of its millenarian civilization, having risen [to the challenge] in the battlefield, finally, after long centuries of ignominious bondage and pavid inertia, to affirm its place in the world with the vigor of arms and a heroic will; and the past, which always looked toward this future in the ardent phantasms of the poets, in the thought of jurists and philosophers, in the martyrdom that the apostles encountered in jail, exile, death; the past, that produced the national Risorgimento longed for during the entire modern era, and with Mazzini, Gioberti, and Cavour, with Vittorio Emanuele and Garibaldi grafted onto the robust trunk of the Dynasty, which since the middle ages had been educating at the foot of the Alps a live nucleus of living Italians, armed with weapons and civic pride, always ready to fight for the Fatherland symbolized in the King; of the Dynasty, which the Italian revolution magnanimously assembled, defended, and fortified in a constitutional State, capable of attracting an entire nation and unifying it in freedom. This past is truly our intangible story; it is the most sacred thing we have nationally, because it forms our being and our personality: that which for seven centuries we aspired to be: that which for sixty years we are proud of being.

This past lives again and is perpetuated in the sacred person of the King. To whom at this moment our devout mind turns with unshakeable faith, that above the dissensions and the fights, which shake the Fatherland's viscera, he is and will always be in his serene firmness, which is the strength and the consciousness of the national destiny, the supreme guarantee of this one and free Italy, which our fathers bound us to and which we live by. But in the King we see likewise the courageous interpreter of the new Italy, which the war wanted and sustained and conquered with the spirit absorbed in the vision and in the feelings of a fatherland greater not just in material extension, but in character, discipline, dignity: Italy, which all of us saw before us, after the war, at first uncertain of ourselves and as if lost in the first sensation of exhaustion and regrouping, and in its momentary weakness exposed, and inclined to rash temptations of absurd and fatal novelty, then thrown all of a sudden into the revived and quasi exasperated consciousness of the ideal and inevitable goal, to which the nation was marching and needed to march so as not to be unworthy of the 600 thousand dead, nearly lost already in the opprobrium of oblivion, but then quickly reclaimed and consecrated to the worship of future generations. This young Italy, reanimated by the mystical spirit of Giuseppe Mazzini, returned to inculcate in people's hearts the prophecy of the nation which alone is the aim, of the nation that individuals must serve, in order to live or die; this young Italy, Vittorio Emanuele III led it to Vittorio Veneto. And it turned to him with Benito Mussolini in October 1922, to reunite itself with him in the venerable Italy of the Risorgimento and to be merged with it, and to walk with it to its new history. This is the faith of Benito Mussolini; this, Gentlemen, is our faith. Monarchical faith, loyal and conservative faith, but courageously constructive faith too.

To construct in order to conserve, to conserve in order to construct. These, in two words, are the problems presented by the March on Rome, which was certainly an insurrectional act, as the Prime Minister defines it in his message. And yet these problems, whether today, at two years of distance from the March, after two years of Government, which wanted to be an essentially conservative reorganization of the life of the Country, focused on raising the tone of this life and giving it health and rhythmical vigor again, – they want to be resolved in their fundamental terms, and will need instead to effect a revolution; but a revolution that cannot but have all the earmarks of a normal evolution. And the very composition of this Committee, from which the Fascist Party wants clear direction for the most appropriate means of development for this essential part of its program, can seem like the most evident proof of its proposal to realize such a revolution by means of the legal albeit profound transformation of the same in-force laws of the State, as might be suggested by the citizens, who recognize the existence and urgency of these problems and have the capacity to advise it in the most convenient technical and political way to resolve them.

In truth, the problems that fascism intends to confront were not invented by fascism. Which can be said to be the only political force that emerged out of the war, but which had already been invoked for many decades; the force that can pull the Italian people up out of the stagnant water into which, before the war, they had fallen and struggled in vain to get out of, and which after the war they risked being completely stuck in. But these problems were the torment of those Italians who failed to see in politics that miserable field of competition of persons and parties in which the great majority of politicians operated since the days of *transformismo*; of those who saw that the constitutional mechanism of the State had begun to rust, and was almost no longer capable of functioning in the interests of the Country; of those who felt that the Country no longer nourished trust in the Parliament and had no respect for it. And every day they saw a corruption of political consciousness growing – which is the same active and concrete feeling of the public good – through the game of the parliamentary system, which easily subordinates the Senate for life[82] to the Lower House, and the Lower House to the Government, while the Government of the King to the majority even, which has become a rabble of

[82]House for life: during this time, Senators held their office for life.

groups and individuals representing solely their own interests. They were the torment then of those who, in the preceding years, with infinite stupor saw solemn deliberations that bound the life of the Nation adopted by large majorities whose constituents openly declared their hostility to the object of those deliberations; and then to reign over the lie and ambush in the days of the most serious dangers to the Fatherland; and then Governments, propped up by the so-called confidence of the House, unable to obtain so much as the discussion of laws announced and promised to the Nation, let alone their approval; and every fruitful legislative effort hobbled; and the use of decree-law, invalidated by necessity, condemned naturally in very learned but academic debates, but the Government also solicited in secret and *coram populo* to appeal, in the impossibility of regular legislative measures; and the entire constitutional organism paralyzed finally and discredited.

It was not a fascist, but a moderate of the old liberal Right, and it was not a revolutionary but a conservative, Bonghi, who launched in 1893 that desperate and heartfelt appeal in the *Office of the Prince in a Free State*, which sounded like an irreverent rebuke of the "supreme magistrature of the State" in the mouth of one of the most faithful servants of the Monarchy. Nor was fascism born in 1887 when, right after the death of Depretis, that is, the person most responsible for the corruption of the constitutional system, Francesco Crispi, initiated his ponderous action of reinvigoration of the national consciousness and of the State, affirming the necessity of freeing the House from servitude to the Ministry, and the Ministry from servitude to the House – two servitudes that made one, in that the Government's domination over its deputies is the effect of a mutual haggling – with the giving of strength to the power of the executive, which is the power of the King, supreme leader of the Nation, conscience and will of the unity and continuity of the Nation; and with a return to the old idea of electing members to the Senate; because even the Upper House should acquire the strength necessary to its eminent office.

But perhaps the Italian liberalism of the prewar years, when nobody spoke about fascism yet, had its greatest and most authoritative champion, because of his high genius and faultless character, in Sidney Sonnino, the silent and tireless guardian of Italian interests in the difficult years of the war? And who has forgotten that article: *Let's Return to the Statute!* – bold but inspired by his pure love for the fatherland, which in 1897, as was natural, dismayed the constitutionalists, but appeared on the political scene of Rudini[83] like a dead letter? And in that article, insofar as concerns the relationship between the executive and legislative powers, perhaps it did not ask any less than might be desired today for continuity and productivity in governmental action.

Since it is a curious thing to note when the Committee shows signs of the fear of reports or the consequences of reports; which is to say that it pre-

[83]Rudinì: Antonio Starabba di Rudinì (AD 1839-1908), prime minister of Italy from 1891-2, 1896-8.

tends to speak in defense of the State and against the profaners who dare touch that sacred ark, as if its entire parliamentary life, against which fascism revolted, were spent protecting this sacred ark; as if instead it were not consumed by punching holes in it in every sense, and as if someone hadn't attempted ultimately, by notorious attempts on article 5, to destroy it completely. In fact, instead, it is just the opposite; so that every time someone tries throw a wrench in the demagogic degeneration of parliamentary institutions, someone else is bound to raise Sonnino's cry of: *Let's return to the Statute!*

Let's return to the spirit, is the intent, to the essential and politically significative nucleus of the Statute; which alone, on these terms, can be conserved and live, as was always clearly seen and proclaimed by anyone who had sincerely prized it and defended it. Given that the Statute of Carlo Alberto and the plebiscites is immortal, o Gentlemen, just like the Fatherland; but on a par with all immortal things it is a cell or organism that develops and survives by itself, perpetuating itself in the perpetuity of the spirit, which is incessantly renewed, and renews itself in its own memories even. The thing, doctrinally, is so obvious and evident that in good faith only a fetishist immersed in the blindest materialism can doubt it. The Catholic Church itself, which is usually put forward as the typical example of a institution that perdures on the basis of an immutable credo, lives by means of a tradition that is a continual revival and interpretation; whose risks cannot be ignored, but insurmountable obstacles cannot be opposed to those same risks, which would be absurd.

Moreover, in theory probably no one will be disposed to swear on the material intangibility of the Statute, for no other reason than that the facts demonstrate *ad oculos* the contrary; and whoever today attempts to cast a quick glance at those articles, it is uncertain whether he will have a harder time finding those that are in full vigor or those that have expired or are substantially modified. One might even say that what is contested is rather the right or political opportunity of an explicit and systematic revision of the constitution made without too much concern for the general opinion or feeling and for the normal or ordinary development of our public institutions. The which contestation evidently cannot concern this Committee, which is not convened to prepare bills of law, but rather to "examine questions from the point of view of their principle" (as was also said authoritatively), in order to present "simple conclusions of principle." Nor will these conclusions – even this is evident – blow up unexpectedly like bombs to frighten and rout the cohorts of distracted sentinels of the sacred ark. If accepted by the Party that asks us for them, they will develop into a plan put before the King's Government and before the two Houses, and hence to be discussed without haste, in broad daylight. And we are here with a desire to serve the Country. Which is suffering in a crisis that it must exit from; and must exit without losing any of its acquired strengths; indeed, acquiring still other strengths that it needs as a result of the progress reserved to it, and which is a matter of life or death for it. And we have the certainty here to be on the right path, historically and legally, of the constitutional development of the State, which we are the faithful servants of.

The declaration, already opportunely remembered in the present debate, [put forward] by the illustrious President of the Senate, or rather by the most patriotically conservative institution that the Country has, would be enough to exempt us; that declaration of his in Manziana's discourse given in June 1923:

> *Regarding the possibility of modifying the Statute, in my opinion there can be no doubt about it. As for constitutional theory, I have already had to write that in States with flexible Constitutions like Italy, the Lower House, the Senate, and the Sovereign, when there is a prior accord amongst them, can always derogate from statutory dispositions in the forms and by ordinary procedure; and it is to be noted that this English theory had authoritative supporters among us, in Cavour, Boncompagni, Pisanelli, Minghetti, Bonghi, Crispi, and Zanardelli.*

But we cannot forget that on May 8, 1848, the Lieutenant of the King, Prince Eugenio of Savoy-Carignano, in the inaugural discourse of the first session of the first legislature of the subalpine Parliament, amidst applause from the Assembly, announced: "If it should happen that the desired fusion with other parts of the peninsula be achieved, those mutations in the law that are worthwhile to make our destinies great will be promoted." Hence, since then, within the Upper House itself, one began to consider a reform of the Senate. So that since then it was obvious that the enlargement of the State had to lead to some changes to the constitution.

One will say that this idea of the opportunity for eventual alterations was natural and justified in the beginning, when the Statute, just born, like all things new, could not have that character of high authority that little by little begins investing institutions that are shown to be historically vital, when the spirit began to expand from little Piedmont to a much broader horizon because of enlarged borders and new national tasks. But I will say rather that by that time they had seen and knew how the Albertine Statute had been born; and how, therefore, they could not be the pillars of Hercules. Whoever has read the minutes of the proceedings of the Council from February 3 to March 4, 1848, made public for the first time on the fiftieth anniversary of the Statute and recently republished more fully and with greater explanations by the Piedmontese Committee of the Historical Society of the Risorgimento, can understand the spirit with which members of parliament of '48 had to protect the most recent Constitution.

When, during the dramatic session on February 3, Carlo Alberto submitted to the considerations of his ministers, who were unanimous in representing to him the need to concede the Constitution before it could be torn up, the first order he gave was "to be occupied meanwhile on a plan that took care not to imitate other Nations servilely." But in the successive session on the 7th, the Count de la Tour could find nothing better than to point to the French Constitution of 1814, modified after the July Revolution, as something that presented less inconveniences; and the Count Borelli, Minister of the Interior, reinforced the idea that there was no time to lose, nor was it the case to mind imitating foreigners or not.

It is necessary to note, he said, the difficulties of finding an Italian Constitution. If one has to adopt one, why not take the most monarchical one, the one most studied for sixty years? It is urgent. This is not a time when the people will be content with vague hopes, the King needs to declare what he wants to do, this needs to be an established principle. And the Count Revel, Minister of Finance, added that from his point of view, once the principles were established, which were needed, of a strong government, with an Upper House [of senators] appointed by the king in order to counterbalance the power of the Lower House, for these were the bases of the French Constitution and it was a matter of working from these principles, deducing and applying the consequences, and it was dangerous to study new dispositions instead of conforming to what in France had been the result of long experience, long study, long discussions by more competent men, more versed in the theory and practice of the representative regime. So they needed five other sessions only, and keeping in mind and slightly modifying the French Constitution, on March 4 it came to an end, they were ready to sign. Rapidity, necessary haste; but who could have imagined, fixing his gaze into the distant future, that in 1924, after the miraculous event of the Kingdom of Italy, after so many great events in the whole history of the world that there would still be someone to say: take care not to touch the Statute of Carlo Alberto?

I will note one more particular only. In the same session on February 7, the Count de la Tour spoke of the "system of introducing into the House, people who represented special interests and corporations, like universities, commerce, the clergy, etc." and he cited England, where corporations sent delegates to Parliament. And the response? The Count Sclopis observed that the English example was not to be followed because in Piedmont these corporations didn't exist. So the authors of the Statute themselves recognized that when these corporations peradventure should arise, they would have to have their voices [represented] in Parliament.

And what happened to the publication of the Statute? The progressive parties were not content with it, and rained down criticisms, varied and acerbic criticisms. Cavour says it himself in an article of his from those days (March 10); where one may read those memorable declarations against the presumed inviolability of the statutory provisions, which today hold value for us as a solemn historical document, coming from a man who was the greatest interpreter of the Statute and remains in modern Italian history a quasi tutelary numen of its free institutions. One needs to re-read here what he said in response to the critics of the Albertine Statute:

Finally the discontented, not satisfied with interpreting many of the provisions of the Statute in a leftist manner, raise their voices to high heaven against the phrase that declares it a fundamental and irrevocable law of the monarchy, as if with that the path to any future progress was impossible and a system of absolute immobility was established, contrary to common sense and the needs of a modern society. Such an imputation stirs up dangerous unrest, either by someone who is in fact ignorant of constitutional theory, or by someone who seeks to rouse by false pretexts.

How ever can one pretend that the legislator had wanted to commit himself and the nation to never bringing the slightest direct change to effect the minimalist improvement to a political law? But this would be to wish to make constituent power disappear from the heart of society, it would be to deprive it of the indispensable power to modify its political forms, according to new social exigencies. It would be so absurd a concept that it could not be conceived of by anyone who cooperated in the redaction of this fundamental law.

A nation cannot deprive itself of the

> *ability to change its political laws via legal means. Nor can it in any minimal way abdicate constituent power. This [power] is placed, in absolute monarchies, in the legitimate sovereign; in constitutional monarchies... the King and the Houses are fully vested with it...*
>
> *We consider the condition that sanctions the Statute as an irrevocable law that could not be violated without perjuring ourselves and being guilty of the most monstrous ingratitude. But that does not mean to say that the particular conditions of the condition are not susceptible to progressive improvements operated by common accord among the contracting parties. The King with the assistance of the nation will always be able in the future to introduce into it all the changes that are indicated by experience and by what makes sense for the times.*

And Cavour himself, when he recognized the eventual opportunity for a reform of the Senate in the Senate's response to the discourse by the Crown, on May 27, – he did not hesitate to write an eloquent article to demonstrate that "a House chosen by the power of the executive branch among certain categories established by the law will probably be a political body respected for its intelligence, its integrity, but it will never exercise an influence such as to able to counterbalance the action of the Lower House." In this way the French Chamber of Peers "was never a real political power, and kneeled before the changeable majorities in the Chamber of Deputies." And he was championing already, only two months after the promulgation of the Statute, the elective system as "the only rational one, the only opportunity in the actual state of current affairs and in Italy."

Gentlemen, I have no need to remind you precisely how often this topic of the reform of the Senate has given occasion to discuss again the legitimacy of eventual modifications to the Statute. An expert of constitutional law, a man of true genius, the Hon. Arcoleo,[84] in his report in 1911 for the reform of the Senate, warned that one must distinguish between organic reforms of institutions that find in them the seeds of their development, and radical changes that shake the origins and structure of them; and that a dispute can arise on the exercise of constituent power only in this second case, when one creates more than one innovates, when there is more upheaval than reform. He warned that

> *institutions are not transformed in any useful way by the sole virtue of doctrine, violence of the crowd, or the advent of improvised deeds; these are signs of changed conditions, the stimulus of new exigencies; but they become fecund seeds only when they derive*

[84]Arcoleo: Giorgio Arcoleo (AD 1848-1914), an Italian jurist and politician.

> *from the inherent development of the same organisms. There is a historical climate that puts out new branches on old trunks, and to this natural process the political orders owe solid resistance and also continuous luxuriance, in which the institutions, while abiding by their origins and their character, changed form and attitude.*

So, with regard to Senate reform, Arcoleo believed it had to do with one of those spontaneous, but necessary changes that reflect "in political orders the changed economic and social conditions of the country"; warning that the Statute is a limit, which prevents turning back, not proceeding forward. In fact, as the same Arcoleo observed, the Senate rules had almost all been modified in various States of Europe with reformative laws of statutory dispositions.

I believe it equally superfluous to recall that the problem of its same reform which has been so many times brought up but never resolved, – the Senate took it up again in 1919, when the obscure politico-social agitations of the post-war years appeared to threaten the very existence of the Upper House; and the Hon. Tittoni was president of the special Committee, and it included the Senators Greppi, Mazziotti, and Melodia, whom we have the honor of having with us, the greatest jurists of the Senate, one of whom had proven himself from the start as being among the most staunch conservatives; and it was the speaker, together with the Senators Greppi and Ruffini, who continued even outside the Senate to champion bold reformatory ideas, which it will devolve on us to take up again perhaps. And that committee, in its reports, focused its attack on what it too called

> *the supposed inviolability of the Statute; as if (the committee said) it were not by now on everyone's mind that it drew a line, beyond which it is not permitted to turn back to the restricted forms of absolutist government, nor to proceed forward through the broad ways of freedom, which the same Statute has gloriously made available to us. As if, again, for lack of any constituent power whatsoever, the reforms, which gradually are presented as necessary, are not to be achieved through ordinary lawmaking. As if, finally, this necessity and the consequent legitimacy of such a process could not by now be counted among the issues theoretically overcome in Italy, by the nearly unanimous consensus of the most serious public law experts and men of State, and practically superseded by the numerous cases of derogation and mutations to the Statute that have gradually taken place.*

It noted that Giuseppe Saredo had listed and illustrated as many as twenty-five of these cases in his report of June 28, 1894, compiled under the charge of a committee of senators who were also intent on Senate reform, which included men like Vitelleschi, Alfieri di Sostegno, Cremona. And it could have noted the more numerous list of names attached by Arcoleo in 1911; as he points out, moreover, that the old list could be enriched by now by "many others."

All that then was before October 1922, when the Italians who were not blind could already see what was very easy to see: that is, that the institutions needed to be updated in order to correspond to the real needs of the country and to contain within the legal structure of the State all the real strengths of the people; and they felt therefore the need to raise their voices in time. The fact then that these repeatedly submitted problems remained unsolved tells us two things, which are however intimately connected.

The first is that the powers of the State were so weakened that they did not have the necessary strength to resolve them; the second is that these problems were poorly submitted. But they were poorly submitted because those strengths, which would have given the State the indispensable vigor and effective power to reorganize itself into forms adequate to the new social and political exigencies, remained outside of it. In fact, for nearly forty years now, we have been deploring the weakness of the State, the radical and socialist character of the so-called democracy of all leftist governments; which is an accepted lie and immoral transaction between a State which has no strength and a social movement that acquires an ever growing strength, remaining institutionally outside of and in opposition to the State; with parliamentary and reformist socialism producing the extreme degeneration of parliamentarianism on the one hand and the most fulsome falsification of the great proletarian movement on the other. Such a lie however has been denounced and fought against by the fierce criticism of this pseudo-socialism, which is parasitical of capital and of work, nourished on the otiose, flattering, and perverting intellectuality that rages in parliaments; critical and practical theory, achieved in our century by syndicalism, which spilled over from Russia in a revolution that will always be highly instructive for every intelligent conservative. Syndicalism will be able to please or it will not, according to one's taste, or, better, according to the culture of each person; but it is one of those grandiose facts with universal and necessary character, solemn, which sooner or later one needs to study and understand.

Syndicalism before the war emerged from its Marxist origins, from the abstractness of its economic conception, and from the same first impulse and ardor of its proletarian faith towards internationalism. But then the war came. Which, among other things, demonstrated the ineffaceable reality of the Nation in the economy of work as well as in production; and it gave a fresh start to this new fact, which in Italy is by now impressed on everyone's mind: National Syndicalism, because of which even the workers are now starting to acquire the concept of, and a feeling for, the Fatherland, which their destiny is bound to, no more no less than that of all other citizens; and Fascism, which has collected and given consciousness, voice, and political efficiency, thanks to the faith of its martyrs, the courage of its supporters, and the most lucid intuition and inspiring words of its Leader, to all the forces unleashed by the war, both moral and social, – fascism has one merit, which history will indubitably acknowledge when a just judgment can be pronounced on it: the merit of having conjoined and fused in one and only one spirit *res olim dissociabiles*:[85] national ideality, in Italy the richest patrimony of a people in the history of the world, with all the splendor of the purest kind, of the loftiest traditions and with all the beauty of the values created by an exquisite culture, and the strength, powerful because disciplined, of the masses. Whom we see today gathered under their pennons marching, inspired, they too, by a new consciousness behind the national flag. These corporations of people, whose organization progresses day after day with a constantly accelerated rhythm under the moderating guidance of the Hon. Rossoni, – they rally before the powers of the State, as never before seen, the masses, no longer dispersed and confused in the amorphous quantitative accumulation of abstract individuals all the same, postulated by the old atomistic and naturalistic liberalism of the XVIIIth century, but real people, the real citizen, such as he is and deserves to be, and makes himself worthy of, in the organization of productive forces that is dependent on the State to recognize, guarantee, and promote it, according to its supreme ends, always essen-

[85] *Res olim dissociabiles*: Latin for "things that could not be united in the past." Tacitus, *De Vita Iulii Agricolae*, 3.1.

tially ethical, if it does not wish to be swept away by uncontrollable adverse forces.

Liberalism of the XVIIIth century sort, which didn't recognize anything but individuals, has had its day. The individuals remain, but they are regrouped, united, and therefore promoted to a greater economic, moral, and intellectual potential, by the laws themselves inherent in their social activity. Civil society abstractly conceived is replaced by a real civil society, concrete, the only one that exists, which is the true content of the State. The representative system, in consequence, must develop and adapt to this new reality, whose lineaments will not yet be defined (what thing is definitive in history?), but already they are glimpsed clearly, and constitute the greatest political problem of the day. And this development and adaptation will be the life of the system, and will demonstrate in fact its vitality. It will be a highly patriotic work and as boldly innovative as it is boldly conservative for all our fundamental institutions, put in a position to recapture lost vigor as instruments of efficacious discipline and the powerful unitarian direction of all the forces of the country.

We do not forget the preoccupations and anxieties of orthodox legal experts regarding recognition of the unions; but we cannot, today, remain silent when the reality that stands before our eyes is already set in motion: because with the laws that are being introduced into our legal system with respect to the professional orders, all prejudices can be said to be overlooked. It depends on fascism, it will depend on us, to inform conciliative bodies about the particular interests of the unions with respect to those of the general interest, and therefore with respect to the supreme authority of the State; a pacifying conciliation of the social classes through debate and the legal resolution of all conflict, and therefore an enhancement to the State's power.

The strength of the State, at least verbally, is desired by everyone today, and one would hope, at least in this part of our program, which is therefore essential, that applause and encouragement were shown to our Committee. But one knows that all too often this sovereign force is invoked against others; and as for itself, it prefers a freedom of exception. All that is human, and not to be marveled at with the candor of eternal radicals ready by their own account to exercise the dictatorship at the expense of conservatives! We retain that there is no true freedom without a strong State: a State that is capable of making laws, and making them respected. Capability that does not mean tyranny, and which is exceptionally well reconciled with the division of powers, in their distinction, whereas the parliamentary regime has a tendency to confound them, and therefore it is really an insupportable system of tyranny and of violent tampering with that delicate mechanism of the State, which is the guarantee of every freedom.

Strong State, which should really be sovereign, above factions; conscious, proud, jealous of its sovereignty; vigilant, ready to intervene with its action which will always be the action of peace and civility. State, which ceases to be the fragile little boat with torn sails, missing a rudder, in the middle of the waves; and it feels its own immortal personality, custodian and avenger of the rights and duties, of the glories and missions of the nation, which was, is, and will be, while the single generations come and go, and parties rise and fall, swept away in the inextinguishable flame of history that continues and proceeds: unity of interests, which below appear entirely economic, and above entirely moral. State, which cannot be mistaken for the petty bickering and plotting of ephemeral groups in an interminable exhibition of ambitions which are vanities; because it is represented instead by the august person of the King, strong in historical consensus of the entire nation, with his dynasty bound in perpetuity by a community of spirit and fortune. This State, the Fascist Party, which for that reason has ambitions to be national, is firm in the intent of restoring and lifting this State to the splendor of its incontaminable ideality, in the minds and hearts of Italians. This is the revolution; this the goal of the March on Rome.

But was this not the goal of our Risorgimento? And was it not the goal then of all those who saw the tradition of the Risorgimento broken to pieces, and who strove to solder it back together? Will this not need to be the ideal of all those who, within and without the fasci, have given some thought to the fate of the fatherland? Of all those who with unbiased good sense have meditated on the history of our country and are not disinterested in its actual politics?

We prepare for our work secure in the knowledge of working for the active and hardworking peace of this great people, who are always threatened by the old, maleficent germs of decadence, fomented by unrestrained individualism, for the power and prosperity of this Italy made great by the war and already on its way to a new history. We set to work with the profound conviction of fulfilling, as far as we are concerned, our intransgressible and imperative duty towards the dead who expected to be forgotten, but who have risen up and demand from the living that promised Fatherland, which they immolated themselves for.

II. Inaugurating the Work of the Committee of Eighteen[86]

Your Excellency,

This Committee is grateful to you for the honor you bestowed on it by attending its first session and bringing the Government's greeting to it. But it is also grateful to you for the clear and firm words with which, interpreting the thoughts of the Prime Minister, you defined the character of the work that the Committee prepares. There are still many people, and also some in good faith, who go about repeating and insinuating into the minds of the usual right-minded people, that the work, already initiated and with resolute energy brought to important results by the preceding Committee of Fifteen, appointed by the National Fascist Party, and which our Committee now continues the mission of and proceeds with the authority conferred on it by governmental nomination, – that the work is a subverting work. Instead, it is, must be, and wants to be an exquisitely conservative work, if it is true that not even monuments are preserved without restoration, and that preservation is always life and development and continual adaptation to always new conditions.

[86]Original footnote: Response given to the greeting brought to the Committee by the Government's representative, the Minister of Instruction, Hon. Pietro Fedele, February 28, 1925.

Your Excellency, we entreat you to tell the Prime Minister that this Committee sets down to work today with the sure and unwavering intent of serving the King and the Fatherland; with the resolve to contribute, for its part, to ensuring the soundness of the institutions and the greatness and potential of the Italian people on the path it has gloriously embarked on, and on which it is not in our character ever to need or be able to recede, not one step even.

III. Declarations[87]

National Idea: We wanted to interview Senator Gentile about the work of the new Committee, but he was induced, after our insistences, to make only these declarations, which are however of precise clarification:

Gentile: I ask you please not to insist on attempts at interviews, which I absolutely cannot grant for obvious reasons of appropriateness that you cannot fail to appreciate. The Committee that I have the honor of presiding over is a consultative Committee of the King's Government, and it cannot communicate except with the Prime Minister's office. On which every decision will depend as to the proposals that by the result of our studies might become bills of law and government project, in the more or less near future. And it understands that the political valuation of the opportunity to put, or not to put, certain problems before Parliament and the Nation not only strays entirely from our Committee's competency, but can only be made by the same Government at a time that it alone is capable of determining as the most appropriate.

National Idea: So the Committee is responsible for completing studies simply?

Gentile: Exactly. Which does not mean however that it is a kind of academy invited to deliberate on abstract questions of a purely theoretical nature. The

[87]Original footnote: An interview published in the *National Idea* of February 28, 1925.

problems proposed for our study are current problems, present on the national mind (as the presidential decree that instituted the Committee says); those, that is, which have already been formulated more or less clearly, and have become subjects of debate amongst the parties who square off in the field of today's political battles. They are the main problems put forward by the National Fascist Party, but which all parties have implicitly accepted as they discuss and take position already with respect to the eventual solutions for which tomorrow one will have to fight. The adversaries of Fascism or some skeptical, indifferent spectators who always judge from the vantage point of their profound sufficiency, accuse fascists of lacking clear ideas on this or that matter.

Well, they will be the first, I imagine, to declare themselves satisfied today if the fascist Government, welcoming the aspirations of the Party, resolutely begins on a path to define, based on the studies of this Committee, a precise plan for a conclusive discussion, whatever that might to be. Problems meanwhile exist, and whoever does not see them does not want to see them. And those fine fellows in the House who show surprise that others might think to tackle those problems, gave another proof of their not excessive, I don't say political, but historical sensibility. And if their surprise was a polemical gesture against the future legislation of the National Government, their gesture has already fallen into the void given that the Government, for its own part, has shown that it did not even notice, and to start with it has presented to the House a law on the secret association. Which only a huge partisan with an intent to deceive can interpret as repugnant to any disposition whatsoever or to the spirit of the Statute, which it is a simple complement and genuine perfection of, however annoying it might seem to so many people. Typical example this of the reality and determination of the problems whose study the Committee of Fifteen occupied itself with, and which are now taken up again by the new governmental Committee. Or does anyone wish to affirm that this question of factions is an invention by the fascists? I do not believe that the naïve souls of the populists would even come to that [conclusion], despite all their improbable confidence in forming and reforming opinions and facts!

National Idea: We saw in the greeting given by you to the Minister Fedele in the inaugural session, how much energy it took to repel the double accusation that the Opposition levels at the old and new Committees; to set about the work of reform directed at tampering with the essential provisions of the Statute, whose inviolability has always been held as indisputable; and to obey reactionary and illiberal criteria and tendencies, which would have menaced the fundamental freedoms of the Albertine Statute.

Gentile: I'm afraid, however, that these accusations will continue to be repeated, because it is too much in their favor that unintelligent folk might believe it. But I and my illustrious and authoritative colleagues of the old and new Committee, we have never become aware of someone who works for or who might ask us to work for removing any one of the freedoms in whose shade some of us were born, and some of us were already able to participate in the Italian people's joy when they were won. Not a man among us has a preference for going backwards however. The Italian people have such a long way to go! But the path will not be certain nor level nor even pointed out by certain zealots disinterested as to its freedoms; and the people know this, and they no longer believe in the sermons that are preached from certain pulpits. And I can pledge to them that no single freedom is in danger, by us at any rate; except the freedom to disrupt this State, which is the platform of all freedoms. And anyway, they must have patience; in any case, surprises are impossible. In good time, Italians will know what laws we will have proposed; and they will have the means to accept them or reject them. Any skirmish today is pointless, and it does not demonstrate a great interest in the public good. Some people find an argument even in the responsibility given to our Committee, to make a rather gross and provincial joke out of it. To each his own; and Italians have laughed for centuries more or less coarsely over so many serious things, so that there is really nothing to be astonished at if they demonstrate also in this case that there is an old Italy, still alive, that was thought to be finished at Caporetto; a weakened, stupid, Italy, which young people disdain and which, I am certain of it, they will destroy. And our Committee will give a hand to these youth, who will be the strong and really free Italy that we desire.

And with that, the Senator Gentile rose from his seat and, smiling, invited us to come back again when the work was accomplished, when the Committee will have been dissolved.

IV. Work Accomplished[88]

We managed to meet with Senator Gentile today and put some questions to him about the work of the Committee of Eighteen. It would have been his desire, since the time the Committee was appointed, that the most absolute reserve be maintained around its work. He retained that it was the strict duty of an advisory Committee appointed by the Government to let the Government itself decide whether to communicate or not to the public the conclusion of its work, and whenever it seemed the most opportune time to do so.

Gentile: But, unfortunately, my desire and intent was frustrated by indiscretions, which it was impossible to prevent in fact, because of the journalistic ambushes that individual members of the Committee were continually exposed to; and also because, I have to say, of the great interest and fascination raised by the character of the work commissioned by the Eighteen. And now we are at the point where I must instead desire that all reports and bills and the same orders of the day that were gradually approved by the Committee be made public as soon as possible.

Popolo d'Italia: And why?

Gentile: The problems are by now collectively on the nation's mind; the press and the parties are in possession of them, and the polemic spreads with the result to be expected from a discussion in which great warmth is placed of course, but which lacks the indis-

[88]Original footnote: Interview published in the *Popolo d'Italia*, July 2, 1925.

pensable basis of precise knowledge of the matter under discussion. I do not believe that any other outcome can be expected than this: that people once and for all stop sneering at the Solons, given that these Solons with their proposals are beginning to disturb the sleep of so many patriots thinking of the future of the Country. Certain newspapers will not stop sniggering perhaps with the usual clumsy vulgarity that in them accompanies the most impudent bad faith. But there will also be one indisputable fact finally, that these Solons are and will be a real problem for these newspapers. Don't you think? Did you see the long disquisitions recently imposed by the Eighteen on the antifascist Congresses? This is already something. But nothing can result from these discussions for now except the need, which will have to be felt generally little by little, to study what precisely the Eighteen proposed, what the reasons for the proposals formulated by their majority are, what the observations opposing those reasons were by members of the Committee itself who were in a minority; and finally what the terms of the actual problem are.

Popolo d'Italia: But in broad strokes, the Committee's thinking, thanks to what it has been called our ambushes, can be said to be already known?

Gentile: I confess that I have no idea what might be printed in the newspapers; and I have consequently no way of judging whether what has been said is correct or incorrect. What I do know is what I happened to learn from some newspaper – things I supposedly thought, but was in fact ignorant of: to read my thoughts there, that I never knew I had, let alone formulated, nor that have even entered into my head. And what struck me even more was a fact, because of which I agreed to the conversation you asked of me today. And that fact is this, what politicians and parties in documents, which aspire to have a historical significance and which can be seen printed, in very big, bold type in the large newspapers of Italian liberalism, give glaring proof of, something that those who should have understood better than others did not understand: that is, they *couldn't* understand a thing. Since I could never say that a Vittorio Emanuele Orlando, or an Umberto Ricci, are incapable of realizing the nature of a proposition like that of the Corporative System of the State, about which by now rivers of ink have been spilled. I have to say, however, that ink on paper was spilled; and nothing has been read since then. Words, words, words, and a great confusion of ideas.

I read, for example, the following words in the letter by the Hon. Orlando to the National Liberal Council: "Today through the announced reforms we still hear the unity of the people being denied, even formally, substituting corporative plurality for it." And I asked myself how in the world could someone accuse the Corporative System of fracturing the unity of the people when it is an organization formed of all the real elements of the people, specified in fact according to their natural functions but precisely, because of it, harmonized in the intimate cohesion and unity of a sound organism? The only answer that can be given is to suspect that the Hon. Orlando confuses the corporative State with the syndical State. One will say: "But explain to me then your corporative State."

It is what we want to create, provided you have the patience and do not succumb to the suggestion of journalistic quibbles and hastily-anticipated criticisms that tilt at windmills.

Popolo d'Italia: But the Ricci agenda, approved by the liberal Congress, when it affirms that "the legal recognition of the Unions would provide for defending their rights and sanctioning the responsibility of them," makes an affirmation of principle and program that does not contradict the postulates of your Committee.

Gentile: It does not so much contradict them as one of the plans that we presented to the Government refers specifically to the discipline of this legal recognition of the Unions. But recognition without the Corporative System appeared dangerous to the Committee with respect to that sovereignty and strength of the State, which liberals as well say they are concerned about: with respect to that unity of the people that even the democratic Hon. Orlando speaks about. But what made me doubt even more the quality of the information given by the Professor Ricci and all the members of congress is to hear him speak against the deprecated reforms because "obligatory Unions and their representation in a political assembly would fracture the unity of the State, by substituting them for the sovereignty of monopolistic bodies at war amongst themselves and would considerably reduce the individual initiative of production and national revenue," in order then to declare "incompatible with the essential principles of the modern State, any project whatsoever to realize the indicated program."

Obligatory Unions? But this was an idea aired in the Committee, and shot down. The Committee retains that in economics there could be spontaneous events to be regulated legally within the confines of the State, but not events to be created by the programmatic action of the laws. Therefore no obligatoriness of the Unions, but only awareness of them and therefore a staying in contact [with them] and discipline.

Popolo d'Italia: But the Corporations?

Gentile: I'm getting to it: they are not Unions, just as Chambers of Commerce and Professional Orders are not Unions; and they will be even less so when these already existing institutions become part of a system, in which are included all the elements that now, deprived of any organization, have no means for coming together to stabilize that social and economic equilibrium which is not only a free economy produced by a spontaneity outside the law; but an economy already disciplined by that awareness of the general aims, or rather by the interference and with the necessary accord of all interests, which transcends the sphere of the simple economy, and is the State. The Unions are outside of the Corporation as intended in the proposals put forward by the Committee, and can for that reason be controlled by the Corporation and maintained in place by means of the State powers, where Unions and individual forces will be able to deploy a legitimate action and live a sane and prosperous life.

So, for us, neither obligatory Unions, nor State Syndicalism. Our aim was to strengthen, not weaken the State. For that reason, we have acceded to the idea of an organic constitutional representation; which is not an invention of Fascism. And there was in the liberal Congress some political writer who put in a good word for this idea in the past.

The which (I don't hesitate to admit it) has some very honorable precedent in the Italian liberal tradition. Which does not mean that it is in line with the liberals gathered around the Hon. Borzino; democrats all of them, and melancholic adulators of a tradition that I would call pseudo-liberal rather than liberal: the tradition, for example, of Giolitti and Orlando, but not of Sonnino.

I will go even further. This reform of ours, quite a bit more complex than meets the eye for whoever fixes his attention on this corporative matter, could also be called totally liberal; in many points it was warmed up to more than once by the more sensible liberals, when Fasci were not spoken about. And yet, if we are in agreement, it will be the fascist reform *par excellence*.

The same thing will happen to it as happened to the school reforms, against which the liberals and populists fight tooth and nail today in vain, after having for so long a time invoked it... in words. It will happen, in other words we will do what others said it would have been good for us to do. It would have been, yes, of course; but... if only.... There were so many *but*'s and *if*'s for something that, in the past, in theory anyways, everyone was in agreement with, and then in practice nothing was to be done about it, and do not even think about touching certain buttons if you don't want agreement to be scuttled.

Today, agreement has become a little difficult because one does what one says. It is Fascism's style: perhaps its only originality. But everyone will realize, a little bit at a time, that that is no small matter.

VI. To His Excellency, the Hon. Benito Mussolini, Prime Minister[89]

Your Excellency,

The Committee appointed by Your Excellency by presidential Decree on January 31, 1925, composed of eighteen senators, deputies, and political and social science scholars, that it might study "the problems present today in the national consciousness and pertaining to the fundamental relations between the State and all the forces that it must contain and guarantee," resumed the work initiated and already conducted by the Committee of XV, which in September of the prior year had been charged by the National Fascist Party with studying the problems relative to the Constitution of the State deriving from the revolution of October 28, 1922. That Committee had in fact assembled on the same day as the anniversary of this historical date; and, taking note of a clear message by Your Excellency, leader of the Fascist Party, it formulated the main themes of study entrusted to it. And these themes were two: the first had to do with the relationship between executive and legislative powers; the other had to do with the relationship between the State and individual and associated citizens (in other words, the State and secret associations, the State and

[89]Original footnote: In order to present to him the actions and conclusions of the Committee of Eighteen.

unions in private law and public law).

That Committee immediately set about looking into these themes. But it maintained, from the beginning, the suitability of removing from the second of them the part about secret associations; and that was for the not negligible reasons of political opportunity, given the extreme warmth that awareness of such a problem had assumed in the Party, from which the Committee had emerged. On which subject, I do not need to recall that, in my capacity as president of the Committee of XV, I had the honor of presenting to Your Excellency the conclusions that were rapidly arrived at, in the form of a bill of law backed by a full report, wherein all the historical, legal, and political reasons of the provision were clearly exposed. By now that bill, favorably received by Your Excellency and presented to Parliament with minor modifications, has been discussed and approved by the House of Deputies, and will before long be a law of the State, which Fascism intends to create in a regime of superior freedom.

The Work of the Committee of XVIII

The Committee of XVIII, which nearly all the members of the previous committee returned to be part of, reunited on February 26 for the first time, approved the list of problems taken up for study; and confirmed the two Subcommittees that were already working on those themes: one presided over by Senator Melodia, responsible for the first; the other, presided over by

Senator Corradini, responsible for the second of the two important themes mentioned above; adding some new members to each of them, in that the number of members had grown and new technical competencies were added to those already possessed by the Committee of XV.

The two subcommittees and minor commissions formed for special tasks within them, worked intensely and indefatigably with studies and individual research and collegial discussions, with inquests and interrogations of experts, in order to accomplish their mandate. In the Committee's brief span of time, 77 meetings were held, despite the impediments and difficulties that the ordinary and indispensable duties of the commissioners who were not residents of Rome put in the way of frequent gatherings. But, thanks to their alacrity, to the patriotic zeal and absolute abnegation with which they attended to their work, and above all to the great political experience of the more expert among them and to the doctrine and great skill of everyone in the matters in which one had to deal, they could in so short a span of time prepare and present to the plenary Committee the proposals and illustrations that I, in turn, am pleased to be able to submit to the judgment of Your Excellency. Seeing that those proposals and related illustrations, in the twenty sessions held by the plenary Committee between February 26 and June 24, after full and laborious debates in which all aspects of the individual questions were examined with great care and from every point of view, resulted in the bills of law and Reports that I have the honor of presenting to Your Excellency.

Executive Power and Legislative Power

From the enclosed minutes of meetings it becomes clear how such conclusions were reached. Here I think it necessary to note only that, in all the conclusions regarding the relationship between the executive and legislative powers, the Committee found itself quasi unanimous, and that the report by committee member Barone, in a form in which only some nuance reflects the particular personal ideas and tendencies of the speaker, expresses what the thought of the entire Committee was, with the exception of committee member Gini, whose ideas are developed in a separate report, which is also attached. In the conclusions, however, regarding relations between powers of the State and citizens, the Committee was divided into majority and minority opinions; and the thought of the majority is in the report by committee member Arias, and that of the minority, or a least a part of it, in the minority report by committee member Coppola, to which the Hon.s Mazziotti, Melodia, and Suvich acceded; and to which are to be added the verbal statements partially in accord, or analogous, by committee members Lanzillo and Rossoni, and those contained in the aforementioned report by Gini, although Gini had agreed with the majority on the most important ideas in the proposals related to this second topic, which concerns the Corporative System of the State.

The Corporative System

This in fact was the topic that divided the Committee, which was nearly unanimous on another main point of the same topic, namely the unions. The Committee unanimously believed that legal recognition, if requested, was to be granted to the unions; but it also believed that not only were unions not to be made obligatory, but that those recognized were to be reduced to only one per category.

The Corporative System in truth is the most innovative idea among those that prevailed through the studies and debates by the Committee. And for that reason it was natural that it should raise doubts, perplexities, preoccupations, and objections within the Committee itself. The same proponents or adherents of this idea considered it for a long time before embracing it. Some of its most ardent and staunch supporters and elaborators were at first its most radical critics and opponents. Nor can the Committee hope for a prompt and easy assent by those who receive the first notice of it of these its conclusions; because it has to do with a complex idea, which for one or another of its elements or aspects, separately considered, risks being mistaken or confused with other ideas, which, in the Committee's understanding, it somewhat opposes. It is certainly an idea that merits attentive and serious consideration, because, in the Committee's opinion, it is the only one that could indicate a means to effectively contain within the sphere of statal action the national forces of production; therefore to make the State adhere to the reality that it is the form of, and from which it cannot abstract or separate itself (as the liberal State tends to do on account of its origins and its nature) without losing its concrete basis together with it its own organic and organizing force. Aside from this idea, there are only two paths forward: either the abstract State of individualistic liberalism is firmly held on to; but this is not the fascist State, in that Fascism since the beginning has had an actual political signification: to fight and beat liberal individualism, having judged individualism to be abstract, and therefore false. Or pure syndicalism is adopted. But pure syndicalism is not the syndicalism of obligatory unions; whose obligatoriness presupposes a principle of obligation superior to the unions, or rather a State in opposition to and situated above the unions, and hence it contradicts the pure syndicalist principle, which does not recognize any legitimate force external to the union, nor can it admit therefore anything but the spontaneous and free union; whence also it must prefer, as it does prefer, the *de facto* existing union to the legally recognized union. Pure syndicalism, at the end of the day, leads to the union that absorbs the State in itself; and which in its fragmentariness and spontaneous and inevitable multiplicity has consequently shattered and destroyed the essential unity. Ideal postulate, it is too antithetical to the principles and profoundest inspirations of the fascist State.

The Fascist State

The fascist State is the sovereign State. Sovereign in deeds, and not [just] in words. A strong state, whose strength admits no equal and limiting peers, although it too, like every moral force, gives freely of itself but has its own self-defined limits. The fascist State does not want to be the State superimposed on the citizen, but rather a State that invests in the citizen and is actuated in his consciousness; and in order to be present, it promotes and educates, knows and recognizes, and treats the citizen for what he is and for what he must be, historically and economically, morally and politically, with all his fundamental interests which determine his orientation and impress a special activity on him. The fascist State, in order to permeate and direct the consciousness of citizens, wants to organize them in national unity; for it too is a soul, a person, a powerful will, aware of its aims. Because the State has its aims which are not those of any particular citizen, nor of any class of citizen, nor of the sum or total mass of individuals who on any given day live within the territory of the State joined together by a common legal bond. National unity (fascists know it and feel it strongly) is not something that already exists at a given moment in time. It has its roots in the past and from the present it stretches out toward the future; and today it lives insofar as, with the vitality that is the fruit of centuries, it turns to the near and distant future and projects itself, and intuits there, and yearns for its greater destiny, which is its plan, the mainspring of its every effort, the *raison d'être* of its very life.

The fascist State is an idea that is set vigorously in motion; but it is an idea; and as such it transcends every present and every contingent and materialistically defined form. For that reason, it emphasizes more duty than right when addressing the citizen; and urges him to exceed himself and to seek his present interest in the future, his personal advantage in that of the Fatherland, to which every sacrifice is owing and from which every reward is to be expected.

The Committee, composed of fascists and old liberals who look to fascism with sincere attachment and trust, is inspired with fullness and a unanimity of feeling for such a concept, which is the plan of the National Government and the Fascist Party.

Launching the Fascist State

Not for a single moment however did it think that it was going to subvert the Italian State coming out of the revolution of the Risorgimento. And so it thought that it would be the faithful interpreter of the spirit of Fascism, born to build, not to destroy. And it is convinced that the State of the Risorgimento and of the glorious national Monarchy, which accompanied the liberation from the pre-dawn hours and bore the Italian people with magnanimous faith to the high noon of the great victorious war and the restoration of Italy to its longed-for borders, this State is by now, by dint of traditions that have become sacred to every Italian heart, a solid construction to be respected, and a solid base on which to build the State of the fascist revolution. So that, in the series of proposals related to the organization of the supreme powers of the State, which it is honored to submit to the Your Excellency's judgment, the Committee believed it needed to restrict itself to freeing that antique and venerable constitutional basis of the Italian State from the superstructure that slowly, in the corruption of our parliamentary system, had been placed on it, and which had little by little made it serve aims far removed from of the thought of its founders.

It is enough to remember the declaration that Carlo Alberto's Minister of Foreign Affairs gave, on February 8, 1848, to representatives of foreign nations, announcing the Constitution granted "as the most monarchical possible," and then to recall the modifications to the same Statute that ministers of His Majesty the King, in the inauspicious year of 1919, had come to consider mature, in order to measure the long path travelled by our institutions in the opposite direction from which it believed itself at first to be moving.

Legal Reforms and Political Praxis

The measures, then, in this respect, suggested by the Committee are limited in their particulars, which to an inattentive judge could appear secondary in importance. But it will certainly not escape Your Excellency's attention that – although modest in their appearance, cautious in their arrangement, inspired with a rigorous, realistic criteria of practicality and possibility, – they touch on very delicate and essential points of constitutional design, on whose recovery the State can depend in its return to a correct development. Which then is all that is expected, in this regard, from the auspicated foundation of the fascist State; the rest, in the Committee's judgment, depends rather on political customs, in other words on the praxis in which constitutional principles are applied. Since all principles are forms that receive meaning and concrete value by the spirit that is applied to them, by the force of will with which they are asserted, by the rigidity with which these forms are expected to be observed, by the faith that animates those whose concern it is to observe them or have them observed, which is the same thing finally. In this respect, Your Excellency, the Italian people cannot expect true reform, nor can they expect it from the Committee of the XVIII, unless it comes from You, from Your Government; to which the Committee can do no more than indicate only a few means, which certainly are of no use unless a strong hand seizes them and adopts them with sincere energy.

The New Constitutional Problem that Fascism Must Resolve

The liberal State, which we inherited from our fathers, is not however capable of satisfying all the exigencies of the modern State. Our society is no longer that of 1848. In conferences in which the Albertine

Statue was prepared, a minister of the King asked whether it was not the case to bring corporations into the House of Representatives; and he was told that it was not the case, in that in the Sardinian State there were no corporations. So the problem to be resolved was not that of the relationships between the State and categories and classes of citizens, but between the State and individual citizens. Today the problem is different; and Carlo Alberto's Statute is inadequate for the actual structure of the State, which happens to regulate a society where the individual citizen no longer counts as such. The big economic, social, and political movements of the second half of the last century, and the first quarter of the present century, have profoundly changed the structure of the greater part of the Italian Nation. Corporations, unions, professional orders, associations of special interests, are established or on their way to becoming established. The political parties no longer address the individual, but categories of associated individuals. Whoever happens to read the descriptions of electoral contests from the past, e.g., Francesco de Sanctis' *Viaggio elettorale* (which is from 1875), gets the impression of looking at a world that ended centuries ago. And the State today instead ignores categories; and as happens with all forces that are ignored, one cannot subject them as would be necessary, one cannot guarantee to them that freedom that is possible only within the State.

The categories, unions, *extra lege* because ignored by the State, are by nature anarchic; they move outside the orbit in which sovereign power makes itself understood and asserts itself. All the strength they have at their disposal is strength taken from the State. And for this reason the State in these last few decades of social conflicts and consequent political contrasts has demonstrated an impotence, which is by now universally considered characteristic of the liberal democratic State. Against such impotence fascism has rebelled, as it wants to be the avenger and restorer of the strength of the State, sovereign and unequaled.

To restore the independence of the executive power from the legislative branch, ensuring the legitimate functions of both; as a result, to organize for greater unity and efficiency the executive power, as the direct emanation of the King's sovereignty, and therefore the active and responsible consciousness of the superior unitary personality of the State; to restore the two Houses, singly and combined, to their original and right physiognomy, and the activity of the integrative organs of sovereignty to the only legislative function wherein the supreme power, by its essentially executive nature, is limited, defined, and ascertained, and thus is controlled and made responsible effectively: all that is not enough. The powers of the State are not the State. Every reform that uniquely addresses them cannot fail to be abstract and practically to no purpose. For this reason the Committee considers the second part of its work a necessary complement to and integration of the first; and it found itself in near total agreement not only by acknowledging the appropriateness of the legal recognition of unions, encouraged in that way to enter into the sphere of statal action, but also by holding such provision insufficient by itself to its purpose, the attainment of which could and ought to be the differential character of the fascist State; the coordination of the State with productive national forces, unions or no, unionizable or not, or even with all the existing and operative forces in the nation which, for the State, is its content. The agreement that existed in this negative judgment did not persist when it passed into a proposal, which to the majority of the Committee appeared that it should do, in the most suitable manner possible, even if susceptible in some particulars to variations and improvements, to bring about that communication and coordination, and therefore the deep internal organization, of the nation in the State.

Consider, Your Excellency, whether this or some other can be the solution to the problem that fascism and the Government feel they want to resolve; which the Committee has studied with fervent desire without prejudice to the genuine and vital traditions of the Italian people, nor to the keenest and most powerful aspirations with which it looks confidently to its own future.

* * *

Your Excellency,

The Committee has completed a body of work that has from the beginning, as a result of its program, provoked pavid suspicions, strange misunderstandings and aversions, and even contumacies and derisions among the largest part of this old Italian people who appear modern at times but only in a small number of youthful groups. Never before has a consultative committee of the Government been made the target of a war similar to that which the Committee, which I have had the great honor of presiding over, sustained in the Italian press, agitated in recent months by the boiling over of embittered passions of highly politicalized delusion, faction, rhetoric, egotistical and lazy individualism, blatant skepticism, diffident towards every idea not literarily exalted but served by a purity of faith and resolve of the will: by all the detritus, in short, of the old Italian soul, which fascism slowly and painstakingly pursues and corrects. Although this war has demonstrated once again that negative spirit, which the Country cannot hope any good will come from, the Committee was often tempted to see in it the greatest reward it could hope for from its work, because nothing flatters men of faith more at times than incomprehension on the part of the demos. But the Committee rejected this temptation. It aspired to one reward only, placed higher than any personal satisfaction: to the advent, that is, of that well-ordered and powerful State, on which it kept a fixed eye in all its studies, whether it meets its expectations, or not. In that State, desired by all Italians, everyone will come around to be of one single mind.

– Rome, July 5, 1925.

Appendix:
Thoughts from the Evening Before

Political Realism and Fatalism, or the Philosophy of the Hon. Nitti[90]

Realism, as it is spoken about in politics, can be understood in two diverse ways, and it is spoken about in very different ways in fact. But the two meanings are not easy to distinguish in a clear and concise manner because the reason for the distinction is not within everyone's grasp. Whence it happens that many believe there to be just one concept of realism, just as there is only one word; and from this confusion arises frequent misunderstandings which give rise not only to abstract theoretical errors, but to uncertainties and practical disorientations and to deplorable deviations of political conduct.

The confusion of realism however becomes rather convenient in polemics, given the power that words always have, not to mention banners, insignia, and all the labels and exterior and abstract countermarks in the field of political battles. Where the number of those who speak, for example, about socialism, or democracy, or liberalism, etc., is far greater than the number of those who are able to give, even approximately, the meaning of each of these terms;

[90]Original footnote: Published in the review *Politics*, April 30, 1920.

around which terms however these individuals rally, with all their social energy, forming the strength of parties and deciding the fate of the community. Thus it is also always convenient to appeal to realism for whoever has to combat the ideas that adversaries put in one's way; as it will always be convenient to attack whoever has his ideas to champion; and in the one case as in the other it is no use to inquire what exactly is to be understood by realism. Yesterday, – that yesterday that already appears so remote! – everyone had a problem with realism, which was the abhorred Germanic *Realpolitik*. Today, the wind has shifted, and those ideas or ideologies that were previously worshipped on the altars have fallen into discredit; and it is a contest to see who is the greater realist, with eyes wide open to the hard reality that politics must conform to; and whoever has less illusions feels and promotes a greater sense of responsibility, which the huge difficulties of the post-war years, and the ever darker threats of an imminent future, imposed on those who survived the war: to the victors no less than to the defeated, joined together in the fatal law of a life economically and morally impoverished and depressed by the strains they had gone through. But the present exaltation as with the previous condemnation of *realpolitik* refer to the same indistinct concept of realism, which pays the price for the empty ideology of the war years and the political cynicism that lies in wait for us, now that we must overcome the crisis produced by the war.

Cynicism will not prevail. Indeed, one needs to realize the misunderstandings that lurk in mental positions, in which it thinks it can plant roots and sprout and flourish; because these mental positions correspond with broadly diffuse spiritual tendencies, against which one must react. The reality, in fact, whether that be the concrete and factual reality, or a fictitious reality, in which nevertheless there is a faith for lack of insufficient criticism and reflection, always exercises an irresistible fascination on the conduct of a man, who always acts as he thinks: certainly not as he thinks superficially, or as he believes he thinks, but according to his deepest convictions, which are his attitude itself in the face of reality.

* * *

Today, to be more frank, we are witnessing a rather curious spectacle, offered by Italian political life. The maximalists of socialism cry out that the times are ripe for the social and political transformation yearned for by them; and that there is no other possible way to resolve the problems that the country is afflicted with. They shout it, but they do not believe it; because if they really believed it, they would have no choice but to act in consequence. And instead, they shilly-shally; and there is no indication that the proletariate is going to ruin it, unless their brightest and most reliable representatives rush to throw themselves between the revolution and the bourgeois regime, virtually done for and condemned to being swept away; they are against an accord that satisfies as best it can the working class in rebellion and saves that regime. The most reasonable or least unreasonable among them, invited to participate in the Government, pull back, convinced evidently that even having a free hand they could not fail to demonstrate through action that their program is unrealizable. Constrained to steer a middle course in Parliament between a Government that cedes to them everything that can be ceded and the enraged who are most inclined to echo without thinking the unseemly cries of the anonymous class of irresponsibles, they say something and then retract it, they rise to speak and then sit down again before having spoken, and they profess finally a faith that they do not hold. They do not have it in any way, shape, or form; because if they had it, they would speak and act before companions whom they accept; or rather they would separate from them, they would leave Parliament, and they would in this way certainly contribute to make their thoughts clear, even to the masses, much better than they can do with the *ibis redibis*[91] of their actions and words, two terms they consider irreconcilable. So, they do not have it. And there is nothing strange or new in this; given that it has always been like this and is quite natural in fact for people to say, and try in every way to make other people believe, that they possess a strength much superior to what they actually do. Nor is there anything to be surprised at in the submissive and contrite attitude of the so-called middle class when faced with the subversive threat; seeing that even this cannot be considered a new occurrence, that the boldness of the ones is made possible by the timidity of the others; and that whereas the former affirm resolutely what they themselves do not believe, the latter are ready to believe what they hear them affirm. A curious case is

[91] *Ibis redibis*: Latin for "you will go, you will return" literally. But it is short for the phrase "*ibis redibis numquam per bella peribis,*" a phrase that is intentionally or unintentionally equivocal or misleading.

that of the philosophy that serves to season the bitter condescension of this submissive attitude. Whose cowardice could be demonstrated, if it weren't for the repugnance and reluctance of their adversaries to take the State's power in hand.

* * *

This philosophy is easily formulated: it has nothing to do with choosing between this attitude or that other possible one, and then discussing *quid faciendum*:[92] but to open one's eyes and see the unique way that is before us. The leader of the present Government has said it so many times before:

> *I do not believe that anyone could do differently than I see myself constrained to do. If there is someone who thinks differently, let him come forward. A sense of reality is needed: which is what it is. A very hard reality, which is not timidity, but rather virile courage, to bow before and render homage to. We need to be realists, and to brush aside whim or fancy, sentimentality, ideals. We must demobilize our minds.*

It is a philosophy that has its good name, Manzoni would say; and it would be pointless to go into the psychological genesis of it, which others, in our case in particular, could attribute to it. It is a philosophy that, according to the political point of view, can also set us up for contempt or ridicule: in that it can really

[92] *Quid faciendum*: Latin for "what to do."

seem ridiculous, the situation of someone who, stepping back, protests that that is the true sign of courage of a wise man; and it can also elicit a feeling of repugnance, of acerbic reprimand, this recognition, this insistent proclamation rather of an ugly reality, which is all the uglier and all more real as the mind is disposed to bend before it. But in conclusion it is a philosophy, even this one: the which can also be baptized as realistic, but must, as every philosophy, be understood, and also judged and criticized before it is accepted or refuted. And it is all the more timely to understand it, as it begins effectively to diffuse that disposition of mind that it is the manifestation of. Seeing that, when we are truly convinced that reality is what it is, we would have no choice but to abandon ourselves to the current, fatalistically, in order to reach as soon as possible the deep maelstrom that is bound to swallow us. That said, may it not be displeasing to philosophers of the simple philosophy typical of daily politics that it be defined with more rigor than they give to it themselves, this philosophy of theirs.

* * *

It is realism, of course, as well. Which cannot be practical without being theoretical, and vice versa. And the first dross that we will need to free our minds of is this: that to make an affirmation of realism in politics is possible without at all making an equivalent one in philosophy. A political realist is someone who, in the circle of relationships in which the life of the State is realized, acts by relating to a historically determinate reality, which is the sole reality conceivable as a concrete reality. But to relate to this reality is to know it; and to know it as the reality that one must relate to in practice: or to conceive of reality, which our personality in its effective operation is tied to, as reality not abstractly conceivable, but conceivable only insofar as historically determinate: that reality. A political realist is someone who sees the reality that he operates in as that reality. That reality is his. And this understanding of reality as our reality, or understanding our reality, the world in which we live, as a reality conceivable in a certain way, this, and no other, is to assert a philosophy. The realist philosopher understands his reality exactly as the political realist does: as a concrete, historical reality.

Except that, reality being identified with history or, as might also be said, with a fact, there is no telling what this history, or fact, might yet properly consist of. And history can be understood in two ways: either as a fact that does not depend on us, – indeed, as a fact that we depend on; or as our fact, that will never be a fact had we not acted to effect it. Sometimes, history is conceived of as a fact of nature, materialistically; at other times, as a moral and assessable human fact, idealistically. Fact of nature, in the first case, even if performed by men; but by men who are outside the sphere of our action, as, typically, those who lived before we were born and before we began to perform some action in the world. By men, that is, who speak of and take into account their fact necessarily, belonging to a reality that is just as foreign to us as natural reality is, inconceivable unless determined in its essence and in its action by an inviolable law, which absolutely limits our will, because it conditions it. Between the man who looks around and sees the inexorable and tyrannically dominating nature of his life and destiny; and the man who looks around and sees, beyond nature, the multitude of other men competing with nature in this work of inexorable and tyrannical dominion over him, there is evidently no essential difference. The one as well as the other comes to find himself alone and lost in a world that is different from what he would realize by himself in the free expansion of his personality. Freedom, for the one as well as for the other, is limited, and therefore impeded, or annulled by the world, at least by the effects in which it ought to be manifested. Which, insofar as it is opposed to the liberty of the spirit, becomes a natural mechanism.

Realism, then, having as its basis the concept of historical reality, and able to be measured against this reality, understood as a natural fact one moment and as a human fact the next, can be and is in fact conceived of as materialistic realism one moment, then as idealistic realism the next. One can in fact profess, with the greatest good faith, to be irreducible adversaries of every materialistic system and advocates of the radical difference between the mechanism and freedom, and to consider this an incontestable attribute of our most solid and certain personality, without however escaping, despite every good intention of ours, the logic of materialism, every time we believe that we need to refer, for our consciousness or for our behavior, to an already existing reality and placed there like a condition of our activity. Indeed, with respect to that concrete affirmation that we make of our personality, whatever our abstract conviction might be, in relation to that reality that conditions it with its existence, we effectively put our freedom to one side and consider as the only existent thing, and the only thing to be taken into account, that mechanism in which we presume ourselves bound, before those conditions that limit us and point out the way.

* * *

Last July, for example, we heard the head of the Government begin the announcement of his program with these exact words: "Every Government that is formed can choose a program. We find a program *sketched out by necessity, which we cannot escape and within whose confines we must remain.*" We have heard him repeat similar words since July, every time he has had the occasion to present Government proposals. It is the central idea, the method, the philosophical principle of his politics. Realistic, to be sure, and he is proud of it. But it has to do with a materialistic realism, in which the program is no longer the thought of the man who creates his own reality, but a necessity that the thought of the man must observe, abdicating the individual power of initiative. A wise man's program, without a doubt; and it is the praise that was bestowed on him by whoever was disposed to praise him because he liked him or because of an analogous spiritual attitude, which is the attitude of the so-called liquidators (passive liquidators) of the war; that diffused state of mind, superficial skepticism, which we have pointed out on a previous occasion.[93] But this is Guicciardini's wise man; the notorious "wise man" of

[93]Original footnote: "The Moral Crisis" in *Politics*, November 1919 issue, a. I., n. 7; reprinted in the volume "After Victory," Florence, La Voce, 1920, pp. 69 ff.

our skeptical and materialistic Renaissance, of decadence, of that period of exhaustion and shameful cynicism in Italian history. The wise man, who, as Guicciardini taught, attends to his own interests and does not bother with the State's, gives no thought to the Fatherland, which will then be fatally abandoned; not exactly to that operative idea that it is or must be, but to the clash of those social and individual forces against which, abandoned to itself, like every idea, it breaks, becoming disorganized in the atomistic material multiplicity of interests. The public good then becomes a vain abstraction; and the only concrete, real and solid thing that remains is that private one. Which, in the long run, will naturally recognize its own insufficiency and return to feeling the profound necessity of being organized as the public good; but, meanwhile, in the myopic eyes of those who are tired of working for a general and higher interest, for the State, it is everything. And so it is no wonder then that the concept becomes lost, and, above all, the feeling for the State's value; and that the country becomes prey and victim to the disruptive passions of individuals and categories; no wonder that the very concept of right becomes clouded, while everyone vigorously affirms his individual rights (as if there were a right for the individual or for the social class when there is no right, but law, the administration of justice, and the power that guarantees it, in other words the State).

Before our very eyes, we see this madness raging in the most impressive form. Whoever today does not walk out on strike, whoever does not think that he needs to remain at his post because of a higher interest, which is more important than his particular abstract reasons (which have no concreteness, unless they become reconciled and therefore coincide with that interest), but uniquely because he believes himself unable to strike; in the best of cases (a very rare case!) because of a certain external modesty; for the most part because he is afraid that nobody will notice his strike, or even think about it. And it does not matter that the strike, further impoverishing those sources that the striker wants to access, results in substantial damage to himself. He does not care about those sources, not because of malevolence, but because the general disposition of minds is this: that everyone has to think for himself, letting God take care of the rest. And this disposition is explained only by observing that before or within the political consciousness of the many, of the Government that they express from their heart, there is not that idea of the State, of the community, as a sovereign idea, from which inspiration would need to be drawn and strength for political action. There is not, and there cannot be, until one believes that our program can and must be dictated uniquely by a specific situation based on fact.

* * *

Socialists, to be honest, do not accept it; and they speak of *achievements*. So that for them reality should not be and cannot be what exists, but what they yearn for as the ideal. And yet they inevitably refuse to move within the orbit of a political movement that surpasses their program and will, and does not permit achievements or an efficacious and positive activity, but a simple operation of social disintegration and destruction instead. In Russia it appears that they have woken up, and have felt therefore the impelling need to restore the basis of the social edifice, which they had shaken in the first rash impulse. A Russian friend and very competent judge of his country assures us that Russia is tirelessly reorganizing itself along the path to imperialism. Be that as it may, an Italian Socialist who speaks of acting and building has a single strength in hand; and it is what is given to him by organizations like the organizations of class, whose strength, in turn, is not positive, but negative. It is the only strength, not of someone who has the ardor to construct, but of someone who is dominated by the impatience to destroy. It is the strength of battle: the strength that his valor has as long as there is an enemy with whom to fight, but who is inspired today rather by the intent and the faith to do away with the enemy; not to build up his strength for an always nobler, more difficult, more fertile battle, but to fall and collapse at the end of the battle itself. Nor is it worthwhile protesting that in this way the country will be saved. It will, but meanwhile all the socialist's strength derives not from the desire to save the country, but from that of conquering the conditions for a better life for himself. And every strike or manifestation of that strength is not accompanied in fact by a serious, collected, and quasi religious consciousness of someone who feels himself to be the creator of a new world, but by celebrations, trips to the country, and din, like people who are happy with the world as it is. This wobbly shack that, as a congressman compared in very expressive terms to this carefree and childlike state of mind, one would straightway like to see fall and break to pieces.

A negative strength, then; a negative attitude: in which socialists are in perfect accord with their adversaries, who can often appear as their secret allies. Since, if socialist congressmen believe they represent the country honorably by giving vent to sneers, shouts, whistles, and other sounds even less noble and less worthy of men who have a serious thought in their head, the so-called liberals resign themselves to hearing those sounds and keeping quiet. The first do nothing, and the second do nothing. And they are equals. In total accord, in substance, because the system is that, and there is nothing to do about it. In other words, what needs to be done is not up to us to say, but things speak for themselves: *rebus ipsis dictantibus*, just as the Minister Fossombroni believed, when he was laying down the law: the world takes care of itself. With a different emphasis they repeat it today, in their own way, revolutionaries and conservatives.

* * *

Well now, we do not want to point out a program, only to say that its spiritual attitude is absurd. Absurd politically, just as philosophically and morally it is absurd. Yes, even morally. And one needs to spur on the Italian spirit, and shake it out of this fatalistic inertia, which hides behind the pompous title of realism. This is the realism of Guicciardini, not that of Machiavelli, the only one that has real meaning, or the only sustainable one. That other, I repeat, even politically, is absurd. Whoever speaks about politics does not speak about the surrender of the human will to a situation of fact; but about the creation of reality. Or if this expression offends the modest ears of our politicians who, like Salvemini, are beset by headaches when one adopts a rigorous philosophical language[94] with them, let us instead say the transformation of factual reality. Inconceivable transformation, if we must derive principles not from our thought, but from reality itself.

In morality (seeing as even politicians must obey a moral inspiration, and Machiavelli in fact obeyed it) there is no action, at least for the modern conscience, unless as the negation of the reality of fact; and whoever adapts to it, and does not see or does not feel primarily that everyone has his own factual reality before him, and has it before him therefore also like a hard, rigid, and necessary reality, or like a ductile and domitable reality, and manageable like an instrument of the human will in accordance with the energy of one's own personality, he will never open his eyes to the light of good. Philosophically, a reality (at least for those who do not suffer from headaches), to which the will, and in general the human spirit, must refer and which is meanwhile to be considered as the antecedent, in and of itself, of the human spirit, is an inadmissible reality by whoever recognizes the necessity primarily of admitting the spirit, or perhaps even only the thought, in order then to be able to think with this whatever it is; also an error.

True realism is not only knowing the reality on which one had better act, as is commonly said; but also and in the first place knowing another reality,

[94]Original footnote: See *Unità*, March 6, 1920.

without which there would be no human life, nor politics, nor anything else: that reality, let's say, that reacts at first glance; and which is our true and proper reality; that internal energy, by which everyone takes his place, big or small, in the world and contributes, a little or a lot, to history in the specific and proper sense of the word: which is not the history that a man (or each man) finds already done, but what he makes instead. Energy, which is will insofar as it is thought: a system of ideas, a program to be put into action; what is called a personality, a man.

So there is reality, which a man must work on, and there is man. The one cannot be confused with the other. "Virtue" is one thing, Machiavelli said; "fortune," which virtue must dominate, is another. And the problem consists precisely in this task that virtue must execute in order to overcome, subject, and then reduce beneath itself, or resolve within itself: fortune. Whoever relies on or submits to fortune does not have virtue, is what Machiavelli meant. Not only is he not a statesman, he is not a man. The true statesman does not whimper over reality, he does not give jeremiads on the shortcomings of men, whom he must govern, and he does not preach. His realism, his virtue, has to make use of that reality and the shortcomings themselves: he must not idly deprecate, but he must industriously put to good use. His nobility needs to show through here. It is not the other things – the things that he must act on – that give him the idea. He is a statesman insofar as he has an idea, and an idea that is realizable. Not a utopia, but a realizable idea. So realizable that he can demonstrate to possess it in one way alone: by realizing it.

The reality that the statesman aims for is the one that he is responsible for: dynamic reality, and not static reality. Not what he finds, but what he puts into being and promotes. Thus the statesman, with respect to the State; thus every man, in general, towards the reality that in practice he refers to and which he cannot presuppose – because then the motive of his practical action would come up short – but that he must realize. Thus the statesman who has the reins of the Government in hand, and stands at the center; thus, with respect to the State, every man who, from every point of view, even from the periphery, participates in it. Because neither the head of the Government nor any citizen has the right to refuse the responsibility of the State, which he is, for his own part, to contribute to; nobody can speak of it like a reality that he has outside himself, in spite of himself even, for the State is what we achieve in our political consciousness, at the core of our being.

Machiavelli, the greatest master of realism, is actually an idealist. The reality that a man knows and studies is not the one he recognizes in order to bend to its law, but rather the one that the more he knows it the more he invests it with his own thought and will. Whoever calls him a naturalist or a materialist does not understand why the greatest thought in his head is this idea, so remote from the *de facto* condition of the Sixteenth century: Italy's unity; a great fatherland, not only in the abstract dominion of thought, but in this world, which men contend over; positively great, as a State that is strong in arms and strong in the awareness of the national ties binding its people. In Machiavelli's mind, there is no discontinuity between the reality that he calls effectual and his well managed State, such as he longs for it with anxious speculation. And there is no discontinuity because between the one and the other he is there, the man. The man who knows (in the Renaissance he begins to know) how to be the creator of his own destiny; as he can be, if he makes an instrument out of reality for his own purpose, raising it thus to a superior level of existence, which is not necessity, but freedom; not fact, but action.

So there is a realism that looks backward, like the diviners in Dante's *Inferno.* Those diviners that the Malebolge of Montecitorio also teems with, where every speech that is given now has a tone of prophecy to it. And it is the realism of the inept or the inert. And there is the realism of the hard-working spirits, those who look forward and instill into souls a faith in their plans and the courage to achieve them. Dante today would return and see such a one with the image

> *... sì torta, che il pianto degli occhi*
> *Le natiche gli bagna per lo fesso.*[95]

Until when?

---

[95] *Sì torta... lo fesso*: Italian for "so contorted, that their tears bathed their buttocks through the crack." Dante, *Inferno*, 20 23-24.

Other Books by the Publisher

Fanchette's Pretty Little Foot by Restif de La Bretonne

Je M'Accuse... by Léon Bloy

My Hospitals & My Prisons by Paul Verlaine

Salvation Through the Jews by Léon Bloy

Words of a Demolitions Contractor by Léon Bloy

Cellulely by Paul Verlaine

Ecclesiastical Laurels by Jacques Rochette de la Morlière

Flowers of Bitumen by Émile Goudeau

Songs for Her & Odes in Her Honor by Paul Verlaine

On Huysmans' Tomb by Léon Bloy

Ten Years a Bohemian by Émile Goudeau

The Soul of Napoleon by Léon Bloy

Blood of the Poor by Léon Bloy

Joan of Arc and Germany by Léon Bloy

A Platonic Love by Paul Alexis

The Revealer of the Globe: Christopher Columbus & His Future Beatification (Part One) by Léon Bloy

An Immodest Proposal by Dr. Helmut Schleppend

The Pornographer by Restif de La Bretonne

Style (Theory and History) by Ernest Hello

On the Threshold of the Apocalypse: 1913-1915 by Léon Bloy

She Who Weeps (Our Lady of La Salette) by Léon Bloy

The Sylph by Claude Prosper Jolyot de Crébillon (*fils*)

Voyage in France by a Frenchman by Paul Verlaine

Ourigan, Oregon by William Clark, Richard Robinson, and anonymous

Drowning by Yu Dafu

Cull of April by Francis Vielé-Griffin

The Misfortune of Monsieur Fraque by Paul Alexis

Fêtes Galantes & Songs Without Words by Paul Verlaine

Joys by Francis Vielé-Griffin

The Son of Louis XVI by Léon Bloy

Septentrion by Jean Raspail

The Resurrection of Villiers de l'Isle-Adam by Léon Bloy

Poems Saturnian by Paul Verlaine

The Biography of Léon Bloy: Memories of a Friend by René Martineau

Fredegund, France: A Book of Poetry by Richard Robinson

The Good Song by Paul Verlaine

Swans by Francis Vielé-Griffin

Constantinople and Byzantium by Léon Bloy

Enamels and Cameos by Théophile Gautier

Four Years of Captivity in Cochons-sur-Marne: 1900-1904 by Léon Bloy

Dark Minerva: Prolegomena: The Moral Construction of Dante's Divine Comedy by Giovanni Pascoli

www.ingramcontent.com/pod-product-compliance
Lightning Source LLC
Chambersburg PA
CBHW022044020426
42335CB00012B/537

* 9 7 8 1 9 5 5 3 9 2 3 6 5 *